RUTH MONTGOMERY
Herald of the New Age

Books by Ruth Montgomery

ALIENS AMONG US
THRESHOLD TO TOMORROW
STRANGERS AMONG US
THE WORLD BEFORE
COMPANIONS ALONG THE WAY
BORN TO HEAL
A WORLD BEYOND
HAIL TO THE CHIEFS
HERE AND HEREAFTER
A SEARCH FOR THE TRUTH
FLOWERS AT THE WHITE HOUSE
A GIFT OF PROPHECY
MRS. LBJ
ONCE THERE WAS A NUN

RUTH MONTGOMERY

MONTGOMERY

Herald of the New Age

RUTH MONTGOMERY
with JOANNE GARLAND

DOUBLEDAY / DOLPHIN
Doubleday & Company, Inc.
Garden City, New York
1986

133
mon

Library of Congress Cataloging-in-Publication Data

Montgomery, Ruth Shick,
  Ruth Montgomery, herald of the new age.

  1. Montgomery, Ruth Shick 2. Psychical
research—Biography. I. Garland, Joanne. II. Title.
III. Title: Herald of the new age.
BF1027.M66A36 1986   133 [B]   85-25424
ISBN 0-385-23311-6

CONTENTS

Introduction *vii*

I First Lady of the Psychic World   *1*

II Early Years   *15*

III The Newspaper World   *27*

IV Washington Career   *47*

V A Taste of the Psychic   *72*

VI A Search for the Truth   *89*

VII Reincarnation   *114*

VIII Off to Mexico   *134*

IX A Glimpse Beyond Death   *146*

X The Healer and the Companion   *163*

XI Atlantis and Lemuria   *178*

XII Walk-ins?   *191*

XIII More Strangers Among Us   *205*

XIV Extraterrestrials   *218*

XV The New Age   *233*

XVI Beyond the Bend   *253*

INTRODUCTION

    To relive one's life through the pages of a book is a nostalgic journey backward through time. Reading again of my initial reluctance, lagging feet, recurring doubts, and plaintive resistance as my spiritual mentors propelled me into each new stage of psychic unfoldment evokes a smile of fond remembrance. If it is true, as many thousands of fan letters attest, that my books have forever changed the lives of readers and helped them to understand the deeper meaning of life, then the credit should go to those unseen mentors whom I call "the Guides." I have simply been the chosen instrument for their imperative project to enlighten humanity about everything from spirit communication and reincarnation to Walk-ins, extraterrestrials, and the New Age that is beginning to dawn.

    I was ever the skeptical reporter, requiring convincing proof before taking my readers along with me on each of the quantum leaps into a largely unexplored and mysterious realm. But if we are to grow and develop spiritually, it is essential that we maintain an open mind and a willingness to begin tapping into that 90 percent of human brain capability that scientists tell us is currently unutilized by most of us.

As the Guides gradually stretched my own thinking to encompass these new realities of time, space, and eternity, my faith in a benevolent Creator unfolded and expanded, as it inevitably will do for all who sincerely seek a richer purpose for living. During the past quarter century I have pursued an often lonely search for answers to some of life's most impelling questions: Why were we born? Do we have a mission in life? If so, how can we determine that mission? Did we live before? Are we forever? Is there a divine plan for us earthlings? Then what is our ultimate goal?

The Guides, in my previous books, have provided many thought-provoking answers to these posers that have long perplexed humankind. The intent of this biography is therefore to inspire others to set forth on their own voyage of discovery, to awaken the slumbering awareness within, and to realize that we are not our *physical* selves, but individual sparks of the Creator. Our bodies die, but *we* are eternal, and it consequently behooves each of us to begin now to prepare ourselves for this New Age that the Bible calls the millennium. Otherwise we will surely miss out on the greatest adventure of all!

My sincere thanks go to Bill Carter, the literary agent who conceived the idea for this book in order.to disseminate the Guides' teachings more widely, and to Jim Fitzgerald, the editor who not only waved the magic wand to make it possible, but generously allowed me to select an unknown writer to chronicle my story.

This brings me to Joanne Garland and my book *Strangers Among Us*, which first presented the concept of Walk-ins—a theory now being considered by some outstanding psychologists and psychiatrists as a possible explanation for the dramatic alterations in personality and ideals of certain patients who had undergone deep depression or a near-death experience. Joanne was my first Walk-in acquaintance, the one who introduced me to this fascinating concept, as you will read here in Chapter XII. In *Strangers Among Us* I called her "Laura," to protect her privacy until first dozens and then hundreds of other Walk-ins bravely elected to make their identities known.

Long before we met, Joanne was an avid reader of all my psychic books, had become thoroughly grounded in their philosophy, and possessed an unusual awareness of life's purpose on planet earth. She is now the narrator during my stroll down memory lane, and I hope that you will enjoy it with us. Do come along!

Ruth Montgomery
Washington, D.C. 1986

CHAPTER I

First Lady of the Psychic World

A hushed silence swept through the packed auditorium as people of all ages, from young college students to gray-haired grandparents, expectantly turned their attention toward the podium. The excitement, almost electric, seemed even now to build in intensity. At center stage the announcer paused, cleared his throat, and began.

"For most of you, our guest tonight needs no introduction. As you are aware, she has already changed our lives in vital and meaningful ways. The author of fourteen books, most of which have forever altered our perception of psychic phenomena, death, rebirth, and the meaning of life, Ruth Montgomery began her career as a newspaper reporter whose insight and integrity won the respect of colleagues and news sources alike."

The large audience listened attentively as the announcer continued: "A recipient of two honorary doctor of laws degrees, winner of numerous journalism awards, former syndicated political columnist and foreign correspondent throughout the world, former president of the Women's

National Press Club, and White House and State Department correspondent, Ruth next turned her investigative skills to a twenty-five-year exploration of the psychic field. A born skeptic, she sought to dig out the facts and then to test them. What she found and subsequently reported—from clairvoyance, life after death, reincarnation, and planetary prehistory to extraterrestrial visitors and predictions of an approaching cataclysm—has revolutionized our perception of ourselves, of our universe, and of our purpose for living. She has been a pathfinder along a once lonely trail, and has lighted the way for others to follow.

"Those of you who have been aware of Ruth's early career as a highly respected journalist know that she checked her sources carefully, producing fact, not fiction, and that she wrote the truth. It was with this same standard for accuracy that she approached the psychic field, and she has uncovered truths so profound that they have deepened and strengthened the religious beliefs of millions.

"Ladies and gentlemen," the announcer concluded, "please join me in welcoming the First Lady of the Psychic World, Ruth Montgomery."

The audience erupted at once into thunderous applause, as a petite figure dressed in a soft pastel suit moved quickly to her place at the podium and flashed a loving smile. Yet the applause continued, delight warming the faces of hundreds of men and women whose lives had already been deeply touched by this writer.

Slowly the crowd's welcome quieted to an expectant hush. All eyes focused on the speaker, who after a few words of greeting began: "I doubt if there's a person in this room who has not had a psychic experience, or who at least has a family member with a baffling story to recount. That's because psychic phenomena are real, and tonight I want to tell you about some of my own adventures in this fascinating realm that lies beyond our five senses and our three-dimensional world."

The speaker's voice, warm and confiding, continued as she recounted how her twenty-five-year career as a syndicated Washington columnist gradually gave way to an absorbing interest in the psychic field. "I was a newspaper reporter, as skeptical as the average member of my profession. We have covered too many political huddles in smoke-filled rooms and exposed too many chicaneries to believe all that meets the eye. But a good reporter must also have an open mind, and little by little, through my extensive investigations, I finally became convinced of the validity of communication between the living and the so-called dead, who have simply moved on into a different vibratory level of eternal life."

Ruth carried the rapt audience with her through those initial delvings into séances, her first encounter with the famed trance medium, Arthur Ford, her dogged insistence on checking out the truth of the many assertions relayed through the sleeping Ford by his spirit contact (an entity called Fletcher), and her ultimate astonishment on finding that Fletcher's declarations proved stunningly accurate in every detail.

It was Arthur Ford, she continued, who told her that she had the innate ability to do automatic writing, a mysterious process of communication in which one first meditates and then, still in the alpha state that it produces, holds a pencil lightly poised above a sheet of paper.

Ruth delights in poking fun at herself, and her blue eyes sparkled as she recounted her early attempts to comply with Ford's instructions. "Nothing happened. Simply nothing," she ruefully confessed, "and after giving it a few minutes each morning I would throw down the pencil and dash off to the Capitol or the White House to earn an honest living. At last, on the tenth morning, some otherworldly force of herculean strength seemed to grasp my hand, and although my eyes were closed, it propelled the pencil into circles and figure eights with such pressure that I thought the lead point would break. I could not have dropped it if I'd tried."

Later that day a friend who was more experienced in the psychic field told her jubilantly, "That's the way it always begins. It's their way of expressing joy that contact has at last been made. Be sure to continue it."

The following morning the pencil began, haltingly at first and then with vigor, to write messages from Ruth's father. Next came funny little drawings of children that were signed with a flourish by a long-dead aunt, and finally the introduction of an entity calling himself "Lily," who announced that he would now take over the regular sessions as her spirit mentor.

Thereafter, beautiful philosophy began to flow through the racing pencil until one morning it spelled out in bold letters, "GO TO YOUR TYPEWRITER! WE THINK NOW THAT WE HAVE DEVELOPED THE STRENGTH TO TYPE THROUGH YOU." Dutifully crossing the hall to her electric typewriter, Ruth rested her hands lightly in touch-typing position, closed her eyes, and allowed her fingers to enjoy a seeming life of their own. With scarcely a moment's hesitation, the keys began tapping, and, on later opening her eyes, she read: "Yes! Yes! We can type! From now on this is the way we will communicate with you!"

The inspiring messages continued each day, as they had earlier with the pencil, describing the meaning of life, our original beginnings as sparks from the Creator, our missions and eventual goals. The Guides also began urging that Ruth disseminate their teaching through a book, so that it would help others as it had already begun to revolutionize her own beliefs and ideals.

Since Ruth's career had heretofore centered on political

and international affairs, and her byline had earned wide recognition and respect in what is largely a man's world, she naturally hesitated to reveal these philosophical messages that had come to her through such an unorthodox source. Following each morning's session with the Guides, she would hurriedly scan the new material, deposit the typewritten pages in a drawer, and rush off to her desk at the National Press Building, or to a congressional hearing, or a White House press conference.

But this strangely inspiring material continued to grow in volume, as well as in insistence that it be published for all to share. It stressed the power of prayer and of love, the need for soul development, and the truth of eternal life. It even hinted at something called reincarnation—an odd notion to a newspaper reporter who had become somewhat of an agnostic during her college years and doubted that there was even a hereafter. "Yet I had never before read or heard such beautiful philosophy as the Guides were busily writing on my typewriter," Ruth acknowledged. "It seemed selfish to keep it to myself."

Meanwhile Ruth's mother, who objected strenuously to her growing interest in the psychic, voiced even graver concern over her tentative decision to write about it. "Oh, Ruth," she begged, "you've done so well in your career, and people have grown to respect and trust you, and even presidents call you by your first name. Don't write that book or they will think you're a *kook!*"

"Because of Mother's objections, I dallied for a year," Ruth continued laughingly, "while she said, 'Don't,' my strong-minded Guide said, 'Do,' and my husband maintained an uneasy neutrality. At last the question was resolved in my own mind. If I were to live comfortably with myself, I had no right to suppress great truths that were important for others to know. They were not intended for me alone."

The books that Ruth finally dared to write aroused a tremendous outpouring of enthusiasm from people of every
religious faith, including members of the clergy who invited
her to speak from their pulpits. Both Catholic and Protestant universities asked her to address their student bodies.
Jewish organizations also extended invitations. The concept
of reincarnation began to gain broad acceptance by people
who reported that for the first time they now understood
this ancient belief, whose tenets may be found in nearly
every religious philosophy on earth.

But what of Christianity, and how does an understanding
of the psychic square with Christian beliefs? Anticipating
the frequently asked question, Ruth explained: "I was
reared a Methodist, but never was I as deeply religious as I
became after studying the material from my spirit Guides.
That really brought home to me the meaning of Christ's
mission, the reality of God, the oneness of all great religions,
and the purpose for which we live. I realized that we are all
one—that each of us is a part of our Creator. An understanding of the psychic has made me a better Christian, but it
transcends the boundaries of all religions. It is universal."
Citing a number of verses from the New Testament, Ruth
remarked: "It seems to me that the only way these various
exchanges between Jesus and his disciples can be inter-
preted is in terms of reincarnation."

Smiling reassuringly at her attentive audience, she continued: "The concept of reincarnation is an ancient one that
is embraced by two thirds of the world's peoples. It was
accepted as a matter of course by the early Christians, including St. Augustine, until the Second Council of Constan-
tinople in the sixth century condemned the teaching because it seemed easier to control the masses if they believed
that they had but one lifetime in which to behave before
facing the Judgment Seat. That council was not even attended by the Pope of Rome, and St. Francis of Assisi and

many other famous Catholic monks, bishops, and Christian theologians have publicly espoused reincarnation in the centuries since then.

"To me it seems the only logical explanation for the seeming inequities of life," Ruth pensively observed. "Can we really believe that a just and loving God permits one soul to be born to wealthy, loving parents who will give it every advantage in life, while simultaneously consigning another soul to an unwanted birth in a city ghetto? Except through a belief in reincarnation, how can we justify the fact that one baby is born perfect in mind and body, while another comes into this life blinded or maimed? The Guides say that it is not God who thus punishes these helpless babies, but that they themselves elected to be born into a situation of hardship or physical handicap in order to make recompense for mistakes committed during earlier incarnations. Needless to say, all of us have transgressions to repay, so perhaps those whom we call 'the unfortunates' are actually the more courageous ones who have chosen to clear their spiritual slates faster than the rest of us. The Guides stress that we must understand this concept if we are to recognize the true meaning of our earthly lives and to prepare adequately for the massive planetary changes that are to come."

According to Ruth's Guides, planet earth will undergo a sudden shift on its axis at the end of this century (a change that many scientists and geologists agree has occurred numerous times in ages past), sloshing the oceans over our coastlines, causing land masses to sink or rise, effecting drastic climatic changes, and plunging our modern society into a period of chaos until the emergence of a golden age of peace and understanding in the twenty-first century. They stress that this chaotic shift will tax us all. Those who choose to survive it in physical body will need to tap their reserves of intuition, ingenuity, and cooperative energy, while those who will inevitably pass into spirit at that time should understand that with such massive numbers of souls arriving simultaneously in the spirit plane, confusion will reign for a while unless we begin now to understand the true nature of our being.

"Again I want to stress that there is no death," Ruth concluded, "that when our bodies die we simply change our energy frequencies. The ultimate goal, for all of us, is to live such loving, helpful lives that ultimately we may be re-united with our Creator. We began when the Creator cast off the sparks that became our souls. He gave us free will, and as we misused that precious gift, errors inevitably crept in, but now is our opportunity for a new beginning. The New Age to come, the Age of Aquarius, is foretold to be an era of such love and understanding that those of us who will be here to experience it, whether in this lifetime or the next, will indeed be blessed. And thank you all so much. You're wonderful!"

The audience, which had sat virtually motionless in utter fascination throughout this forty-five-minute talk, suddenly burst into enthusiastic applause, nodding their heads to one another, beaming, their eyes shining with appreciation. Some reached across to touch loved ones. Others applauded with renewed gratitude. Not a soul rose to leave, but anx-iously awaited the start of the question-and-answer period that would continue for another fascinating hour and could have gone on all day had not the announcer returned to assure the enthralled participants that Ruth would be avail-able immediately after the program to autograph books.

Applause filled the jam-packed auditorium, and people rose and gathered their belongings, not to leave but to join the swarm of well-wishers who began to surround Ruth, to reach out and touch her hand, to embrace her and thank her for the way that she had changed their lives. One after another approached her, anxious for just a brief moment to offer a warm hug and a word of gratitude. Finally realizing that many more people were waiting patiently, someone urged them to form a line, one which soon extended the length of the hall. While many fans requested autographs, some sought only a chance to meet this person whose work had so deeply affected them. There were such remarks as these:

"Ruth, I can't tell you what your writing has meant to me. It has completely changed my life, and given it meaning and purpose."

"I was on the verge of suicide when, like a miracle, one of your books came into my hands. It's the most important thing that has ever happened to me."

"I just wanted to get where I could hug you and tell you about my daughter. She was making a mess of her life, and I got her to read your books. Now she has completely turned her life around, and I'm so grateful to you."

"My husband died this year, and I thought I would lose my sanity, but then someone gave me one of your books. Now I know that he's just as alive as I am. I can't tell you what a change it has made in my life."

"Before I read your books, I didn't realize what life was all about. Now I have found a richness and a purpose I never knew before."

"Thanks to what you've written, I've lost all fear of death. How can I ever thank you for the serenity you've given me?"

These comments mirror the thousands of letters that pour in to Ruth every year from all over the world. Many people ask for information about their own past lives, or their major purpose in this lifetime, while an enormous number seek some message of comfort from a deceased loved one. The Guides have made it clear that their purpose in communicating with Ruth is not to serve as a medium for individual contact, but rather to disseminate vital information affecting all mankind. The brief daily sessions of automatic writing that began a quarter century ago leave little time for anything else. But occasionally she is so moved by her deep concern for others that she does pose a personal question.

One such event occurred in February, 1985, when Ruth received a call from her longtime friend, Martha Rountree, co-originator and former moderator of TV's "Meet the Press." Almost in tears, Martha recounted heartbreaking news that she had just received from her dear friend Carolyn Brady, wife of former assistant secretary of commerce Lawrence Brady. That morning Carolyn had found their seventeen-year-old daughter Melissa dead in the family car in the garage, a suicide by carbon monoxide poisoning. The Bradys were deeply upset. Could Ruth *please* ask the Guides for any word of Melissa. Carolyn Brady had been an avid reader of her books for many years, and she trusted the Guides. "I knew that Ruth refrained from seeking personal messages," Carolyn says, "yet we were distraught, grasping at straws, desperately seeking some answers to our question of *why* this terrible event had to happen."

Ruth felt reluctant at first. She did not know the Bradys, and not wishing to risk receiving a message that could cause further unhappiness to grieving strangers, she said that she would prefer not to ask the Guides. *"Please,"* Martha entreated her. "Please, would you do this as a personal favor to me, just this once? You are the only one Carolyn believes in."

Relenting, Ruth assumed her place at the typewriter for her daily session, first typing out a brief question for the Guides. Did they have any word from a young girl named Melissa Brady? Then she began her slow, deep breathing, her silent prayer for protection, and her period of meditation. Finally, after resting her fingers lightly on the typewriter keys, the automatic typing began.

"Yes, she is here, Little Melissa, and so sorry for what she did," the Guides responded. "Teenagers have a hard time keeping balance in today's world, and she was emotionally unstrung, but should have thought more before acting. She loves her mother dearly and worships both her mother and father. She is saying: 'Why, why, why was I such a fool? Oh, Mother, please don't blame yourself or Daddy. It was a crazy kid thing to do, and I love you all so much. Forgive me. I'll be near you often for a while, before I choose my project to work on here, so love me and trust me. Adieu but not goodbye.' "

Ruth had known nothing about Melissa, so she had no means of knowing whether the message was valid until Carolyn confirmed it in every detail. "This had to be from my daughter," she later declared. "It includes too many key phrases typical of Melissa." Among the evidentials are the fact that Larry Brady had always called his daughter "Little Melissa" when speaking either to her or about her. Melissa had been "emotionally unstrung" after watching a television documentary about teenage suicide the evening before her death. The phrase "It was a crazy kid thing to do" sounded exactly like Melissa, according to an aunt who often had heard her employ that choice of words, and she invariably referred to her plans as "my next project." But most striking of all, her mother says, was the phrase "Adieu but not goodbye." Melissa was proud of her French, which she had studied for three years. She loved Paris and looked forward to returning there with her grandmother that summer. Whenever she would leave a room or go off somewhere, she would always flip her head back over her shoulder and say "Adieu." It was never "Goodbye," or "I'm off," or "See ya later," but always "Adieu."

Carolyn's relief and gratitude for this message has been immense. "I no longer feel as hopeless as I thought I would feel," she says. "I know that Melissa is indeed very much alive." Yet Carolyn adds that it is not merely this personal message which has brought such comfort. "All of Ruth's books have awakened me to the reality that life never ends, that we all return again and again, to learn and to grow." A practicing Catholic, she began reading Ruth's books ten years ago after becoming interested in the late seer Edgar Cayce. "When I first came across a book Ruth had written, I found it so fascinating that I started to read everything I could find by her. The messages from the Guides are obviously coming from a very special source; they helped me to see my Christian faith in an entirely new light. Words and phrases I had read in the Bible had always seemed to be mere words, but now they took on a whole new and more logical meaning and made perfect sense. Ruth's books give people inner strength and an understanding of why we live and die—what we're all striving for. I only wish more people knew this truth about life."

Through the weeks after Melissa's passing, Carolyn and Larry have received countless messages of comfort from friends and strangers alike. "People have asked what they can do to ease our grief," Carolyn says. "I tell them not to send flowers or money, but to please just go out and read Ruth Montgomery's books. 'Do that for me, in memory of Melissa, and that will help me more than you could ever know, because then you will share my understanding of the truth, that life continues without end.' "

Similar sentiments have been expressed by Frederick Von Mierers, an internationally known psychic-astrologer whose life and philosophy are described at length in Ruth's most recent book, *Aliens Among Us.* According to Frederick, "Ruth has done more to popularize the ideals of universal religion with the masses than almost any other author. Her bestselling books have brought this universal view to many who were previously aware only of the sectarian, dogmatic view of their own particular churches. This is a great service rendered to mankind in this time of world crisis. The ideals that she perpetuates help to bring all of us to a greater understanding of our relationship with one another and with our Creator, thus strengthening the bonds of brotherhood that must be made stronger if we are to progress as a civilization."

Frederick emphasizes that through her Guides Ruth has, without realizing it, rewritten the ancient Hindu scriptures, the Vedas, in a way that the Western mind can comprehend. "She is a great servant of the light, who is helping all mankind to grow in awareness and understanding of the divine principles." Referring to the dawn of a New Age of awareness on the planet, Frederick stresses that these highly energized ideas are coming to the forefront of the consciousness of her readers and are acting as beacons of light, guiding them along the highway to ultimate self-realization. "This has always been the message of the East," he concludes, "the great Yogi-Christs of India, and now Ruth is helping to popularize these sacred ideals among the Western peoples."

According to the Guides, Frederick in previous earth lives was a high priest in many different religions, who has returned at this time to train young leaders for the New Age. He considers that his special mission is to help unite the major religious philosophies with science under the banner of the one eternal truth.

And what of Ruth's own purpose for this lifetime? As a child she dreamed of becoming a foreign missionary. Yet life led her through a stunning career, first as a widely respected and accomplished journalist who traveled the world to interview presidents and kings, then as a skeptical reporter of things supernatural.

"I believe that I came into this life with a definite mission, as we all do," she began softly. "I think mine was to dispel the illusion that there is such a thing as death. I wanted to spread the word that life is eternal, and that there is continuing communication between the living and the so-called dead. When I was a little girl, those subconscious promptings came as suggestions for missionary work, but as I look back over my lifetime, I realize that it was necessary for me first to establish my credentials as a widely syndicated newspaper reporter who wrote truth, before the path could be opened for me to help others accept the still greater truth that we are all one, and as such, we are all a part of God."

In the view of readers whose lives have been deepened and enriched by her work, Ruth Montgomery has succeeded far beyond that childhood dream and become a true missionary to all of planet earth. But her road to this fulfillment has been a long and winding one, littered with obstacles that she has learned to view as "stepping stones." Her life story begins in the rolling hills of southern Illinois, in the heart of America's Middle West.

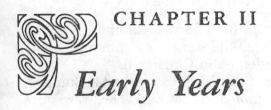

CHAPTER II

Early Years

Sumner, Illinois, was a lovely little town back then, with fewer than a thousand souls and with rows of neat frame houses set well back from streets lined with majestic old shade trees that have since fallen victim to elm blight. The sidewalks were smooth stone, and perfect for roller skating.

Inside one of these sprucely kept cottages, Bertha Judy Shick was impatiently awaiting the birth of her second child, and until her own death at the age of eighty-nine she always insisted that it was a ten-month baby, despite the admonition of her village doctor that she had simply miscalculated. "But I *know*," she would blushingly argue.

A former schoolteacher until her marriage to Ira Whitmer Shick, Bertha had lived in Sumner all her life, the youngest of four children of Charles Clayton Judy, Sumner's well-liked and respected station agent for the Baltimore & Ohio Railroad, and himself a scion of the old Swiss Tschudy (Judy) family of historians and educators whose history, recorded on nearly five dozen parchment scrolls inherited by

Ruth, traces back to A.D. 870. Bertha's mother, Caroline, was the daughter of Dr. David Burget, a Sumner physician who took his medical degree in Cincinnati.

At the time of his marriage Ira Shick worked in Sumner's only bank, actually a combination bank and hardware store. One of nine children born to former schoolteachers Jane Whitmer and Peter William Shick, he had grown up in a large Victorian house on the 360-acre family farm five miles south of Sumner. His father was the unquestioned leader of the farming community, and his grandfather, John Vandament Shick, a Civil War veteran and a Republican since the founding of the party, had descended from a line of early eighteenth-century German settlers in Pennsylvania. Ira's mother's earliest American ancestors had arrived in New Amsterdam, as New York City was then called, in 1636, only sixteen years after the Pilgrims landed at Plymouth Rock, buying a large property in lower Manhattan near present-day Wall Street, and also establishing a mill at Rensselaerswyck (now Albany), New York. Both Ira and Bertha therefore descended from old Colonial families, with eight direct ancestors who had fought in the American Revolution.

Now they were anticipating the newest addition to the family, a child who would grow up to become one of the most thought-provoking writers of our time. But if Ruth was indeed late in arriving, it was probably the last time in her peripatetic career of meeting newspaper deadlines. Musing about the inconvenience that she seemed to have been inflicting on her family, Ruth says: "My grandmother and Aunt Mabel Judy had been delaying a train trip from Sumner to St. Louis until after I was born. We had well-to-do cousins there whom they visited rather frequently, since Grandfather's position entitled them to railroad passes. But as days turned into weeks, they finally gave up waiting because of some pressing business in St. Louis."

Their train had reached Flora, some thirty-five miles west

of Sumner, when a messenger boarded with the news, relayed by telegraph, that Bertha's baby girl had at last arrived. They promptly changed trains and headed back to care for two-year-old Paul Judy Shick during his mother's convalescence. No name had as yet been chosen for the seven-pound, blue-eyed infant, but when Bertha suggested Elizabeth, Ira promptly vetoed it. "How about Ruth Whitmer?" he asked. And so it was agreed.

"We were always a very close-knit family," Ruth recalls. "Many of our cousins seemed almost like brothers and sisters because we played with them so often. Mother and Dad were devoted to their own siblings, and Grandmother Judy and my spinster Aunt Mabel were wonderful to us all of our lives. It was a happy childhood."

But there was sadness, too. An outbreak of pneumonia swept through Sumner the year that Ruth turned three. "It was an unusually severe winter, I am told, and of course in those days there was no penicillin. Both of my grandfathers and my dad's twenty-three-year-old sister Mae died within the space of two weeks. My mother's father had served as station agent for forty years and was also the longtime president of the Sumner school board, so when he died that bitter January, the B & O Railroad sent a special train from St. Louis to carry the mourners to the cemetery only a mile down the road."

Ruth hastens to add that her immediate family was never particularly prosperous. "But we didn't realize it in those days," she muses, "because both the Judy and Shick families were so highly regarded that they had friends and contacts wherever we moved, and we were always welcomed socially. Money was not the criterion then that it seems to be today."

The Ira Shick family moved rather often during those early years, first to nearby Lawrenceville, Illinois, and then at the urging of an old friend to Princeton, Indiana, where

Ira sold Velie and Maxwell automobiles. "Dad was always an adventuresome man." Ruth smiled nostalgically. "He had never before driven a car, but ever since his youth, sitting on a rail fence to watch one of the new contraptions go by, he said that he would think to himself, 'If ever I could get my hands on one of those!' Now was his chance!"

Ruth's sister Margaret was born in Princeton when Ruth was four and soon became her lifelong confidante, and closest pal and ally. Their father had briefly taught school after a year at a state teachers college in Illinois, but without a college degree or specialized training he could not aspire to a high-paying job. "But he always worked very hard and was a devoted family man," Ruth reminisces. "He was a loving, kindly father, and Mother was a very self-sacrificing, wonderful woman who was extremely ambitious for her children. She sewed most of our dresses, as every penny had to be watched. We children knew that we couldn't have everything that we wanted, nor did it occur to us to ask for luxuries."

The year that Ruth would have started kindergarten a measles epidemic occurred in Princeton, so Bertha kept her daughter at home to avoid exposure. Having been a schoolteacher, she made up for those missing months of play school by starting to teach Ruth the first-grade basics. "I learned not only my letters, but to read and write, and even to do some simple arithmetic," Ruth recalls. "By the time I started school at the age of six, I already knew most of what was being taught, so I naturally made all A's and was promoted directly to 2A, skipping 2B."

In those days, when the population was smaller, the same teacher taught both the A and B classes in the same classroom, and the pupils necessarily learned to concentrate on their studies while the other group recited lessons, "something that came in handy in later years when I had to write breaking news stories in the middle of a noisy press room " she adds.

Ruth recalls her early love of reading. "I remember when we were given the Heidi book as an assignment in the fourth grade and were told to read the first five pages. Well, I found the story so engrossing that I devoured the whole book that day. Obviously I was less than brilliant in the next day's discussion. How could I remember exactly what was in the first five pages when I'd read it all the way through?"

While the family lived frugally, Bertha Shick made certain to budget enough for her children to have some special advantages. In Ruth's case, that advantage came in the form of weekly elocution lessons, starting at the age of six, and later piano and dancing lessons as well. "That's why I've never had any fear of audiences," she says with a laugh, "because from that time on I was a strutting little star on center stage. With no television, people in small towns must have been desperate for entertainment, or I'd never have made it."

Until she eventually rebelled at the age of fifteen, she regularly memorized lengthy "pieces" that her mother had ordered by mail, and acted them out before audiences in various small towns of southern Illinois and Indiana. "Hear Ruth Shick, the Child Impersonator," handbills advertising the event would read. Except for shorter recitals given at grown-ups' luncheons, clubs, and teas, Ruth's performances often made up an entire evening's entertainment at various churches attended by her grandmother and aunts. "People would pay twenty-five cents, or make a 'silver offering' at the door, and fill the hall, if you can imagine it," Ruth quips. "Mother arranged that 90 percent of the proceeds always went to the church, and only 10 percent to me. I often thought that it was the opposite of tithing, but there it was I who had the joy of showing off!"

Bertha assembled all of Ruth's costumes for these programs, which were in three acts and ran for a couple of hours. For the first act she would appear in normal attire for humorous recitations, often in dialect. Next, while a local person played the piano, she would change quickly and then somersault onto the stage dressed as a boy in overalls for character performances. Finally she would appear in a dainty evening dress, to play roles out of Dickens or from some other work of fiction.

Many years later, after Ruth had become a top-notch Washington writer, columnist Malvina Stephenson wrote an article about her in which she declared: "Her knack for impersonations, which trace back to her childhood lessons in elocution, adds flavor to the Washington stories she often tells."

The Shicks were a churchgoing family, and Ruth took religion seriously as a child. "I became enamored with the thought of becoming a foreign missionary," she recalls. "In Methodist Sunday School I would hear about the missionaries in Africa or China, and it sounded terribly exciting to travel to far-off countries and live among the natives, telling them about God and Jesus." Contribution envelopes in those days were divided into two pockets, one for local church expenses and the other for missions, and Ruth begged her mother to put all of her offering into the mission pocket, until Bertha explained that the local minister also had to be paid.

The year that Ruth turned five she and her seven-year-old brother Paul joined a group of other children at the Methodist Episcopal Church in Princeton for the rite of baptism. "Our mothers knelt with us at the altar, and after the pastor asked our full names he baptized each of us by sprinkling water on our heads, as was the custom in the Methodist Church. Paul, like most first-born sons, had as his second name our mother's maiden name—Judy—but he hated it because he thought it sounded sissy for a boy. I was kneeling between him and Mother, and when the minister asked his name he promptly replied, 'Paul Whitmer Shick.' 'Judy,' hissed my mother. 'Whitmer,' Paul firmly insisted, swiping my own middle name. Thoroughly confused, the minister compromised by saying, 'Paul Shick, I baptize thee . . .' It was hilarious."

Not long afterward Ruth learned in Sunday School that Jesus had been immersed in the river Jordan. Therefore, sprinkling was not sufficient baptism, she decided, and began clamoring to be totally immersed. Her grandmother and Aunt Mabel Judy belonged to the Christian denomination, and fortuitously their church in Sumner had just completed a new edifice to replace the old one that had been there since Ruth's great-great-grandfather and other members of the Judy family founded the congregation in 1860. The church had a spanking new baptistry, and the minister announced that because her ancestors had been its founders, Ruth would be the first to be baptized in the new facility.

"Mother made me a pretty new yellow voile dress to wear for the ceremony," Ruth remembers, "and I was led down into the baptistry, where I forgot to hold my breath and choked on water as the minister immersed me I heard the poor man say, 'Oh, pshaw!' But I took the ceremony so seriously that although we had few extra clothes to spare, I would not let Mother wash that dress, and I never wore it again. I insisted that the holy water should stay in it forever."

Just as Ruth took religion seriously at a young age, so she also began early to respect the sanctity of life. As was the custom in small Midwestern towns, the Shicks kept a few chickens penned in a corner of the backyard. They were intended for the table, but their clucking and scratching provided occasional entertainment for Ruth and Paul. "Sometimes we would stand by the wire fence and watch the chickens, and there was one that we could recognize because of a particular marking on its head," she remembers.

One Sunday after dinner the two children wandered out to the backyard and noticed that the hen with the special marking was missing. They excitedly rushed back to the house to tell their mother, who casually replied, "Yes, that's the one we had for dinner today."

From then on Ruth became a vegetarian, much to the consternation of her mother, grandmother, and aunts, all of whom cautioned her that she would "never grow up big and strong" unless she ate meat. "They tried all manner of persuasion to get me to change my mind, even to stuffing mashed potatoes with meat gravy into my mouth one Sunday, hoping that I'd realize how delicious it was," Ruth relates. "But I cried bitterly and refused to swallow, until at last Mother allowed me to leave the table and spit it out. From then on my patient mother had to serve me butter beans—my favorite food—every single day to ensure that I would get sufficient protein."

Ruth remained a vegetarian until adult life, when she married a "meat and potatoes" man and decided that if she had to cook meat, she might as well eat it. "But I still feel qualms," she admits, "and can't bear to eat it if I allow myself to think that it used to be alive."

All during her life Ruth has had many friends, but in each new community there seemed to be one very special one. "The families of my closest friends were invariably more affluent than we were, but it never seemed to make any difference," she says. "I stayed all night at their houses many times, and they often stayed at our house, and Mother was always so good at planning little treats for us."

Ruth's best friend in Princeton was a girl named Katherine Weese, and when they were eight years old, Katherine's father gave her a pony and cart, which the two girls drove all over town, sometimes taking little Margaret with them. Katherine also had a miniature child's house in the backyard, where they often played after school, but one day they decided to climb to the dome of the county courthouse. "An elderly caretaker led us up the winding stairs and out onto the observation platform," Ruth recalls with a shiver. "The view was exciting, but when I looked straight down at the lawn far below, I suffered the most horrible dizziness and fear—as if I would have to jump, but didn't want to."

She had never heard of acrophobia, and learned only much later that this fear of heights carried a name of its own. It has continued to plague her throughout her life, in helicopters, on the balconies of tall apartment buildings, on ski lifts in Europe, wherever it is possible to look straight down, although the broader view from airplanes does not bother her. She now believes that the acrophobia stems from a traumatic death scene in a previous Egyptian incarnation along the Nile, a lifetime that will be touched on later in this story.

After five years in Princeton the Shicks moved twenty-seven miles north to Vincennes, Indiana, where Ruth lived from the age of nine until her senior year in high school. "Almost immediately I had a new 'best friend,'" she says, "and although Katherine and I continued to love and visit each other, Gladys Marie Sargent and I became almost inseparable. Both of our mothers belonged to the Eastern Star, and Gladys and I were initiated into the junior organization called Job's Daughters. We rode bicycles and went everywhere together."

As usual, Ruth's schoolwork was outstanding, but she claims never to have been the favorite of her teachers. "I lacked the apple-polishing disposition to be a teacher's pet," she says with a chuckle. "I was too independent. But I must say that I was much better behaved at school than in the bosom of the family. As a tiny tot I remember refusing to take one of those little Pierce's Pleasant Purgative Pellets, and running around the living room screaming 'No, no, no, no, no' until Dad removed his belt and strapped my legs. But Dad was always so penitent after spanking me! He would sit on the side of my bed, stroke my hair, and tell me how sorry he felt at having to punish me. Frankly I preferred his method to Mother's. She would sometimes slap my face, and still stay mad at me. I loved her dearly, but we had clashing temperaments. 'You're just like your father,' she would chide me. 'You both flare up and say angry things, but two minutes later you've returned to your usual sunny disposition and have forgotten all about it.' Mother couldn't forget that easily."

But Ruth's independent nature carried its positive side. At the age of eleven she secretly entered a writing contest intended for adults, omitting the fact that she was a fifth-grader. The electric company had invited contestants to submit their descriptions of proper home lighting, and several weeks later, to Mrs. Shick's amazement, a check arrived in the mail. Her little daughter had won first prize!

While all schoolwork came easily to Ruth, English classes were her favorites, and she loved to write compositions. By the time she entered high school she had abandoned her childhood fantasy of foreign missionary work and decided that she wanted to become a newspaper reporter. "I thought it would be an exciting kind of life," she recalls, "a way to write while also earning a living, because if you start out just to be a writer, you can starve to death."

Ira Shick by this time was manager for the Vincennes branch of the L. B. Price Mercantile Company, a firm that sold household goods door-to-door throughout the country. The summer after Ruth's junior year in high school he received a promotion to manage the company's larger office in Terre Haute, sixty-seven miles north of Vincennes, and the family moved again. Ruth, who genuinely liked people and always made friends quickly, soon found herself in the midst of a bustling social life. "A girl named Martha Jane Wheeler immediately became my new 'best friend' in Terre Haute," she says. "She had an older brother named Ralph who began escorting me, and we often double-dated to movies, or played games at each other's houses."

The two girls began their senior year together, but Ira had longed to live in Texas ever since his youth, when he had worked one winter on an uncle's large farm outside of Waco. "As we were growing up, Dad kept talking about how he'd love to go back to Texas. He would even buy us 'hot tamales' from a peddler in Vincennes, of all places!" Barely six months after the move to Terre Haute, Ira found his opportunity and happily accepted a transfer to the Waco branch of L. B. Price, packing up his family and moving them midway through Ruth's senior year.

Waco provided an unexpectedly warm welcome to this newest member of the senior class. To her astonishment Ruth found herself elected at once to the presidency of the civics class. "I was surprised even to be nominated by these nice strangers," she remembers. "It was my first week of school there, but the election was unanimous. That was a true demonstration of southern hospitality."

Ruth's new friends promptly invited her to write for the *Daisy Chain*, Waco High School's award-winning weekly. Her two high schools in Indiana had not published school papers, but her byline articles began to appear regularly all through that spring semester.

She graduated from high school at the age of sixteen, a straight-A student. But the Great Depression was beginning, and even though prestigious Baylor University was located in Waco, not too many local families could afford the high tuition. Her brother Paul was already a Sigma Chi at the University of Kentucky, and, having done so well all through school, Ruth also longed to go on to college, but the prospects were bleak.

She muses about those Depression years: "So many of the very bright boys and girls of that era who graduated when I did were unable to attend college because their fathers had lost their jobs or suffered business reverses. It was such a pity, because college would have changed their whole lives thereafter."

Eager to continue learning, she returned to Waco High School that fall for postgraduate courses, "things that I wanted to know but had not been able to work into my curriculum, such as French, more history, and typing. Having taken extra courses throughout high school in order to graduate in three and a half years—at June graduation ceremonies—I was still younger than most of the seniors, so I felt reasonably comfortable with the class behind me."

Among the courses for which Ruth signed up during the spring term that postgraduate year was public speaking, a subject that she enjoyed after her early years as a child elocutionist. One of the assignments was for each student to interview a prominent businessman of his or her own choosing, and then make a speech about it to the class.

For Ruth Shick that assignment was to change her life.

CHAPTER III

The Newspaper World

For Frank Baldwin, editor of the Waco *News-Tribune,* the four o'clock appointment would provide an amusing diversion. "I need to interview someone for a school assignment," the young female voice had explained over the telephone, "someone prominent in the community. May I come in to see you?"

Recalling her decision to contact Frank Baldwin, Ruth explains: "We were instructed to select someone from a field in which we were interested, and since I wanted to become a newspaper reporter more than anything, it seemed only natural for me to find out who ran the local paper, and then to interview him."

That afternoon Ruth went directly from school to the office of the Waco *News-Tribune,* bid goodbye to the young beau who had accompanied her for the walk, and climbed the dingy steps up from the street to Frank Baldwin's office off the city room.

"He was a small man, and rather feisty," Ruth recalls fondly. "I asked him about himself and the workings of a newspaper, and at the close of the interview, when I was thanking him for his time, he said, 'Are you going to Baylor this fall?' "

"I don't know," Ruth replied hesitantly, not having told him that she was already a postgraduate student in high school.

Baldwin, always abrupt and direct, pressed her further. "Is it money?" he demanded.

"Yes." Ruth's subdued admission embarrassed her.

"Well," he offered, "how would you like to become a reporter here and work your way through Baylor?"

Stars in her eyes, she managed to reply, "I would simply love it!"

Baldwin went on to explain that every four years the *News-Tribune* hired one Baylor student to work for the paper, and the one they'd had was about to graduate. "You can study anything you want to at Baylor except journalism," he warned, "because they always come out of that with highfalutin ideas that they know all about running a newspaper. Now send your father in to see me, and we'll set it up."

"I walked out of there on air," Ruth remembers, "and absolutely floated all the way home. Looking back, I believe a guardian angel must have taken me in hand that day, because Mr. Baldwin didn't even know whether I could write."

As soon as the school term ended, she reported to work at the Waco *News-Tribune* for $12.50 a week, but barely a month later Baldwin summoned her to his office with disturbing news. The Depression had forced the owner of the newspaper to make personnel cuts, and he could not afford to keep her on through the summer.

"I looked at him with panic in my eyes," Ruth recalls. "I asked how I could possibly save the money for my tuition if I couldn't work again until September."

But Frank Baldwin had already figured that cut. "When you register in the fall, just refer the tuition office to me, and you can arrange to pay it as you go along."

Ruth dreaded telling her mother of this setback, but Bertha reacted with loving reassurance. "I'm glad," she said, "because you need a summer to relax and have fun before you start to work."

"And I did have a wonderful summer," Ruth remembers. Popular with boys as well as girls, she never lacked for dates, and there were dances nearly every week. "I was just a happy (although never happy-go-lucky) teenager, who loved to dance and laugh."

Autumn arrived soon enough, and with it an intensely busy schedule. As a Baylor freshman Ruth enrolled only in morning courses so that she was free to work each afternoon. "I would go to classes from eight in the morning until noon, then without a study break I'd cover the speeches at luncheon clubs like the Kiwanis or Lions or Rotary, and return to the *News-Tribune* to write up the story. After that I'd be on general assignment until six in the evening."

Being a female, Ruth was at first expected to handle society reporting, but to her great relief she soon proved herself capable of writing regular news stories and interviewing notable persons who visited Baylor, among them poets Robert Frost and Carl Sandburg.

"Sometimes I would be given an evening assignment as well," she recalls, lamenting her loss of precious study time. "Among others, I remember covering a speech by Norman Thomas, the socialist leader who was always running for President." Following such a late event, she would return to the newspaper office about ten in the evening, write up her story, and only then be able to call it a day. Even so, she managed to keep up with her studies and earn all A's.

By her second year at Baylor Ruth found that money had become even more scarce. All employees at the Waco

News-Tribune had taken several pay cuts, and Ruth's starting salary of $12.50 a week soon fell to $10.80. "I also became a grader for one of the professors in the English Department, at thirty cents an hour," Ruth adds, noting that
her newspaper duties continued to demand six or more
hours of attention each weekday, and all day on Saturday.

The Depression had by now brought student enrollment
so low that Baylor began paying its teachers and graders in
vouchers which could be applied only to housing or tuition.
"Many professors moved into Baylor-owned facilities, and I
was given no money for grading papers, only scrip," Ruth
explains. "It was rather grim for everybody in those days."

During Ruth's third year at Baylor Ira Shick lost his job
when the southern branches of the L. B. Price Company
were forced to cut down their staffs. But by then the Depression, which started in the nation's industrial North and
spread southward, had begun to ease somewhat, farther
north, so Ira found an opening in the company's Louisville,
Kentucky, branch.

This job transfer meant that Ruth's family had to leave
Texas, "but my brother Paul and I stayed on at Baylor and
moved into the separate dormitories for men and women,"
she explains. "Paul was by then in law school there, and also
grading papers for thirty cents an hour, in scrip. We borrowed a little money for his food and cash expenses, and I
had enough with what I was getting from the *News-Tribune*
to pay mine. Then we combined our scrip to pay our dorm
rent and tuition, and with that we managed."

At the end of the school term they rejoined the family in
Louisville, and Ruth immediately applied for a newspaper
job there. By this time she had accumulated a file of news
stories written in Waco, and many of them carried her byline, rare for those days and certainly contrary to Frank
Baldwin's established policy at the *News-Tribune* of "no
bylines, period." The bylines were acquired one summer

while he was on vacation and the news editor was left in charge. "Mr. Baldwin put an immediate stop to it on his return," she says ruefully, "but those bylines helped enormously in getting another job."

To Ruth, who loved the stimulation of newspaper work, and the writing, the job she landed on the staff of the Louisville *Herald-Post* seemed like a miracle in that era of scarce employment. She handled general news reporting and for a period served as women's editor. But the miracle proved short-lived, as the Depression relentlessly continued.

"They reduced the news staff by the last seven who had been hired, because they were in such financial difficulty," Ruth recounts, "and the *Herald-Post* finally folded six months later. I was out of a job."

Determined to pursue this elusive career, Ruth visited her grandmother and aunt in East St. Louis, Illinois, for several months and wrote free-lance articles for the St. Louis *Post-Dispatch*. Then the L. B. Price Company promoted Ira Shick to manager of the branch in Lafayette, Indiana, home of Purdue University, and Ruth moved back with her parents, fervently hoping to finish college at last. The government had newly established a national youth program to assist those trying to go to college, and after enrolling she started work in the publicity department of Purdue at thirty cents an hour. Fortunately the tuition was much lower there than at Baylor.

But more stumbling blocks soon toppled into her path. Ruth's eyes had begun to trouble her, and family finances, stretched to their limit by the continuing Depression, could not cover an expensive eye examination and glasses. "Then at a roller-skating party with girls from the Alpha Chi Omega sorority that I had pledged, I fell and broke my wrist," Ruth adds. "Between my strained eyes and my broken arm in a sling, I couldn't type and keep my job, so I had to drop out of Purdue."

Frustration seemed to pile on frustration. That summer she was hired as a social worker with another government agency, the Federal Emergency Relief Administration, but after only a year of this work, first in Anderson and then in Richmond, Indiana, the program was severely curtailed. Once again out of a job, she returned to live with her parents in Lafayette.

"I went to work as a secretary in a local insurance company, but hated it," Ruth recalls with a grimace. "I thought, 'If I have to be a stenographer for the rest of my life . . .'" Her voice trails off, the frustration that she felt still vivid in her mind.

It was then, however, that tall, handsome Robert H. Montgomery strode into her life. "I had been having a lot of dates with a nice young man from Anderson whom I'd met while a social worker there," Ruth recalls. "One weekend his best friend, Bob Montgomery, who had been his college roommate, came to visit him from Detroit. They picked me up in Lafayette and several of us went for a chaperoned two-day outing at Lake Manitou."

Upon returning home she found her mother all smiles. "Oh, Ruth," Bertha exclaimed, "I don't know what you can see in Jim after meeting Bob Montgomery. I just loved Bob, and he has such beautiful manners!"

Shortly after that weekend Jim suffered a slight injury in an auto accident. Hospitalized, he asked Ruth if she would kindly write to Bob in Detroit and assure him that he was recovering nicely. Bob's reply to her letter arrived by return mail, with the teasing comment: "I've highly recommended you to Jim. Do you have a sister just like you?" Their correspondence continued, and led shortly to an invitation from Bob's older sister, Rhoda Montgomery, a school principal, to visit them in Detroit.

"I thought, '*What* an opportunity to have a free place to stay while trying to get a job on a newspaper again!'" Ruth

smiles impishly in remembrance. "I immediately telephoned a news vendor who handled out-of-town papers
and asked if he could give me the names of any Detroit
newspapers."

The man on the other end of the line thought for a moment and replied, "Well, offhand there's the Detroit
Times . . ."

"Okay, thanks." Ruth couldn't wait for him to think of
more; one name would be enough. Having no street address
for the paper, she fired off a letter to "Managing Editor,
Detroit Times, Detroit, Michigan," describing her newspaper experience and expressing her wish to return to the
field.

"A crazy, delightful letter came back!" she chuckles. "It
was from a Mr. Ed Lapping, who was the city editor: 'Can
you climb through an upper window to steal a photograph
of somebody who doesn't want his picture published? Can
you force your way through a battling crowd to get an
interview we need for the news?' It went on at length in
that vein."

Intrigued, Ruth wrote back that since she weighed only
ninety-five pounds, she doubted if she could force her way
through a maddened crowd. And as for climbing through
an upstairs window to steal a picture: "No, I wouldn't do
that, but there are other more tactful ways to get stories,
and I'm sure that I can do it that way."

Ed Lapping must have found her response equally intriguing, because he replied, "Well, come in and see me
when you're up here and we'll talk about it."

Having arranged this much, Ruth happily accepted
Rhoda's invitation for the following weekend. The overnight train to Detroit arrived at eight on a muggy Saturday
morning. "It was an excursion rate, and not a sleeper, so I
sat up all night," Ruth explains. Bob met her train and
escorted her to the beautiful breakfast room of the Book

Cadillac Hotel. "I was very impressed," she admits. "Bob was *such* a good-looking young guy, and I'd never seen such a glamorous dining room."

"What would you like to do today?" Bob asked over breakfast, and named several possibilities.

Ruth came right to the point. "I'd like to go to the Detroit *Times*, because I have a job interview with Ed Lapping."

"Ed Lapping? My brother Burke works for the *Times*. How do you know Ed Lapping?" Bob exclaimed, and listened in amusement while Ruth recounted her wacky correspondence with this curious stranger. "Okay, fine. I'll wait for you at my brother's desk. He's off on Saturdays."

The Detroit *Times* bustled with activity that August morning. An afternoon paper, its most hectic hours took up the first half of each day, and Ruth remembers the scene with nostalgic amusement: "Ed Lapping was seated at the city desk, with reporters swarming around. After Bob pointed him out, I walked over to him and said, 'I'm Ruth Shick.' He turned in his swivel chair and slowly looked me up and down. Finally he said, 'You look like Norma Shearer. Wait a minute.' "

Lapping finished the copy that he was editing, then stood up and said, "Come with me."

"He was a very tall, white-haired Norwegian," Ruth recalls. "Hollywood would have cast him as a Viking ship captain."

Leading the way to his office, a glassed-in corner overlooking the big city room, Ed Lapping began asking questions; then, reasonably satisfied with the preliminaries, he escorted Ruth to a desk.

"Here's a story you can work on by telephone, because you don't know the city yet," he directed, relating the simple background facts. "Make some calls, get all the information, write the story, and bring it to me."

"So I made the calls, typed out my story, and presented it

to Lapping," Ruth recounts. "He looked it over, said, 'Okay, fine,' and immediately handed me another assignment. I went back to the desk, made more calls, did the interviews by phone, and wrote up this second story."

"Fine," Lapping commented. "Now here's another one."

"Mr. Lapping," Ruth interrupted softly, "how long do you think I'll be?"

"Why? What are you doing?" he barked.

"Well," Ruth began, "Bob Montgomery is waiting over there for me, and if I'm going to be much longer, I'd better tell him."

"*How* do you know the Montgomerys?" Lapping was startled.

Ruth, who never traded on influence with anybody, made it plain that this case was no exception. "I came up to visit Bob and his sister," she explained. "I didn't know until this morning that he has a brother working here."

"Oh, I didn't realize that somebody was waiting for you," Lapping replied. "Well, all right, when can you start to work?"

Delighted, Ruth assured him that two weeks' notice to her present employer in Indiana would cover her obligations there. "All right, then," he agreed. "I'll see you two weeks from Monday. Be here at eight o'clock—sharp."

Glowing with anticipation of the new job, Ruth enjoyed the remainder of her first visit to Detroit, returned home on Sunday's overnight train, gave notice to her employer Monday morning, and then broke the news to her parents.

"Mother probably would have been aghast at my going off to live in a big city all alone if she hadn't already fallen in love with Bob," Ruth says with a laugh. "My parents were delighted about my career opportunity."

Ruth owned a car in those days, a dilapidated Model A Ford which she had needed for home visits as a social worker in Anderson and Richmond. It was a one-seater, not a sedan, and toadstools kept growing out of the wooden frame on the rear ledge. "I had bought it in installments out of my $110-a-month salary, and it had cost $100," Ruth remembers in amusement.

Ira Shick insisted that his daughter get her "jalopy" checked over thoroughly before the solo journey, and the outcome was not propitious. "It has a cracked head," the mechanic announced. "It could give out on you today, tomorrow, next week, or who knows?" Ruth, having absolutely no idea what a cracked head meant, reported the news to her father.

"So what are you going to do?" Ira asked.

Without a moment's hesitation, she announced with a grin, "I'm going to drive it to Detroit."

On a fine Saturday morning in early September, Ruth loaded her few clothes, suitcases, and books into the crazy little car, embraced her parents one last time, pulled out the choke, and started the motor. They stood outside waving goodbye, and as the Model A disappeared around the corner, Ira paid his ultimate compliment: "Bertha, our gal sure has guts!"

For the first few days in Detroit Ruth stayed with Bob's mother and sister until she found a lovely room on La Salle Boulevard. "A widow who had a beautiful home rented rooms to a few young career women," Ruth explains. "It was perfect; I was lucky to find something so nice right away."

Meanwhile Ed Lapping at the Detroit *Times* was putting Ruth through her paces, sending her off through heavy city traffic in her rattling little car to capture urgent interviews or cover a breaking news story. But her most memorable scoop surprised even Lapping.

Word had filtered out that Doris Duke, then the wealthiest girl in the world and heiress to the great Duke tobacco fortune, had arrived in Detroit with her new husband,

Jimmy Cromwell. The couple, still honeymooning, had checked into a suite at the Book Cadillac Hotel, and Ed Lapping sent Ruth over for an interview.

"I thought this was a thrilling assignment!" Ruth laughs. "I was so naive that I didn't know Doris Duke had never given an interview in her life. Lapping had probably sent me as a joke."

Telephoning upstairs from the hotel's lobby, Ruth reached Doris Duke and politely asked if she might come upstairs for an interview. "You know I never give interviews!" Doris exclaimed caustically, and slammed down the receiver.

"I was pretty upset," Ruth remembers. "I still regarded it as my first big break, and was not about to admit defeat." Determined to complete her assignment, she headed upstairs and knocked on the door. No one answered. "So I just waited there, hoping that something would happen."

After about twenty minutes a waiter came down the hall bearing a massive serving tray with breakfast intended for the Cromwells' suite. The man stopped at the door, knocked, called "Breakfast," and the door swung open at once.

Seizing this sudden opportunity, Ruth squatted beneath the enormous tray and followed him through the door. "We went in, and they were seated at a table in the middle of this huge drawing room of the suite, Doris Duke bundled up in a full-length mink coat and galoshes, with massive curlers in her hair. She must have been used to more heat. I walked over to their table and identified myself."

Doris and Jimmy greeted the brash intruder with stunned silence, then began eating. The young reporter stood her ground.

"Can't we have breakfast in peace?" Doris finally demanded.

"Oh yes, I'm sorry," Ruth replied and took a seat on a sofa

across the vast room. The honeymooners continued eating, until Ruth, in a meek, small voice, broke the heavy silence. "Can't I say *anything?*"

Doris burst out laughing, and between bites said, "Sure, what do you want to know?" Ruth obtained her interview, a warm and friendly exchange about the specially ordered Cadillac with brass trim instead of chrome that they had come to pick up, and about the movie they had gone to see the evening before. Ruth then thanked them and sped back to the Detroit *Times* to write her story.

Ed Lapping, anxious to enjoy his own joke, greeted Ruth with a broad grin and waited to hear all about what he was sure had been a wild goose chase. Instead, she began talking about her interview.

"What!" Lapping exclaimed. *"Stop the presses!* Remake page one. Ruth, start writing," and as each sentence appeared on her typewriter, Lapping would pull it out for the printer. The eight-column front-page headline shortly thereafter announced: "Doris Duke Gives First Interview Here."

"Many years later," Ruth recalls with a laugh, "I was to run into both Doris and Jimmy, after their divorce, at separate parties in California and Washington. Each of them had a marvelous sense of humor, and thereafter we all enjoyed retelling the story of how I had slipped into their honeymoon suite behind the waiter. We became lifelong friends."

Throughout that autumn in Detroit Ruth dated Bob Montgomery as well as some news reporters, and Bob began suggesting marriage. "No, I'm not ready to think of marriage," Ruth would counter, realizing only too well that young ladies who married often lost their jobs. Employment remained so scarce that one job per household was deemed sufficient in an era when families had to scrape just to survive. Still, Bob continued to raise the subject.

Ruth's first Christmas in Detroit approached, and she

longed to return to her family in Lafayette for a holiday
visit. By this time Ed Lapping had grown quite pleased with
her work, especially after her coup with the elusive Doris
Duke, and he gave her an extra day off for the weekend trip.
Bob borrowed his sister Rhoda's new Hupmobile and set
out with Ruth for the all-day drive south to her parents'
home.

The town of Angola, county seat of Steuben County, Indiana, had earned a reputation as a Gretna Green, since it was
located just across the state line, and unlike Michigan it
required no five-day waiting period for marriages. Coinci-
dentally Angola lay along the direct route from Detroit to
Lafayette, and Bob Montgomery, without prior announcement, pulled the Hupmobile to a stop and shut off the motor
in front of the Steuben County Courthouse Removing the
ignition key, he turned to Ruth. "All right, let's go in and get
married."

"Oh no, Bob," Ruth protested, as she had so many times
before. "I'm really not ready. Besides, you've only met my
mother once. You don't know the rest of my family, and
they don't know you, and we don't even know whether
you'll like each other."

"All right," Bob said with resignation, starting the motor,
and they continued the drive south.

Christmas in Lafayette turned out to be a joyous family
reunion, with Ruth's brother Paul and his wife and first
child there, as well as Ruth's sister Margaret, to share the
holiday with Bertha and Ira. But a massive snowstorm
swept through the Midwest late on Christmas Eve. Roads to
the north lay blocked, and Paul, who started home early
Christmas Day, phoned to warn Ruth and Bob not to attempt a drive north to Detroit until the storm had passed.
With no other alternative, Ruth dispatched a "snowbound"
telegram to Ed Lapping, explaining that she would arrive

back at work a day late, and she and Bob set out in the
Hupmobile early the next morning.

Snow lay everywhere, piled high along the roadways, but
since it was December 26, the shops and offices had reopened after being closed for Christmas. Also open for business was the Steuben County Courthouse in Angola, and
again Bob pulled the car to a stop squarely in front of it, shut
off the motor, and turned to Ruth.

"I met your family," he began. ' I liked them, and they
liked me. Now let's get married."

Again Ruth protested.

"Come on," he said. "That was why you said you wouldn't
get married on the way down. Now you've no excuse."

Ruth paused, considered the matter, and finally reached
for her boots. "Well, wait till I zip up my galoshes" was her
unromantic response to the proposal.

Looking back on the day of her marriage to Bob Montgomery, Ruth laughingly claims that fate has always seemed
to move her to where life intended her to be. "Without that
blizzard we would have driven through Angola on Christmas Day, and the courthouse would have been closed. Who
knows when I would ever have had the courage otherwise
to say yes?"

But Ed Lapping had once threatened to fire Ruth if she
married. The elopement definitely had to be kept secret, at
least until the newlyweds could figure out how to break it to
him. "We arrived in Detroit about dark," Ruth recounts,
and had dinner together in a favorite restaurant. Then Bob
dropped me off at the house where I was staying, and he
went on home. The next morning we both reported to work
as usual."

That weekend, on the pretext of visiting friends, the new
Mr. and Mrs. Montgomery took off for Toledo, stayed at a
hotel together for the first time, and afterward returned to
their respective homes. They double-dated on New Year's

Eve, at a country club dinner-dance with friends, and Bob again dropped Ruth off on his way home. The following weekend, with another manufactured excuse, they motored off to Pontiac. But as the third weekend approached, Bob exclaimed, "This is ridiculous. Let's announce it. We can't keep taking off for weekends." It was a major decision, but Ruth, after insisting that her mother must be the first to know, went to a public phone booth and called Lafayette. "Oh, Ruth, I'm so relieved!" Bertha exclaimed after hearing the news. "I've been so worried about you alone in that big city, and Bob is such a wonderful man! You couldn't have pleased me more. I'm so happy about it."

Now to tell Lapping, before he heard the news from someone else! Realizing that she would be putting her job on the line regardless of how she handled the announcement, Ruth took a roundabout approach. "May I have Saturday off?" she asked. "I'm going to be married this weekend."

Shocked, Lapping began pacing up and down the big city room, loudly snapping his fingers as he always did when deep in thought. "He was exactly like a Viking sea captain pacing the deck of his ship," Ruth recalls with a giggle. Finally he strode back to where she waited. "I'll let you get married on one condition," he thundered.

"Yes, sir."

"Before you get your mind filled with all these romantic notions of marriage, you'll have to promise me that you will go across the street to that bookstore and buy a book called *What Every Woman Should Know,* and read it all through tonight."

"Gladly," Ruth replied. "I promise you I'll do it."

"Now when are you getting married?" Lapping continued.

"Tomorrow about three o'clock in the afternoon," Ruth

fibbed, hoping he would think that she and Bob were driving to Lafayette for the wedding.

"All right," Lapping finally agreed. "I give my permission."

Ruth bought the book and read it. But instead of going to Lafayette, she and Bob spent Saturday looking for a furnished apartment. Later, other reporters at the Detroit *Times* recounted strange behavior on the part of Ed Lapping that afternoon. He continued to watch the clock; they didn't know why. And at the hour of three he suddenly announced, "Well, Miss Ruth is getting married just about now." It was obviously on his mind.

While marriage agreed with Ruth, she readily admits that cooking and housework did not. Having begun work at the age of seventeen, after memorizing "pieces" throughout her childhood, she had never learned to cook. "I had no idea whether canned vegetables had been precooked, or what you did with them, and, needless to say, I knew nothing about preparing meat," she confesses.

Since her own family lived hundreds of miles away, and she certainly did not want her new in-laws to learn of her total lack of culinary skill, she turned to the next available source. "When Bob and I would go to the grocery, I'd send him down the aisles to pick up canned goods while I'd slip over to the butcher, flash him a winsome smile, and say, 'You know, there are so many different ways to cook this particular meat. How do you think is the *best* way?' Then I'd listen avidly and go home and cook it that way." Ruth laughs. "I didn't even know about cookbooks. Lapping should have told me about that!"

Ruth's husband, Robert H. Montgomery, a management engineer for Ternstedt, a division of General Motors, was the youngest of seven children of a Methodist minister who died before Ruth knew the family. "Bob is a direct descendant of Richard Warren, who arrived in America on the

Mayflower in 1620 and was the twelfth signer of the Mayflower Compact," Ruth recounts, noting that both Franklin Delano Roosevelt and Winston Churchill also descended from Richard Warren. Bob had graduated with a Bachelor of Science degree from Greenville College in Illinois, then spent four years studying engineering at General Motors Institute, GM's training college for young executives. At the time of their marriage he was earning forty dollars a week, and Ruth twenty-five, although raises followed.

In addition to keeping house and learning to cook, Ruth continued her hectic days at the Detroit *Times*, driving her battered Model A Ford all over town to murders and other assorted tragedies. One of her most memorable assignments was posing as a member of the women's auxiliary of the infamous Black Legion to learn what she could of the inside operations of the extremist organization. She it was who established the identity of one of its murdered members, and broke the news to his young widow who was hospitalized for childbirth—an exploit that was later dramatized on a national radio network and won her the Pall Mall Journalism Award. Another time she posed as a policewoman to tell a woman that her husband had just committed suicide after being exposed for embezzling funds.

"I had begun to hate it," Ruth confesses. "The Detroit *Times* was a Hearst paper, and very flamboyant. Its circulation depended on human tragedies, and I disliked my role of invading other people's privacy. It was a matter of personal integrity. If this was all that newspaper reporting had to offer, I felt that I had made a mistake in my chosen career."

Because she was so thin and lacking in energy, her doctor advised that she give up working for a while, and she resigned from the *Times*. "Bob thought that if we built a house it would make me more contented with staying at home."

She smiles in reminiscence. "We found a nice lot, hired a contractor, and eventually moved into a red-brick, two-story, three-bedroom house that cost the to-us-impressive sum of six thousand dollars, financed by a home loan. It was fun settling in and arranging the furniture, but as soon as the last pictures were hung, I was so bored that I went down to the Detroit *News*, a much more prestigious paper, and happily became a reporter again, with more dignified assignments."

Her bylines regularly appeared in the *News* for the next several years, until the kind of job that Bob had always wanted suddenly opened for him. He became a management consultant with the New York-based firm of Stevenson, Jordan and Harrison, and as defense contracts began pouring in, his assignments required frequent moves to various parts of the country. With their house and furniture sold, Ruth and Bob lived out of suitcases in a succession of furnished apartments from New York to Alabama, never staying in one place long enough for her to approach a newspaper editor, although she managed to sell some magazine articles.

"By now World War II was raging," Ruth recalls, "and when Bob's fifth move took us to Chicago, I knew that I simply had to get back into the newspaper business. What an opportunity! A big city with four papers, and male reporters being drafted! Armed with scrapbooks full of my bylines, I applied to managing editor Don Maxwell at the Chicago *Tribune*, and was hired that same day for sixty-five dollars a week. I thought it was a fortune!"

Happily back in her own element, Ruth's front-page bylines appeared with regularity on stories about court trials, war developments, and politicians. She interviewed visiting VIPs from Washington and abroad, and after covering a Chicago press conference conducted by Congresswoman Clare Boothe Luce, she learned that Mrs. Luce had called the paper the next day to say that Ruth's was the only accurate account of her remarks.

The war meanwhile continued unabated, and in 1943 Bob Montgomery accepted a commission with the Navy as a lieutenant jg. Proudly practicing his salutes before a mirror, he announced that he didn't want *his* wife to become a camp follower, and reported for his first "hardship post" in Williamsburg, Virginia. As a management engineer he was assigned to the Navy's Bureau of Ordnance, and since he heard no shots fired in anger, the novelty of wearing a uniform rapidly wore off. Soon he was urging Ruth to abandon the *Tribune* and join him at the stately Williamsburg Inn, where he and some other navy officers were quartered. But Ruth mischievously replied that she was no camp fol- lower, and merrily pursued her career. One day the *Tribune* assigned her to cover a murder trial in Grand Rapids, Michigan, and since she would be out of town for several days, she duly telegraphed that fact to Bob. He meanwhile had been transferred to a different location, missed Ruth's message, and tried nearly all that night to reach her by telephone at her Chicago apartment. That proved to be the last straw. He now demanded that she give up her "silly career" and join him in Washington, D.C., where he was now stationed.

Ruth was willing, provided she could keep on working, but the elderly gentleman who headed the Chicago *Tribune*'s Washington bureau had long refused to permit women in his jealously guarded bailiwick. She therefore wrote to Richard Clarke, editor in chief of the *Tribune*'s jointly owned sister paper, the New York *Daily News*, to inquire about possibilities in its Washington bureau.

Two days later, returning from a local assignment, she was handed a teletype message from John O'Donnell, Washington bureau chief for the *Daily News.* "How much and when can you start?" it asked succinctly.

The most exciting days of her long newspaper career were about to begin.

CHAPTER IV

Washington Career

The pace was frenetic in the wartime capital of the free world that June of 1944 when Ruth Montgomery launched her new career as a Washington correspondent. During her first week she had explored the venerable halls of Congress and covered several Senate debates.

Now, scarcely a week after taking over her desk in the Washington Bureau of the New York *Daily News*—a paper with the largest circulation in America—she was sallying forth to the White House, eagerly clutching her newly issued Secret Service identification card. Passing through the portals of the gracious old mansion, she joined a cluster of other newswomen who were assembling in the Green Room.

"I was all eyes," Ruth remembers with a grin. "I had never before been in the White House, even for a public tour, and now we were about to invade the sacrosanct family quarters on the floor above the public rooms." Promptly at 11 A.M. the signal came, and the "ladies of the press" trooped up the broad staircase to the Monroe Treaty Room, taking their seats decorously. In another moment Eleanor Roosevelt swept into the room, trailed by her social and personal secretaries.

"Hello, hello, hello," the First Lady fluted in her high-pitched voice, extending limp fingers for quick hand touches with each of the assembled journalists before settling down to announce her hectic schedule. Then the questions began to fly, and Eleanor Roosevelt answered them quickly, although some of her weekly news conference responses inevitably caused the President's male assistants to squirm when they read them in the press.

Ruth readily admits to being thrilled at the novelty that day, but her exhilaration was even greater a short time later when she found herself tightly wedged amid a gaggle of perspiring newsmen in the presidential office. Franklin Delano Roosevelt customarily met reporters twice weekly around his gadget-littered desk, behind which he remained seated while they shoved and jockeyed for standing position as close to him as possible.

"The President obviously enjoyed the lively give-and-take of these press conferences," Ruth reminisces. "And the press liked them, too, since they provided an open sesame to front-page bylines. But at my first one I could scarcely concentrate on his words for pinching myself. There sat the President of the United States, grinning roguishly as he emphasized a point with a jab of his long cigarette holder, and here was I—lowly Ruth Shick from Sumner, Illinois—squashed between the top newspaper men of America for history in the making. His utterances about the raging war on two fronts would make tomorrow's headlines around the globe. Was it true that I was actually there?"

One of only a handful of women reporters assigned to cover "hard news" in Washington during that era, she soon became a regular at President Roosevelt's news conferences. Most of her feminine colleagues in the press corps were consigned to covering women's affairs or regional news, but Ruth quickly proved herself capable of handling the top stories of national and international importance, and because she could write so rapidly and accurately, her editors at the *Daily News* soon realized that if an urgent story needed hurried handling for an early deadline it should be assigned to Ruth.

In addition to the White House conferences, she covered major stories on Capitol Hill, at the State Department, and on Embassy Row, as well as interviews with such visiting wartime celebrities as General Charles de Gaulle. It was a far cry from Sumner, or even from Chicago.

Within eight months of her arrival in Washington she was elected by her colleagues to head Mrs. Roosevelt's all-woman White House Press Conference Association, and the First Lady had her to tea. But events in the nation's capital were moving quickly. While the Battle of the Bulge was still claiming enormous casualties, Ruth attended FDR's press conference at which he announced "off the record" that he would meet with Joseph Stalin and Winston Churchill at the Russian port of Yalta.

On his return from that historic conference in February of 1945, Ruth covered his address to a joint session of Congress, and subsequently his press conference at which she noted a dramatic loss in his vitality. That evening she wrote to her parents: "The President looks so gray and drawn that he resembles an old, old woman more than a man." Viewing him at arm's length across his White House desk, she could observe his waxen skin and translucent complexion.

The Allies crossed the Rhine, and the war news began to improve, but Roosevelt's health did not. He went to Warm Springs, Georgia, for a working vacation, with press coverage limited to three men from the news services. On April 12 Ruth was preparing to leave her office in the National Press Building for the day when she heard the ominous three-bell alert of the United Press ticker that signaled an important bulletin. The announcement read: "Roosevelt is dead."

At the direction of news editor Ted Lewis, Ruth dashed off to the White House to cover the press briefing and the private swearing in of Harry S. Truman as President. The next morning reporters regrouped to be briefed on funeral arrangements, and learned that because dignitaries would be arriving from all over the world to attend the solemn ceremony in the White House East Room, news coverage would have to be pooled. Space could be spared for only ten reporters, and one could be a woman.

Board members of Mrs. Roosevelt's Press Conference Association, quickly polled by telephone, agreed that Ruth should cover the event for them, and on the morning of April 14, 1945, she slipped through the throng of silent mourners massed outside the White House to join her nine male colleagues in the flower-bedecked East Room for the twenty-three-minute funeral rite. Immediately afterward she and her fellow reporters met the crowd of newsmen gathered in the West Lobby to brief them on the services before leaving to write their own stories.

The transition from Roosevelt to Truman brought a distinct change in presidential press conferences. "Gone were the long cigarette holder and the jocular fencing with the press," Ruth recalls. "Gone also were the hour-long waits in an exhausting queue outside the Oval Office until FDR decided that he was ready to meet the press. Harry Truman was invariably prompt, and while standing rather than sitting behind the presidential desk he used his two hands like meat choppers to emphasize his points. His trigger-quick replies challenged our racing pencils. They also caused some shattering reactions abroad until his advisors cautioned him to give more thoughtful responses."

The war in Europe ended in May 1945, and with Japan

that August, and gradually travel restrictions were lifted, opening the door for press junkets to other parts of the globe. One of the first such excursions inaugurated Pan American World Airways' direct-flight service to Buenos Aires, and for the initial flight thirty top editors and news correspondents from Washington and New York were invited along on the journey below the equator. Ruth had never before traveled abroad, and with heady anticipation she secured her first passport to join fellow reporters, all of whom were men except for New York columnist Inez Robb.

Their "direct" flight took three days, delayed by frequent refueling stops and interminable red tape before being permitted to land in the Argentine capital. At a welcoming reception hosted by the Foreign Minister that evening, Eugenio de Sosa, a Cuban newspaper publisher who was President Juan Perón's best friend, expansively asked Ruth what he could do to make her stay more pleasant. Inasmuch as Inez Robb had already served notice that it was "every man for himself" on the news front while in Buenos Aires. Ruth demurely replied that she would like to have an exclusive interview with President Perón.

"But the great President *never* grants exclusive interviews," he gasped. "Besides, he thinks a woman's place is in the home."

Ruth smilingly persisted, and the courtly Latino finally suggested that perhaps if she wrote out some questions, he could obtain written replies for her. That was better than nothing, so she agreed to bring them to the press conference that Perón had scheduled the next day for the visiting press group.

Still polishing her questions, Ruth arrived at the Casa Rosada a few minutes after her compatriots, who were already occupying the best seats at the enormous conference table. She tried to slip unobtrusively into a chair near the end of the table, but De Sosa was watching for her. As soon as he glimpsed Ruth, he whispered to Perón, who beckoned an aide to escort her to the head of the table. As cameras clicked, he arose, bowed, and gallantly kissed her hand. Then he directed that a chair be placed for her in the seat of honor on his right, and an existing photograph of the encounter clearly reflects the look of bafflement on the faces of her colleagues.

That evening, while her fellow reporters set out to enjoy an evening on the town, Ruth opted to turn in early, and was just dozing off when the telephone rang. It was De Sosa, who had apparently done his spade work well. First swearing her to secrecy, he said, "Miss Montgomery, the President was very, very impressed with you and your questions. He has decided that if you will not tell anyone else, he will send his car for you tomorrow morning at nine for an interview."

"The next morning I dressed in the darkened bedroom to avoid awakening Inez, who was my roommate," Ruth recalls impishly. "I breakfasted downstairs, and promptly at nine the bulletproof presidential limousine drew up in front of the hotel, to the terror of a gabby desk clerk who had occupied my waiting time by criticizing Evita Perón."

It was Perón's first exclusive interview as President, and with De Sosa serving as translator he expressed his hatred of communism, his detestation of former Ambassador Spruille Braden, and his firm promise to enlist on the U.S. side if we again went to war. This was real news, since Argentina had refused to back the United States in the world war that had so recently ended. "But Miss Montgomery," Perón added chivalrously, "if all *norteamericanos* were like you, there would be no misunderstandings between our two continents."

As soon as the hour-long interview concluded, Ruth stopped at the cable office to write and file her dispatch before quietly joining her unsuspecting colleagues for lunch. "The next morning we departed," Ruth recalls, "and as our plane landed in Rio de Janeiro, Brazil, I was startled to learn that the interview had made front-page headlines throughout South America."

This was by no means the last time that Ruth's reporting would cause an international sensation. Early in January 1947 Eugenio de Sosa telephoned her again, this time from New York, with a cryptic proposal that she fly with him to Havana to cover a "big story." Again she was sworn to secrecy before he confided that a Cuban revolution was imminent and that he was helping to direct and finance it. "I want you to be there to ensure 'fair' coverage," he explained. Pressed for details, he finally whispered that the object was to depose President Ramón Grau San Martín and that invasion ships would be sailing within a week for Havana.

Intrigued, Ruth secured permission from her editors at the New York *Daily News*, and then met De Sosa at LaGuardia Airport for the takeoff. During the long flight the Cuban publisher cautioned Ruth not to "recognize" him at the Havana airport, and on landing she found her own way by taxi to the Hotel Nacional.

"There I waited—and waited," she recalls. "I had been directed not to contact De Sosa, but each day one of his mysterious aides would bring messages to me at the hotel swimming pool. By now I had learned the reason for the planned coup d'état: Grau was strongly backed by the Communist Party. The conservatives feared that he would defy the one-term constitutional limitation on presidential terms, to seek reelection and then turn Cuba Red."

A bit ruefully Ruth observes that basking beside a beautiful swimming pool in January was not an unpleasant way to earn a living, but as a newspaper reporter she yearned for more action. At last she proposed to De Sosa's aide that she seek an interview with President Grau, and when he warmly welcomed the suggestion, she sent off a telegram.

"Grau's answer was surprisingly prompt," she remembers. "I was invited that same evening to the presidential palace for an interview. But unfortunately my eyelids by then had swollen almost shut from the tropical sun at the pool. I telephoned to request a one-day reprieve, while a Cuban doctor treated my eyes. The next evening, wearing dark glasses to hide the swelling, I kept my appointment."

During the lengthy interview Grau spoke of a possible revolution and led her to the broad windows of his office, which overlooked the plaza and beautiful harbor. With a sweeping gesture he demonstrated how easily planes could "swoop down this mall" to destroy him, and since Ruth knew the plans better than he could, she fervently hoped that invading forces would not strike while she was there.

Then she posed her big question. Aware that Grau himself was the principal author of the constitution that forbade a second term, she asked whether he planned to run anyway, as some of his critics suspected. His answer was to capture eight-column banner headlines in all Cuban newspapers for a week to come: "I will not seek reelection next year on one condition; that is, if Batista or any of the old political crowd does not seek a comeback." Since everyone was aware that former President Fulgencio Batista intended to "seek a comeback," Ruth realized instantly that this statement amounted to an intent to defy the constitution.

As soon as she could gracefully conclude the interview, she raced to the cable office, borrowed a typewriter, and sent off her dispatch to New York. By the next day United Press had circulated her bylined account throughout Cuba and South America, and the lobby of the Hotel Nacional was jammed with reporters and photographers, bombarding her with questions and snapping endless pictures. Havana newspapers ran lengthy feature articles highlighting her entire career; politicians and educators sought her attention for interviews, speeches, and dinners in her honor; a Cuban senator interviewed her on radio; and *Time* and *Newsweek* magazines led their press sections with long articles about her startling scoop. In a single session she had managed to capture a story that had eluded Cuban journalists for months, and everyone was gleeful except the left-wingers.

But perhaps the most significant outcome of this entire adventure was that Ruth, by reporting the truth, had prevented a revolution. "We've called it off," a beaming De Sosa explained to her. "We don't need to have it now. You've smoked out Grau's real intention, and now that people know, they will prevent it." They did indeed, and to Ruth's amazement she later received an autographed photograph from Grau, with a warm letter of congratulation.

There are a couple of interesting sidelights on Ruth's love-hate affair with Cuban heads of state. In March 1952, as the only woman in the press entourage accompanying President Truman to Key West for his work-and-play vacation, she had no sooner daubed herself with suntan oil than a telegram arrived from her New York editors: "Revolution broken out in Cuba. All incoming planes and ships being turned back from island, but get there anyway."

Playfully wiring back that she was swimming across, she managed to secure passage on a rickety Cuban plane that landed uneventfully in Havana. There she covered the coup d'état by which General Batista deposed President Carlos Prío Socarrás, Grau's elected successor, and proclaimed himself dictator.

But Batista's luck also turned. Amid mounting pressure against his corrupt regime, he fled the country January 1, 1959, and Fidel Castro with his rebel band seized power. Because of Ruth's superb sources, she immediately began informing her readers that Castro was a Communist. "Not so," CIA director Allen Dulles declared to her in an exclusive interview. "Ruth, I can tell you flatly that Fidel Castro is not a Communist. A liberal, yes, but not a Red."

"Allen Dulles was a good friend of mine," Ruth muses, "but I refused to believe him on that one. I had excellent sources that I had learned to trust, so I continued in my columns to sound the alarm throughout that spring and summer of 1959." Events soon proved her correct. The crisis in Cuba deepened as industries were nationalized and the way opened for Soviet, Communist Chinese, and Czechoslovakian penetration. Cuba was unquestionably Red.

Several years later, at a top CIA strategy meeting, Allen Dulles lamented, "If only we'd known before that Castro was a Communist!"

"Ruth Montgomery knew it," replied Colonel Stanley Grogan, a high-ranking CIA official. Reaching for his briefcase, he pulled out a complete file of her articles on Castro and slapped them on the conference table.

Ruth's continuing quest for truth sometimes brought more personal results. On invitation from the government of Egypt in 1953, she flew to Cairo as one of sixty or so top reporters from all over the world to cover the first anniversary of the ouster of King Farouk by a military junta. "It was my second trip to Egypt," Ruth recalls. "The year before I had met and been entertained there by Prince Abbas Halim, a cousin of King Farouk who was also the former husband of a Washington friend, Princess Tawhida Rediker. I had attended the debuts of their two daughters in Washington, and both girls were then visiting their father in Cairo."

Meanwhile Prince Abbas had been jailed by the military junta as a "political prisoner" for organizing Arab workmen and leading their fight for shorter hours with more pay.

Princess Tawhida, aware of Ruth's upcoming press trip, asked if she would try to get a message to her former spouse that she and their daughters were "pulling" for him.

At the start of Ruth's second, week-long visit President Mohammed Naguib, Colonel Gamal Abdel Nasser, Colonel Anwar Sadat and several other members of the junta conducted a joint press conference to extol the merits of the new regime. Throughout the crowded session Naguib calmly and skillfully handled inquiries from this assemblage of the world's most accomplished journalists, until Ruth stood up and asked politely, "Mr. President, when will your government be secure enough that you can release your political prisoners?"

Instantly there was stunned silence. Naguib turned to Nasser on his right, and to the other colonels on his left. Then they all went into an anxious huddle. It was the first time that the President had even hesitated in answering a question, but he finally responded: "There are two hundred of them, all agents of foreign powers."

Ruth remained dissatisfied. "Is Abbas Halim an agent of a foreign power?" she pressed.

Again there was hasty consultation before Naguib eventually replied, "Abbas and three others, no. All the rest, yes."

The next day Ruth and her fellow journalists boarded a special train that would carry President Naguib, other dignitaries, and members of the foreign press down the Nile to inaugurate Egypt's first massive land redistribution program. Cheering Arabs thronged the station, and the train was barely underway before an Egyptian official sought Ruth out to announce that the President would like to have her join him in his presidential car. Startled, she asked if he were sure that he had found the right person, and received an affirmative reply.

Bidding goodbye to her colleagues, she followed him

through several cars full of inquisitive journalists. "They were no doubt as mystified as I was by my summons," Ruth says with a shrug. "When we reached the private car, Naguib arose, bowed, and indicated that I was to sit beside him. He was a charming, grandfatherly type who spoke excellent English, and since I had been in Egypt during King Farouk's reign, we had a lot to talk about."

The conversation proved so affable that at last Ruth dared to ask once again, "Mr. President, what about Abbas Halim? When *do* you think your government will be stable enough to free its political prisoners, such as Halim?"

"Oh, Miss Montgomery," he exclaimed, "Abbas is a troublemaker! For the year since he's been in jail we've had no strikes. When Abbas is out, we have strikes."

Ruth chided him gently. "In America we have strikes, too, but we don't jail the leaders or the strikers. We feel that they have a right to strike for better hours and wages if no violence is involved. I doubt that Abbas is a violent man."

Naguib stared straight ahead for a time, frowning as he weighed his options. Finally he turned back to Ruth, and, smiling broadly, declared: "Miss Montgomery, for *you* I will do it. I will let him out." The following week, after the world's journalists had departed, Prince Abbas was indeed freed. His Washington family was jubilant, and the prince wrote Ruth a warm letter of appreciation.

"But what I did not learn until I talked to him again, years later in Egypt," Ruth chuckles, "was that the vast estate Naguib was giving away to the peasants that day had been expropriated from Abbas Halim."

Throughout those Washington years Ruth was also covering the headlined stories of the day: the treason and espionage trials of Axis Sally and Judith Coplon, the conversion from a wartime to a peacetime economy, the raucous McCarthy hearings on Capitol Hill, and the visits of Winston

Churchill, Princess Elizabeth and Prince Philip, Lady Astor, and other world celebrities.

"I sometimes felt guilty at being paid for this privilege of occupying front-row seats at the greatest shows on earth," Ruth confesses with a nostalgic smile.

She was also foraging far and wide in search of news. Frequently traveling abroad, she had toured occupied postwar Europe, picked her way through the ruins of German cities, and flown in a coal plane in the Berlin airlift at ceiling zero, "clutching a card printed in Russian, which in the event of a crash would identify me to unfriendly Soviet ground troops as a reporter instead of a spy." In 1955 she circled the globe, and as she landed in various world capitals, she discovered that many of the ambassadors and their wives had cancelled her hotel reservations and insisted that she stay with them at their embassies. Others gave dinner parties in her honor. "President Eisenhower had appointed some of our favorite Washington friends to diplomatic posts in faraway places," she says offhandedly, "and their welcome mat was out for me." Thanks to such long-term social ties with officials who knew and trusted her well enough to speak frankly, Ruth was able to write comprehensive articles about America's diplomatic alliances and the specific problems that faced our foreign missions. Some of these articles also influenced future legislation, as they drew attention to fiscal inadequacies that had remained unnoticed in the postwar years.

In July of 1959 Ruth and a select group of her colleagues from major news services drew one of the most coveted assignments of their careers: the first official visit of an American Vice President to the Soviet Union. "Only a very small number could make the trip," she explains, "because of limited accommodations, and all but three of the reporters were men." Vice President Richard Nixon had been pleading for some time that Ruth be sent on their goodwill trips abroad, because his wife Pat was working hard for improved international relations, and male reporters tended to overlook her activities.

"To say that accommodations in Russia and Siberia were 'limited' became an understatement," Ruth recalls with a laugh. "In one hotel there were only two bathrooms for the entire building, while in another the lavatory was located at the end of a long corridor, with the only shower five floors below, and the elevator would carry passengers up, but not down!" Sleeping arrangements evoked howls of laughter from correspondents who found themselves assigned to bunk indiscriminately with men or women.

"As soon as we checked into the hotel at Novosibirsk, Siberia," Ruth relates, "some wives who had joined their husbands in Russia, plus the few female scribes, began dragging their cots through my door. That night eight of us tried to sleep in a room designed for two. Sleep? No! I tossed all night on my hard cot as I learned that men aren't the only ones who snore."

The single event that the world most remembers about Nixon's Soviet trip was his visit to the American Exposition in Moscow and his confrontation there with Soviet Premier Nikita Khrushchev. "When Nixon and Khrushchev reached the model American kitchen, they fell into a discussion of who was more advanced, Americans under democracy or Russians under communism," Ruth explains. "They began to raise their voices, and suddenly Nixon was shaking his finger in the face of the Soviet leader, while cameras clicked." It became known throughout the world as the "Kitchen Debate." And Ruth holds an official document, framed and mounted on her office wall, designating her as a member of Nixon's "Kitchen Cabinet." The password? *Mir i druzhba*, Russian for "peace and friendship."

With *mir i druzhba*, and with no small measure of curiosity, crowds of Soviet citizens greeted the American officials

and press throughout their tour, but nowhere was this fascination more apparent than in the assemblage of onlookers
present for Nixon's televised address to the Russian people.
No American had been allowed to speak on Soviet television or radio before, and this was during the Cold War,
when tensions between our two countries ran high. As the
"pool" reporter chosen to cover this historic event, Ruth
remembers: "First I was shown the control room and the
tiny studio where Nixon would speak. Then I went to the
adjoining reception room to watch his broadcast on the big
TV monitor and found a large group of Russians waiting
expectantly. When the program came on, you could have
heard the proverbial pin drop. It was total silence as they all
strained forward to catch every word by Nixon and his
Russian interpreter. Their utter absorption was fascinating."

En route back to Washington, during a two-day stopover
in Warsaw, Poland, she was even more entranced by the
heroes' welcome accorded a U.S. Vice President and the
press by Catholic, freedom-loving Poles who took the
Americans into their hearts. This, despite roadblocks put in
their way by the Communist rulers.

Ruth had by now become something of a regular com-
muter abroad, and during an extended trip through the
Holy Land for an eight-part Lenten series, she secured an
exclusive interview with King Hussein at his palace in Am-
man, Jordan. Later she was to dance with him at the White
House when President Lyndon B. Johnson hosted his first
state dinner for royalty. Other monarchs whose state visits
she covered included Queen Elizabeth II of Britain, the
Shah of Iran, King Saud of Saudi Arabia, and King Mohammed V of Morocco, and on a trip to Greece she interviewed
King Paul and Queen Frederika at their palace in Athens.

While the pace of her overseas assignments proved hectic, Ruth had maintained an even more frenetic schedule on

the home front, especially every four years as presidential election fever gripped the nation. She and fellow correspondents hauled their typewriters from summer nominating conventions in Philadelphia, Chicago, or San Francisco to campaign trains crisscrossing the continent to all-night November vigils awaiting the voters' final decision.

"These trips were harried!" she exclaims, remembering. "In 1948 I rode the Dewey campaign train all fall. We lived out of suitcases in tiny compartments, and once a week we would stop long enough at a hotel for a quick shower or a bath." But whistle-stop tours also provided personal moments with the candidates and their families. "On the Eisenhower campaign train Mamie and her mother rode with Ike in the presidential car, and several times they invited me to come and sit with them," Ruth recalls. "Once Mamie reached over to feel the material in my cashmere suit, and told me to go straight back to my compartment and take it off. Cashmere, she scolded, was not durable, and too expensive to wear out while working so hard on that train."

By 1960, presidential campaigns had become airborne— "Much more frantic and exhausting!" Ruth laments. "On the trains we traveled with our luggage and our beds, and since I was usually the only female reporter, I had a compartment to myself. After covering the last speech at night we slept while the train took us to the first meeting of the new day. Not so with planes! Then we often worked twenty-hour days, crisscrossing the continent, lugging our typewriters and suitcases into a hotel at two or three in the morning, only to check out again at six. It was truly grim— but who would want to miss it?"

Long days had also marked Ruth's coverage of the 1951 Japanese Peace Conference in San Francisco, where she was one of only two newswomen, and the sole correspondent for her paper. "Pity poor me," she wired to her editor at the New York *Daily News*, "all alone covering this conference while the New York *Times* has ten reporters here, and the New York *Herald Tribune* seven." His answering telegram came a half hour later: "Our sympathies are all with the *Times* and the *Herald Tribune*, having to compete with you!"

Yet the peace conference also yielded lighter moments. During a rebuke of the Soviets' attitude by a Western delegate, stone-faced Russian delegate Andrei Gromyko suddenly got up and stalked out of the room. "The Czech and Polish delegates exchanged uneasy glances, then followed suit," Ruth recalls in amusement. "Immediately we reporters hotfooted after them, assuming that Gromyko had walked out on the peace conference. Convinced that a major story was unfolding, we trailed him down a long hall and a steep flight of stairs until he abruptly turned into the men's room. We all stopped outside, wondering what to do next. Soon he emerged and made his way back to the Conference Hall, followed by two very foolish-looking Communist delegates."

But not all of Ruth's reporting involved trips away from home. Her primary beat remained the nation's capital, and congressional investigations commanded much of her attention. "I covered the Hiss-Chambers confrontations before the House Un-American Activities Committee," she recalls. "We knew that either the suave Alger Hiss or plump and rumpled Whittaker Chambers had to be lying, but which? Then Hiss claimed that he had no recollection of how he had disposed of his 1929 Model A Ford to which he testified that he had great sentimental attachment. The car had ended up in Communist hands. That's when I began to doubt his honesty. My own first car had also been a 1929 Model A Ford, and I remembered exactly what I had done with it!"

Ruth's keen attention to political and international affairs earned her the respect and recognition of her peers, who elected her president of the Women's National Press Club (the National Press Club forbade membership to female scribes in those years). Likewise "Meet the Press," a weekly news program launched by Martha Rountree and Lawrence E. Spivak, featured Ruth as a regular panelist both during its early radio days and after it became the most popular show of its type on television. She later appeared on similar TV programs, including the Rountree-Spivak "Keep Posted" show, George Allen's "Man of the Week," and Martha's "Press Conference." "I greatly enjoyed these panel shows," Ruth recalls. "We would interview a top newsmaker of the day, and with so many Americans watching on TV, we were soon recognized wherever we went."

In addition to her television appearances, Ruth's byline appeared regularly in newspapers throughout the country. For the New York *Daily News* she wrote her own weekly syndicated column, as well as daily news reporting, and often filled in for ailing columnist John O'Donnell. In 1956, hailed by *Editor & Publisher* magazine as "one of America's outstanding women reporters," she was hired by International News Service's new president, famed foreign correspondent Kingsbury Smith, for "the dream job of all times." Describing that "dream job," it went on to say of her: "This brilliant writer will report in her own bright, distinctive style the important as well as the human interest events on the Washington scene. . . . She has interviewed countless dignitaries here and abroad, and is on first-name acquaintanceship with many of the men and women who are world figures."

Newsweek magazine also carried a long account of the INS coup in luring her away from the *Daily News*. It began: "Ruth Montgomery has a wide acquaintanceship among Washington officials, a handsome residence in the fashionable Northwest section of the capital, a syndicated column, and a notable record of news beats scored for the New York

Daily News. Last week INS added more warming color to the Montgomery story. . . . For a long time Ruth Montgomery has been drawing dream assignments. . . ." And it detailed many of her scoops through the years.

At a salary substantially higher than the *Daily News* could match, Ruth moved her office belongings a block down Pennsylvania Avenue to a desk at International News Service, where her only instruction was to write "a daily feature on any topic of your choice," plus a weekly column. By this time she had become one of the highest-paid newspaper reporters in America. "A far cry," she quips, "from my $10.80 a week salary in Waco, Texas."

Her insight and reportorial accuracy earned Ruth a reputation for trustworthiness, yet she cites "reliable sources" as playing a key role in her quest for truth. How did she manage to cultivate the wide range of news sources that became available to her through a quarter century in Washington? "I had wonderful social contacts," she explains, 'beginning with Cissy Patterson, publisher of the Washington *Times-Herald,* whose brother published the New York *Daily News.*" Redheaded Mrs. Eleanor Medill "Cissy" Patterson, a reigning hostess whose guest lists for lavish dinner parties in her Washington mansion included senators, cabinet officers, and top military brass, frankly loved Ruth's writing and gave it prominent space in the *Times-Herald.* "She invited us to all of her formal dinner parties, and during World War II my good-looking husband, with his lowly first lieutenant's bars, was the only uniformed guest beneath the rank of general or admiral."

Ruth and Bob Montgomery became popular hosts as well as guests on Washington's social circuit, both then and later when Bob became deputy director of the Small Business Administration. They could count among their personal friends many of the major newsmakers of the day "This was unusual for a newspaper reporter in those days," she admits. "We were invited to receptions and parties practically every night during all of those years, including dinners at the British, French, and other embassies, state dinners at the White House, or gatherings at the homes of senators and other officials. Whenever I needed to check out a story, I could pick up the phone and call one of these friends. They knew they could trust me."

She placed one such call to Robert F. Kennedy, an old friend, shortly after his brother Jack's presidential victory in the 1960 election. "What position do you think you'll take in the new administration?" she asked. He thought for a moment, then listed his preferences: "Secretary of State, Secretary of Defense, Attorney General . . ." Ruth managed to suppress a gasp. "Bobby," she counseled, "why don't you decide on Attorney General? After all, you do have a law degree. You'd be criticized for thinking of those first two posts because Jack is your brother. Nepotism, you know. But you *were* his campaign manager, and Eisenhower named *his* campaign manager, Herb Brownell, Attorney General." She wrote a column suggesting that Bobby would be named Attorney General, and the next week the appointment was made.

Personal contacts led Ruth to countless scoops throughout her Washington career, but perhaps the most sensational one had its genesis at a Saturday night party in 1957 given by Barry Goldwater and his wife Peggy. "Hey Ruth, Styles," the Arizona senator signaled to her and Senator Styles Bridges. "Come over here, I've got something to tell you."

"Barry had just returned from the West Coast," she recalls, "where he'd seen President Eisenhower's older brother Edgar. He said that Edgar was hopping mad about the way Ike was running the country—too left-wing—and he blamed it on their liberal younger brother Milton. Barry grinned broadly, and Styles and I laughed with him."

On Monday morning Ruth adhered to her cardinal rule of never taking unfair advantage of confidences imparted at parties, where joviality and friendship often loosened tongues. "I phoned Barry at his Senate office and asked permission to use the item," Ruth relates. "Chuckling, he said he'd just learned Edgar was in town, and suggested that I phone him directly at his hotel."

Delighted to have found a forum for his complaints, Edgar agreed to an interview the next afternoon. But early Tuesday morning he telephoned back. "Miss Ruth," he began, "I mentioned your name to some of the senators at a get-together last night and they all said you're terrific. Could you come over for the interview right now?' He had awakened her out of a sound sleep.

"I'll be there as quickly as I can," she assured him. "I flew into my clothes, called a cab, and rushed to his suite at the Statler-Hilton, where he and his wife were both waiting."

Edgar poured out his gripes as quickly as she could write them down in front of him. The President was spending too much on welfare and foreign aid, he complained, failing to balance the budget, and taxing enough to kill business. He was breaking his campaign promises and leaning way out to the left. On and on he grumbled, until finally Ruth looked up and noticed the time. "Didn't you say you're having lunch at the White House with President Eisenhower?" she asked. "It's nearly noon; you'd better go."

"There's no hurry," he assured her, preferring to continue talking. "Dwight'll be there when I get there." But she insisted that he mustn't be late, and accompanied him and his wife downstairs to the taxi stand, where he refused the first available cab and ushered her into it, over her protestations.

Arriving at the INS office in a tingle of excitement, Ruth whispered to the news editor, "I've got one heck of a story." He followed her to her desk, and began pulling the report of her interview from the clattering typewriter, a paragraph at a time, as quickly as she could write it. "My God!" he kept gasping. Within minutes a three-bell alert sounded on teletypes in client newspapers across the country, signaling a major bulletin that would remake front pages to carry the Edgar Eisenhower interview in eight-column banner headlines. Editors from coast to coast rushed to phone their Washington correspondents to follow up on the story, and newsmen soon filled the corridors of the Statler-Hilton to await Edgar's return. Only Ruth knew of his whereabouts— at the White House lunching with the President, blissfully unaware of the stir his remarks had created.

Three hours later Edgar returned to his hotel, only to find its halls clogged with reporters eager to question his quotes. "Come on in, boys, and I'll pour you a drink," he announced, unlocking the door to his suite and assuring the shoving horde of newsmen that Ruth Montgomery's story was absolutely correct. But as he settled in to continue talking, the phone rang in the adjoining bedroom. It was White House press secretary James C. Hagerty, who had by now seen the story and was reading the riot act as only Jim could do it. At the call's conclusion Edgar rejoined the assembled scribes. "Boys, I've been misquoted," he said, obviously subdued. "I have nothing more to say." Not a person in the room believed him, but they left.

The next morning Ruth looked forward to President Eisenhower's scheduled press conference with some trepidation. "I held my breath as the first questioner asked him for comment on his brother's remarks," she recalls. But the President's reply dispelled her fears. "Edgar," he said with a wry grin, "has been criticizing me since I was five years old." The newspaper audience erupted in gales of laughter, in which Ike joined. Clearly her story had been accurate. Editors throughout the country inundated her with congratulatory telegrams, and *Time* magazine carr ed a long, laudatory article which began:

"Ruth Montgomery of International News Ser/ice, an attractive news-knowing woman, has scored more than one beat with her charm and wide popularity among Washington officialdom. Her enviable talents paid off last week." After several paragraphs describing her headline-grabbing interview with Edgar Eisenhower, the article said: "Such assurance comes easily to Ruth Montgomery. A lively dark blonde married to Robert H. Montgomery, deputy chief of the Small Business Administration, she was good enough at her trade to cause INS to hire her away from the New York *Daily News* in January 1956, and to be the only woman assigned to cover the Anglo-American Conference held in Bermuda this spring."

George Dixon, a fellow columnist and one of those whom Ruth outwitted in Argentina with her Perón exclusive, wrote a long, delightful piece summarizing Ruth's entire career and her unusual popularity with officials and their wives, concluding with, "She's the most wonderful newspaperwoman ever to hit Washington."

The Edgar Eisenhower scoop earned for Ruth the coveted George R. Holmes Memorial Award, "in reccgnition of her consistently outstanding reporting from Washington, and particularly for her remarkable interview with Edgar Eisenhower, judged to be the finest and most distinctive work by an International News Service reporter curing the year."

This award proved to be only one of many such symbols of recognition that have been bestowed on Ruth for her writing. Theta Sigma Phi, the national professional society for women in journalism, honored her with an Award of Appreciation from its National Capital Chapter and the Indiana and California chapters gave her their Woman of the Year Awards. She was invited to address numerous

Theta Sigma Phi gatherings throughout the country, as a woman who had reached the pinnacle of her profession. The Indianapolis Press Club bestowed its annual Front Page Award on her, and Ashland College awarded her an honorary doctorate when she served as its commencement speaker. The Laurel Honor Society elected her as Baylor University's "Most Valuable Alumna," and Baylor also established a special Ruth Shick Montgomery collection to house her papers and manuscripts at its Waco, Texas, campus.

But the honor that has touched Ruth most deeply came in 1956 when Baylor, her beloved alma mater, named her to receive an honorary doctor of laws degree, an accolade the prestigious university bestowed only once a year. "This was one of the highlights of my life," Ruth says in happy remembrance. Congratulatory telegrams and letters poured in from across the country, including a personal note from President Dwight Eisenhower, who himself had received the coveted honor the year before. "As a recent and fellow Baylor 'alumnus,' " he wrote, "it is a special privilege to join in warm felicitations to you on a richly deserved tribute to your outstanding achievements in the field of journalism." He also wrote to Baylor's president, congratulating him for his selection of Ruth to receive that high honor.

But it was Baylor's citation that day which captured the essence of her newspaper career. "Ruth Shick Montgomery," it began, "as an honor student in Baylor University, gained from members of the Baylor faculty an undying love for truth, which has made her a leader in her profession. Mrs. Montgomery has been associated with some of the greatest newspapers in America. She has conferred with Presidents and Kings and other makers of history. She has traveled throughout our country and in many foreign lands, searching always for the heartbeat of humanity and recording it for the information of all who read. Her pen has written accurately, in the confidence that the truth will make men free."

Ruth's quest for truth, combined with a dogged insistence for accuracy, had meanwhile begun to lure her to explore a realm that would forever change people's thinking, and ultimately redirect her own career.

CHAPTER V

A Taste of the Psychic

A thick gray cloud mass hung over Washington, day after dreary day in March of 1956. Yearning for warm sun and sand, Ruth and Bob Montgomery finally telephoned Bob's sister Rhoda in St. Petersburg, Florida.

"Yes, yes, by all means fly down for the weekend," Rhoda exclaimed delightedly. "Say, how would you like to go to a séance while you're here?"

"Quite frankly it sounded like a bore," Ruth confesses. "What we wanted to do was spend all possible time on the beach, but I reluctantly agreed to go, provided it wouldn't take too long."

Rhoda scheduled an appointment with Dr. Malcolm Pantin, a St. Petersburg medium, and at the appointed hour drove her Washington visitors to his parsonage next door to the Spiritualist Church. Pantin ushered them into a brightly lighted, windowless room furnished only with a modest card table and a handful of folding chairs. "At Rhoda's suggestion, while in the car, I had hurriedly scribbled some questions on a scrap of paper," Ruth recalls. "And the resultant scrawl was nearly indecipherable, even to me." Dr. Pantin took a seat on the opposite side of the table and called upon Bob to tie a dark handkerchief over the medium's eyes to block out the light. "There was no way he could have seen anything, much less read my scratchy notes on the paper that was facing me," Ruth continues.

At Pantin's request the group began to sing a hymn as he entered a deep trance, banged his head on the card table, then sat up straight, and with a thick Spanish accent introduced himself as "Pedro," an entity from the spirit world. "If he was only acting, he certainly belonged in Hollywood," Ruth exclaims, remembering her surprise. Blindfolded, Pedro groped for the question sheets that lay on the small table. He held them between his palms and proceeded to bring messages purportedly from the dead.

"First he said he had word from my father, who had died three years before," Ruth recalls. "I figured that Rhoda could have tipped him off to that fact, though she later denied it vigorously. But then he referred to my mother by her nickname, 'Bertie,' and revealed other facts about my family that Rhoda could not have known. He also said that my husband had just received an attractive job offer, a fact that Bob and I had disclosed to no one, and that my father 'knew about' a dark blue-and-green-plaid suit." Then Pedro conveyed a warning from Rhoda's spirit guide—*not* to make the trip north that she was planning before the first of May because of "too many dangers."

By the end of this odd session Ruth had become intrigued. "What was that about a blue-and-green suit?" she asked Bob later in the car. He replied without hesitation: "You sent a suit like that to your sister Margaret just last week. Don't you remember?" It had certainly slipped her mind until then.

"I was frankly mystified by the whole thing," she admits.

"I couldn't understand it, and I wished that I could pursue it further, but we were there only for the weekend."

Four weeks later Ruth found her opportunity, when Bob was unexpectedly summoned to St. Petersburg to address a business group. "Rhoda had mentioned something about 'direct voice' sessions with trumpets in a darkened room, but Pantin had claimed that we weren't ready for that on our first trip," Ruth says. "Now I was really curious, so I agreed to accompany Bob to Florida if Rhoda could arrange a darkroom séance for us. And she did!"

Once again Dr. Pantin led the group into his windowless room, but this time Ruth inspected it more carefully. "I checked the walls, the ceiling, the corners, everything," she confesses. "The room's only draperies were black-velvet ones that the medium drew across the locked door to block out all traces of light. Our chairs sat side by side, facing three funnel-shaped aluminum trumpets on the floor in front of us." Pantin took a seat on the opposite side of the room, facing his visitors, and flicked off the light. In the pitch-black darkness they once again sang hymns while he supposedly entered a trance.

Then a strange male voice, amplified by a trumpet that seemed to float in the air, began to speak from one corner of the room, introducing himself as "Whitecloud," Pantin's control in the other world. From the opposite ceiling piped a high female voice, that of a spirit named "Mazie," who announced that she would usher in some departed family members for this hour-long session. A male who claimed to be "Hiram," Bob's father, spoke next. "The voice cheerfully conversed with Bob and Rhoda about a house where they had all lived many years before," Ruth recalls. "Then Mazie returned and said that she had another visitor who was ready to communicate."

"There's a gentleman here who wants to talk to his girl. He says he's her boy," Mazie proclaimed in her squeaky

voice. No one responded, and when she repeated the re-
mark, Rhoda asked which of them she meant.

"He wants *his* girl," Mazie persisted. "He says she'll
know, because he's her boy."

"Iry Boy!" Ruth exclaimed, genuinely startled, as she suddenly remembered the pet name that she used to call her
father, Ira.

"Of course," Mazie replied with a giggle.

At that, a male voice spoke through the trumpet: "Hello,
Ruth! You don't know how wonderful it is to get to talk to
you at last."

"The mysterious voice continued with personal advice,
using my father's habitual way of stressing points that he
wished to make," Ruth continues. "He also told me to stop
taking so many newspaper junkets all over the world, and
stay at home more with my husband. How like him that
sounded!"

Then the trumpet seemed to pass to her Grandmother
Judy for sentimental conversation, and finally, with a swelling roll of Indian drumbeats, to the thunderous boasting of
one called "Big Chief White Mountain." "Me protect you all
the time," the voice bellowed right into her ear. "Sit still
and I show you how *big* and strong I am!" A trumpet suddenly thumped Ruth three times on the head, evoking in
her a burst of startled laughter.

"At the end of the session Pantin sighed deeply in the
inky blackness, coughed, turned on the light, and sleepily
rubbed his eyes," Ruth recounts. "The trumpets that had
started out in a neat row on the floor now lay scattered
about the room, one resting rakishly against Rhoda's ankle."

This darkroom session hardly satisfied Ruth's curiosity. "If
anything, it raised even more questions in my reporter's
mind," she admits. "No other person had been there, the
trumpets were not electrified in any way, no one could have
entered the room, and the voices had seemed to originate

in various locations, as though the trumpets were floating. If a trick, how could it possibly have been performed? And so much accurate information! I couldn't fathom it!"

"I wanted very much to learn more about all this," she continues, so as we were leaving, I asked Pantin if he knew of anyone in the Washington area who conducted direct-voice séances. He gave me the name of Rev. Hugh Gordon Burroughs of the Spiritualist Church of Two Worlds."

One Sunday afternoon soon after their return to Washington, Ruth and Bob slipped in unannounced at Reverend Burroughs' church in Georgetown to attend its weekly service. "We had persuaded two friends of ours, Hap Seitz and his wife Tania, to come along for company, and they'd agreed with some reluctance," Ruth explains. "I was curious to see what would happen at one of these open gatherings where we were all unknown."

The foursome took seats near the front of the attractive church that had once belonged to a traditional Protestant denomination. "I looked around at the congregation, most of them obviously members of the church, and they seemed no different from a Baptist, Methodist, or Presbyterian group," she recalls. As in any other service the minister delivered a sermon and everyone sang hymns. But at the end of it Reverend Burroughs strode up and down the aisles to deliver "psychic" messages from the "spirit world" to various members of the audience, who gratefully acknowledged these tidings.

"Amelia is trying to communicate with someone here," he announced. There were no takers, so Burroughs moved on to the front of the room and said to Bob, "You have recently received a new job offer." Bob nodded that this was true. Next he stopped in front of Hap Seitz. "William is trying to reach you," he stated. Hap made no response, but the woman directly behind him volunteered that she knew a William. This would have been an easy "out" for a medium seeking to please his audience, but Burroughs stood his ground. "No," he insisted, shaking his head, "I see 'William' written across this man's chest. It has to be for him." Hap said nothing. Frustrated, Burroughs let the moment pass, then continued his message delivery to others who eagerly accepted his words.

On their way home Tania turned to her husband: "Your father's name was William, and your mother's name was Amelia. Why didn't you admit it?" Shrugging his shoulders, Hap acknowledged that he had momentarily forgotten about his father, since he had died so long ago, and that his mother's name was pronounced "Amälia," not "Amélia."

This startling exchange intrigued Ruth even further, since it ruled out conscious mind reading on the part of the medium. "Soon after, Bob and I made a private appointment with Reverend Burroughs," she says, "and in order to ensure that he would give us a direct-voice session, I volunteered that we had already had one with Reverend Pantin in Florida." It turned out that the two men were friends.

Burroughs' darkroom séance proved even more dramatic than the Florida one, with a wider variety of voices and more vivid detail. "First a 'Father Murphy' spoke via trumpet and introduced himself as Burroughs' control in the spirit world," Ruth recounts. "Then a number of Bob's relatives seemingly came through, including a great uncle named John Graves who had disappeared in the 1870s and was never heard from again by his family."

"Sometime when you're driving through Wyoming I'll lead you to my grave," the voice chuckled. Ruth regretted that this detail would be too difficult to prove.

Then the spirit of Father Murphy returned with "a gentleman who wants to talk to his girl—he says he's her boy."

Here Ruth posed her own test. "What's his name?" she asked in an effort to cross-check this otherworld being.

"His name is Ira, isn't it?" Murphy replied, whereupon

the purported voice of Ruth's father took over the trumpet for a cheerful family visit, after which Father Murphy came back, saying, "You used to call him 'Iry Boy,' didn't you, Ruth?" She had to admit that this was true, but wondered if Pantin had tipped him off.

A wheezy-sounding "Uncle Charlie" spoke next, his voice uncannily similar to the one that Ruth remembered from her childhood. Charlie claimed that "Will and Mary" were there, along with "George, Elizabeth," and several other Shick relatives whom she could not place. She later wrote to her mother to ask about these names, only to learn that Will had been Uncle Charlie's twin brother, but that she thought Will's wife Mary was still alive. George had been Ira's favorite cousin, and "Elizabeth" had been the name of Ira's grandmother.

"How could Burroughs have learned these names, when I myself had not known them?" Ruth puzzles. "Uncle Charlie had simply married Dad's sister—I knew nothing of *his* family. Each feminine and masculine voice was distinctly different, and each of those I'd known had the resonance that I remembered." At the end of the session the trumpets landed back on the floor in disarray, Burroughs stirred from his trance, sighed, and at last reached up to pull the light cord. "It was a staggering performance," Ruth exclaims.

But her adventure into the unknown did not stop there. "I went out and bought a Ouija board," she says, referring to the strange device that is sold in toy stores. "I had heard of them, but had never tried one myself. I persuaded Hap and Tania Seitz to work the board while I asked for answers that they wouldn't know. That way I could be sure to eliminate unconscious cheating."

Seated face-to-face with the board perched on their knees, Ruth's two friends tentatively rested their fingertips on opposite sides of the heart-shaped pointer. Suddenly it seemed to move on its own, gliding from letter to letter across the printed alphabet on the board's smooth surface. "First I questioned the name of Reverend Burroughs' control in the spirit world," she says. The pointer correctly spelled out "M-U-R-P-H-Y." Then it continued with a meaningful message for "Ruth" from "Ira." "I was more intrigued than ever," she admits.

The following week Rhoda arrived in Washington for a visit, her arm encased in a cast to support a broken collarbone. She had ignored the dire warning imparted during the March séance and had set out on her trip north before the end of April. Midway through her journey the car in which she was a passenger was demolished and she and her companion only narrowly escaped going over a mountain crest. The séance warning had indeed proved accurate! Ruth invited her to one of Burroughs' direct-voice séances, whereupon Rhoda's spirit guide immediately declared through the trumpet, "I'm not going to say 'I told you so,' but the signs were just not right for you to make the trip north at this time." Then their relatives took over, as usual.

The wealth of evidential material imparted through two mediums in different parts of the country could well have convinced even the most distrustful nonbeliever that spirit communication should be taken seriously. But eleven years of political and international reporting from the nation's capital had endowed Ruth with a streak of skepticism running deeper than it does in most people. "I couldn't accept all this merely at face value," she says. "If the future could truly be foretold, if grief-stricken relatives could actually converse with departed loved ones in the darkened séance chamber, then surely everyone would be trying to do this. Where was the catch?"

With the persistence that only a seasoned journalist could muster, she arranged to attend more séances and began to examine and cross-check each bit of information that came from the mysterious voices emanating from supposedly floating trumpets. "How did you make your living while on earth?" she inquired of the purported spirit of her late father-in-law, Hiram Montgomery—well aware herself of the answer. Yet oddly the disembodied voice seemed confused by her query. Not to be outmaneuvered by an inquisitive reporter, Father Murphy, Burroughs' spirit control, seized the initiative at the next session and mischievously posed the same question to Bob, who saw no alternative but to volunteer that his father had been a Methodist minister. After that Hiram was always introduced by spirits as a "preacher."

Likewise Ruth observed that whenever she informed Reverend Burroughs that she had "heard" from her father through the Ouija board, or that she had seen deceased relatives in a dream, spirit voices would discuss the same matter via trumpet as soon as the medium slipped into trance. "I came through to you on that board the other evening," or "You were actually over here with us for a few minutes last night," the spirit voices claimed. Since these statements proved nothing to Ruth's investigative mind, she thereafter refrained from supplying any information, either to Burroughs or to the mysterious voices, in an effort to eliminate foreknowledge.

Testing further, she once asked Ira's spirit voice, "Have you spoken to Rhoda since she returned home to Florida?" An excited telephone call from St. Petersburg the evening before had announced such a contact, but Ira answered in the negative. "I was puzzled," Ruth admits. "If this was legitimate, how could he not remember speaking with Rhoda only a day or two before? I wondered what was really going on."

Since her exploration of the spirit world had thus far yielded more questions than answers, Ruth determined to "run it to the ground." She therefore placed a call to her boss, Kingsbury Smith, at International News Service in

New York, saying, "I've been to a few séances lately. They've been fascinating and fun, but I'm frankly baffled. I'd like to pursue this subject further, with other mediums, and also do some research. Do you think it might make an interesting series?"

"Sounds terrific!" he replied at once. "Not much is going on in Washington through the summer anyway. Why don't you go ahead with it?"

"Only on one condition," she countered. "I don't know enough about the subject yet, so I won't try to push it as a believer, nor will I deliberately set out to knock it down. Let me just do a straight reportorial stint and tell what happens to a girl reporter who goes to séances. I'll need to spend some time at a spiritualist camp in Pennsylvania to finish gathering material. Is that okay?"

"Splendid! Should make for an interesting feature. Go right ahead, and let me hear from you when you get back."

With the nod from Kingsbury Smith, Ruth arranged with Reverend Burroughs, who was also president of Camp Silver Belle in Ephrata, Pennsylvania, to enroll for several days at that spiritualist enclave, where a variety of mediums and clairvoyants regularly conducted classes, delivered lectures, and scheduled both direct-voice and materialization séances for the camp's enrollees. "I was eager to assemble as much material as possible," Ruth explains, "to convince myself once and for all either for or against the possibility of spirit contact."

Ruth and Bob drove to Silver Belle, a historic barracks that had housed troops during the American Revolution, and checked into their assigned cottage. Their first spiritualist encounter came within an hour, at a public service, with a "psychic" message delivered through Rev. Earl Williams that a preacher named Hiram would want to speak to his son Robert, and that "Iry Boy" sought contact with his daughter. "This proved little," she argues. "Burroughs could have passed that information to his colleague. I don't claim that he actually did so, only that it was certainly possible."

Next, attending a direct-voice séance with a medium named Rev. Elinor Bond Donnelly, they shared a darkened room with three strangers. But the same parade of relatives announced themselves by trumpet. "I asked Ira for news about my sister," Ruth says, confessing that she had earlier tried this ploy with Burroughs. "None of the mediums knew that I had a sister living in Indiana, and I phrased each question so that an outsider could not know whether she was living or dead. The purported voice of my father dodged the matter artfully, as it had before."

Midway through this darkroom session, Ruth perceived that one voice seemed to come from a spot immediately in front of her. Impishly she slid downward in her chair and reached out with one foot. "Almost immediately it struck something solid, which hastily withdrew," she recalls, observing that the medium was supposedly in trance in a chair across the room.

"Did we touch someone with our trumpet?" the otherworldly voice inquired. "We tried."

Ruth kept silent. "After all," she quips, "nothing had touched me. I was the one who deliberately did the touching."

Darkroom sessions at Silver Belle yielded a variety of special effects, whether a darting point of light, a glowing star marking the forehead of an Indian spirit control, or the silent, fluttering arc of sparks resembling a Fourth of July rocket. But by far the most sought-after experience, indeed the most popular of all, remained the widely touted materialization séance to be conducted by Rev. Bertha Eckroad.

"I had heard of these strange phenomena," Ruth says, "where the dead purportedly appeared before the living, mysteriously forming into an ethereal configuration supposedly drawn from ectoplasm of the entranced medium. But in order to write about materializations I had to see them for myself."

Heady with anticipation, Ruth and her husband joined thirteen other adults in a closed séance chamber "At one end of the room a set of heavy curtains formed the standing enclosure known as a 'cabinet,' " Ruth recalls. "I examined it with great curiosity but could find no evidence of hidden stage props or doors, only the simple folding chair that awaited the medium." At the far end of the room a light shrouded in red cellophane would illuminate the spirits as they entered. The medium arrived and was introduced to the eager group. Miss Eckroad wore only a thin summer dress without pockets.

A second medium, Elizabeth Giberson, instructed those present to take their places in folding chairs that were arranged around the room in a horseshoe. When summoned to meet a spirit form, they were to approach the apparition and converse with it, but under no circumstances, she warned, should they pass between the figure and the cabinet, lest they sever the ectoplasmic connection and thereby cause serious harm to the medium. Likewise they must not touch the materialized figure unless given permission to do so. Instructions complete, the room was plunged into semi-darkness and all joined together in singing a hymn while their eyes grew accustomed to the soft red light.

Then, one at a time, diaphanously clad figures emerged from the dark curtains of the cabinet, and Miss Giberson called the names of those who were summoned to rise and greet each apparition.

"My name was finally called," Ruth says, "and I eagerly moved to the center of the horseshoe to meet a form introduced to me as 'Grandmother Judy.' I peered into the aged face that I could not recognize, but this figure did have the long black hair that I remembered my grandmother retaining until her death at the age of eighty-three. We spoke together, and as she turned to leave, she brushed my bare arm with the lacelike material that hung from her sleeves."

More hymn singing ensued before Bob and Ruth were both summoned to the center of the room. Bob's late sister, Asenath, it seems, sought to meet them together. "This figure was dressed rather like all the others," Ruth recalls, "except with different facial features and hair coloring."

Then Bob's other deceased sister, Ruth, emerged in turn, bearing a strong resemblance to the way she had looked on earth, they later agreed. "I grew bold this time, and asked her if she could kiss me. She answered, 'Of course,' and, cupping her hand to her mouth, she kissed at me through that. Her hand brushed my cheek—and felt suspiciously human!"

Some thirty figures took turns appearing from the folds of the cabinet curtains during the seventy-five-minute session before Miss Eckroad stirred once again and brilliant light replaced the room's eerie red glow.

"Bob and I walked silently back to our cottage through the darkness that evening," Ruth remembers. "We had agreed not to discuss the materialization séance until we could each write down our impressions." Their observations proved nearly identical. While a parade of figures had emerged from the medium's curtained enclosure, they entered the room one at a time, never in pairs. All were either good-sized children or female adults—no men. Their gossamerlike clothing was similar, their height approximately the same, but their hairdos and faces differed, as did their voices.

"The only logical conclusion seemed absurd—that Miss Eckroad had spent a frantic seventy-five minutes making herself over repeatedly, and had memorized all our names and those of our relatives. That made no sense," Ruth concedes. "Yet how could so many other humans silently enter a cabinet that was only a few yards from us?"

The following morning she discussed her questions and doubts with Reverend Burroughs, who urged her to "trust" for now. One more séance session remained.

Virginia Leach Falls, a charming and articulate young woman, had impressed Ruth and Bob during her public lecture earlier in the week. They subsequently requested a private session with her, to take place on the day of their departure from the camp. "Mrs. Falls asked us to say the Lord's Prayer as she entered into trance," Ruth recounts. "Then the voice of her control, an Indian maiden, rattled off the names of relatives who awaited their turn to speak."

First Ruth's Grandmother Shick announced her presence and declared that she had tried to materialize the evening before. Had she seen her? "But it was my Grandmother Judy who had seemingly appeared, not my Grandmother Shick." Ruth pointed out the error, to the obvious surprise of this spirit voice. Then Ira spoke up, indicating that he, too, had tried to appear. "But no men had strolled out of the cabinet," she explains, noting a second serious error of fact.

Bob's two sisters next took turns with the trumpet. *They* had supposedly visited the night before, but now made no mention of it. "Suddenly, while a voice identified as Asenath's emanated from a spot directly in front of us, a strange, misty form began to take shape," Ruth says, remembering her surprise. "It remained stationary for a few moments while conversing with us and then vanished abruptly into the inky blackness of the room."

"Did you see your sister just now?" the voice of the Indian maiden inquired.

"We had certainly seen *something* strange," Ruth concedes, but wondered if the medium had lifted her skirt to expose a luminescent petticoat.

"I'm so glad," the little voice replied. "I sprinkled ectoplasm around her and did so hope that you could see her."

Bob's other sister then made her presence known. "Isn't
this marvelous?" she asked.

"What do you mean?" Ruth prodded.

"That I'm actually able to speak to you," the voice responded.

Remembering that this sister-in-law had purportedly spoken with and even tried to kiss her the evening before, Ruth
could not resist one last reporter's trick question: "Darling,"
she asked, "when will we actually get to *see* you?"

"You must have patience," the voice answered. "If you
study spiritualism in classes, I may be able to come through
to you."

Classes indeed! Ruth and her husband returned to Washington sadly disillusioned. "Surely our relatives have better
things to do than to follow *us* around all the time," she
recalls thinking.

To complete her preparation for the series of articles on
spirit communication, Ruth examined every book she could
find on the subject, both pro and con. "I combed the Library of Congress, but by the time I finished I knew exactly
as much as I had before I started," she laments. "While I
could see how some mediums might be tempted to resort to
trickery or fraud, especially on days when their abilities
weren't up to par, I remained frankly baffled by other phenomena that I could not explain."

Did mediums maintain card files on the families of those
who sought spiritual contact? If so, how could they afford
such a complex information system long before the days of
microcomputers, especially when they charged only three
to five dollars for an hour-long session? And even if they had
such information and shared it among their colleagues, how
could they remember so many details of family names and
connections in a darkened room? How did human sounds or

drumbeats emerge from one corner of the room and then from another. "And how," Ruth wonders aloud, "did Malcolm Pantin's spirit helper, Mazie, know that I had called my father 'Iry Boy,' when my absent sister and I were the only people in the world who ever called him that?" Yet how could those same spirits be so mixed up as not to remember a purported contact that had occurred only a day or two before?

One final experiment with the Ouija board yielded an oddly prophetic message. "I sat with a friend, Lydia Mithoff, and closed my eyes while the pointer glided from letter to letter," she recounts. "It spelled out a warning from Ira to Ruth that said, 'Do not publish writing. You can do one proving life after death.' It was definitely not a message that I wanted to hear, so I did not consciously influence its content. I didn't obey it anyway."

On September 23, 1956, with a great fanfare of publicity, Ruth's eight-part series entitled "My Visit to the Spirit World" began to run in hundreds of client newspapers throughout the country. Beginning with her initial "Pedro" contact in St. Petersburg and continuing from fascination and bafflement to shattering disillusionment at Silver Belle, she carried her readers step-by-step through her own observations, questions, tests, and ultimate puzzlement. She also raised further questions. Cissy Patterson, she observed in the final installment of the series, awakened from a nap one afternoon to find the full-color presence of her former husband standing at the foot of the bed. A cable the next day confirmed the man's death in Poland at the exact time that she had "seen" him. Equally as odd, the U.S. Patent Office often receives nearly identical applications for the same invention long before such a product goes on the market. Something is going on, Ruth suggested, on levels we cannot as yet comprehend. And as for mediums? Should they be able to *prove* that grieving relatives can actually converse with departed loved ones, surely the world would beat a path to their door.

"The next move is up to them!" Ruth challenged as she turned her back on the spirit world. Personally she was finished with the psychic field. Or so she thought!

CHAPTER VI

A Search for the Truth

The New York headquarters of International News Service had never seen anything like it. Day after day, first by bundles and then in weighty canvas sacks bulging at their drawstrings, letters forwarded by client newspapers poured in from all parts of the country. Finally Kingsbury Smith picked up the phone and dialed Ruth Montgomery in Washington.

"We're inundated with letters about your séance series," he began. "Nothing we've ever before printed has generated such a heavy response. What do you want us to do with all this mail? It's addressed to you."

"Please don't send it down here!" she pleaded, lamenting the impossibility of writing thousands of polite replies along with her columns and her moment-by-moment reporting of the final frantic weeks in the 1956 presidential campaign. "Why don't I type out a form letter that you can reproduce in volume and mail out from there?"

"Good idea!" he responded.

Now it was goodbye to the heady psychic diversion and

hello to the hurly-burly of national politics. Before writing the eight-part series on séances Ruth had spent the entire month of August covering the Democratic nominating convention in Chicago and the Republican one in San Francisco, afterward visiting Austine and William Randolph Hearst, Jr., at the fabulous San Simeon castle in California for several days with her husband Bob.

Immediately after dispatching the form letter to Kingsbury Smith, she set forth to cover the Adlai Stevenson campaign train. Then she switched to the two vice presidential contenders—Richard M. Nixon and Estes Kefauver—accompanying them by train and plane, and wound up her frenetic schedule with the Eisenhower swing through the West and South. Lastly she covered Ike's victory celebration at Republican headquarters on election night.

The pace at last became more leisurely, and as Ruth and Bob resumed their accustomed rounds on the Washington party circuit, she was surprised to discover the stir that her psychic series was still creating. "Oddly, people whom I'd known for many years started telling me about their own eerie experiences," she relates. "They confessed that they had believed in the psychic for many years, but hadn't wanted anyone to know about it. At an embassy party the Turkish ambassador cornered me to describe a prophetic occurrence that happened to him while taking an overnight train through Rumania. He said he dreamed that his brother entered the compartment, displaying the dial on his watch, and said he had come to say goodbye. He awakened disturbed, looked at his watch, and noted that it was a few minutes before 5 A.M. On reaching his destination, he learned that his brother had died at that precise moment."

Equally bizarre experiences were related to Ruth by such luminaries as General and Mrs. Nathan F. Twining, Ambassador and Mrs. U. Alexis Johnson, Major General and Mrs.

Leigh Wade, Mrs. William Faulkner, Mrs. Douglas MacArthur II, Ambassador Loy Henderson, and numerous others.

Her best friend, Hope Ridings Miller, editor of *Diplomat* magazine, also admitted that she had been fascinated by the psychic field since she was a little girl, when her mother found a missing diamond ring—thought to have been lost on a cross-country trip—after being told in a dream to look in the fourth finger of a glove. Some years later an odd sense of danger impelled Mrs. Ridings to leave a church meeting early and rush the three blocks home, only to find her fifteen-year-old daughter Hope unconscious in the bathtub. The flame on the room's instant gas water heater had gone out, and Hope would have been asphyxiated or drowned if her mother had not heeded the sudden premonition.

Through previous research Ruth had discovered that it wasn't just loonies or crackpots who were interested in psychic manifestations. Highly educated, extremely intelligent people had written about the subject, among them Sir Arthur Conan Doyle, the physicist Sir William Crookes, Sir Oliver Lodge, and Sherwood Eddy, a minister who founded the YMCA in the Orient. "All had taken the subject seriously and had explored it in depth," she says. "I reasoned that other powers beyond our five senses had to be at work here, or those towering intellects could not have been so utterly deceived."

Meanwhile she was swept into the excitement of a new Congress, which the Democrats still controlled despite the Eisenhower landslide. She conducted numerous exclusive interviews with the top newsmakers, received awards, and continued to turn out headlined stories, but something seemed to be lacking. 'I felt a strange emptiness," she muses in retrospect. "For a few short months I had been caught up in an exciting new world that had nothing to do with politics or world affairs. I was baffled, thrilled, and puzzled by that intoxicating realm that seemed to lie beyond our three-dimensional world. I was convinced that some of the ploys were fraudulent, and I had firmly closed the door on it, yet I experienced an elusive void within. I loved my reportorial work, but a little of the sparkle seemed to have gone out of it."

International News Service merged with United Press that spring to form UPI, and Ruth was one of only five writers retained by the Hearst organization, which raised her salary and gave her the title of chief Washington correspondent for the newly formed Hearst Headline Service. Now she was a widely syndicated columnist who could write about any subject of her choosing, and in 1958 when she noticed a small advertisement for an upcoming speech in Washington, she little thought that her life was about to enter a dramatic new dimension.

The ad proclaimed that Arthur Ford, America's best-known living medium, would be delivering an address in behalf of Spiritual Frontiers Fellowship (SFF), a new organization founded by some outstanding educators, professionals, and clergy to investigate psychic phenomena within the framework of established churches. "This was an encouraging approach," Ruth says. "Spiritualism is a separate religion with its own congregations, but inasmuch as every major religion has had its genesis in psychic phenomena, it belongs within existing churches."

Throughout her research at the Library of Congress, Ruth had continually encountered lengthy references to Arthur Ford, most of them highly favorable even in the books debunking other mediums. She determined to attend his lecture and persuaded Bob to accompany her. Afterward she introduced herself to Ford as a reporter and asked for an interview so that she could write a column about the new organization.

Ford happily agreed, and two days later they met in his hotel suite for a half-hour talk about SFF, after which Ruth closed her notebook and posed a more personal question: "Do you think there's anything to Ouija boards?"

Ford thought for a moment. "Well, some people," he began, "have been successful in discovering psychic ability that way, but it should not be used as a party prank or a plaything, because it can also be dangerous if the wrong type of entities are attracted."

Ruth shared with him the strange message that she had received, purportedly from her father, on a Ouija board two years before: "Do not publish writing. You can do one proving life after death." She explained that the "writing" referred to a series on séances and mediums that had ended up on a rather debunking note.

"I just wonder if there's anything to it all. Some of the séances seemed so obviously phony, but others were quite impressive, and I've read good things about you," she continued, gently alerting him to her native skepticism. If he had anything to hide, she reasoned, he would politely show her to the door.

But Ford made no such move. "If you like," he offered, "I'll go into trance and you can see what Fletcher has to say. Then you can form your own judgment."

Intrigued by his suggestion, Ruth sprang from her chair to help lower the shades and turn out the lights, but Arthur stopped her.

"Darkness won't be necessary," he said, smiling. "I'll just tie a black handkerchief over my eyes. If you'll excuse me now, I'll lean back and make my exit, and if Fletcher comes through, talk to him as you would with anyone else."

He stretched back in the chair and appeared to drift off to sleep while Ruth waited for something to happen. After a few silent minutes his body suddenly jerked, his chin rolled, and a voice with a French-Canadian accent announced, "Good morning."

"Good morning, Fletcher," Ruth replied, greeting the strange voice of Ford's spirit control. The two chatted briefly, then Fletcher got down to business.

"Quite a few friends here want to say hello," he began. Ruth reopened her notebook, thankful that the room's bright light enabled her to write. "This one was an uncle of some sort, a preacher, says he's upset about events in the Congo. His name is Ed—no—Fred Bennett."

"Sorry, Fletcher, but I've never heard of anyone by that name," she responded frankly, disappointed that someone more familiar hadn't come through.

"He says he didn't know you," Fletcher continued, "but to ask your husband."

Moving right along, the voice introduced another stranger, one Spence Irwin, who seemed concerned with the Near East. But these names meant nothing to her. She listened politely and took notes, but made little effort to mask her boredom. "I told Fletcher that this was all very nice, but I had no interest in discussing the Congo or the Near East with strangers. Fletcher apparently took the hint, because he next introduced my father," she recalls. "He described Dad's sudden death of a heart attack with remarkable accuracy, and said that I was away when it happened." Ford, she noted, could have had no way of knowing that she had rushed home from Egypt in 1953, flying two days and nights to make it to her father's funeral. "Ira says he enjoyed his funeral very much and was so glad that you could get there in time," Fletcher said. He also discussed her mother's physical condition, and then he changed the subject.

"Do you remember someone named Jinx?" he asked, describing a man who claimed to have known her during her cub reporter days. "Jinx Tucker is his name, says he used to set his own stories on a linotype machine, keeps talking about football."

Startled, Ruth suddenly recalled Jinx Tucker, who had been the sports editor of the Waco *News-Tribune*. "But I hadn't known him well," she adds. "I knew nothing about his having used a typesetting machine. In fact, I didn't even know whether he was dead."

Fletcher moved on to describe a judge, "someone who once lived near you, in a street or town called Lafayette. He says he disappeared nine months ago, but he's here now. He drowned. He wants you to tell everybody that he's over here."

"All right," Ruth agreed with some reluctance. "I'll tell them."

Other strangers came through, and before the session ended, Fletcher conveyed one last message: "Your father says the most important story in the world for you to write is this: 'I live, and we are in a world of activity and growth. We are not living in a vacuum. I couldn't be happy if idle. I'd rather be out of my body than to be an invalid, and I'd have been pretty much an invalid if I had stayed on there. I'm as vital and just as active now as when I was a boy.' " He continued with personal messages for the family, and at last Fletcher bid farewell. A few silent minutes later Ford took a deep breath and emerged from his trance.

"Later that day I wrote up the interview about Spiritual Frontiers Fellowship for my column," Ruth recounts, "and when I arrived home that evening, I casually asked my husband if he had ever heard of anyone named Fred Bennett."

"I had an aunt who married a man by that name," he replied, "but he's been dead since I was a child. How did you hear of him?"

She ignored his question and probed further. "What did this Fred Bennett do for a living?"

Knowing nothing of Ruth's mysterious morning session

with a trance medium, Bob answered, "He was a foreign missionary in the Congo. Why?"

Startled by this unexpected confirmation, she returned to her notes during the following days and methodically attempted to verify the names that Fletcher had mentioned, starting with the missing judge.

"I telephoned the Lafayette *Courier-Journal* in Indiana and spoke with the editor, George Lamb, feeling rather ridiculous as I tried to explain why I was calling," she recounts. "I asked if he knew of any missing judge from Lafayette."

"Oh, that would be Judge Lynn Parkinson," he replied. "He disappeared in Chicago about nine months ago. They found his hat and umbrella by Lake Michigan and the FBI has searched for him in seven states. Aside from that, there's been no trace of him, and they're still paying his federal judge's salary into his bank account."

"Tell them they can stop doing that now," Ruth offered, "because he's dead."

"What? How do you know? How did you find out?" The editor pressed for details, anticipating a major news scoop from one of America's best-known reporters.

"I heard it at a séance," she replied, unable to suppress a giggle, whereupon he joined in her amusement and listened to the rest of her strange story.

"But two weeks later I picked up the morning newspaper from my doorstep," Ruth recalls, "and on the front page a headline read, 'Body of Judge Parkinson Found Floating in Lake Michigan.'"

Strangely, other details imparted through the sleeping Ford proved to be just as accurate. To check on Jinx Tucker, Ruth phoned the Waco *News-Tribune*, where editor Harry Provence verified that Jinx had died. "I'll never forget him," the editor volunteered before she could even mention it. "He's the only newspaperman I ever heard of who set his own stories directly into type on a linotype machine. He was a printer, too."

Subsequent long-distance calls confirmed all the other names mentioned by Fletcher except for Spence Irwin. Lacking this one detail, Ruth wrote a two-page Sunday spread on Arthur Ford and his uncanny ability, noting the accuracy of each name and fact except that one. But no sooner had her piece appeared in *American Weekly*, the Sunday supplement carried in newspapers across the country, than her telephone began to ring. Spence Irwin, the long-distance callers informed her, had been the foreign editor of the Cleveland *Plain Dealer*, and he had made a trip to the Near East shortly before his death.

"I had to conclude," she says with a laugh, "that whether or not there was anything to the psychic, there certainly was something to Arthur Ford. I also began thinking that there was something terribly important here that I'd better pursue, though at the time I had no thought of making it a career or writing a book about it."

Arthur and Ruth became good friends. He telephoned whenever his travels brought him to Washington, and often the Montgomerys invited him to dinner or to afternoon sessions with friends. "I continued to test him for many years," she admits. "He realized this, and good-naturedly put up with my experiments.

"I would invite a small group of people to our house and ask them to arrive promptly. Then I'd be certain that Arthur came fifteen minutes later. I'd tell him only that these were friends of mine who were interested in the psychic and that if he didn't mind we would wait until later for introductions."

He was fond of Ruth and welcomed her lingering skepticism. "That's all right," he would reply. "I prefer it that way." Then he would tie a dark handkerchief over his eyes, lean back in his chair, enter a deep trance, and allow Fletcher to speak to the assembled strangers.

Invariably Fletcher addressed each person in the room, telling them things about themselves and their families that could not have been known either to Ford or to the others present. They gasped as he identified their departed loved ones, described their childhood homes, or delivered messages of very personal meaning. Clearly Arthur Ford was no fraud.

Ruth's next experiment with the psychic began in 1960, two years after first meeting Ford. "I had tried the meditation that Arthur recommended," she admits. "He said that it helped people to develop their psychic abilities, but my mind never seemed to stand still long enough to achieve more than an occasional sense of deep peace; then I would be interrupted by the telephone or some other household noise. I had also tried the automatic writing that I'd read about, but, having no success, I quickly abandoned it."

One day Ford urged her to try again. "Ruth," he said, "I'm getting vibrations that you have the talent to develop this ability, and I wish you'd try it."

"He told me how to go about it," she recalls. "He said that one should attempt it for no more than fifteen minutes at a time and always at the same hour each day. That's most important!"

Following Ford's instructions, she sat at her desk at eight-thirty each morning, her spine erect. With a silent prayer for protection from evil forces, she entered a ten-to-fifteen-minute period of meditation for spiritual enlightenment. Then while in the alpha state that meditation produces, with eyes still closed and her mind freed from rambling thoughts, she picked up a pencil and held it lightly poised over a sheet of paper.

Day after day nothing happened, until one morning an unseen force seemed to seize her hand and guide the pencil

in circles and figure eights, around and around and around.
"I was puzzled," she admits. "This was supposed to convey
messages, not circles, but I knew I had not know ngly propelled the pencil."

An hour later she called on a colleague who was also
interested in the psychic "Oh, Ruth," the friend exclaimed.
"I've just received a message through automatic writing
that says 'Now Ruth can do this.' "

"Sure, let me show you how Ruth can do this" she exclaimed, laughing at herself as she produced the piece of
paper filled with heavy circles and figure eights.

"But this is authentic," the friend announced. "It always
begins this way. That's wonderful!"

Through the following days, gradually building in
strength, the automatic writing began to convey messages
signed with Ruth's father's name. "I couldn't figure out
what was going on," she remembers thinking. "I supported
the pencil, yet it seemed to write without me. I had no
thought of what was being expressed until I later read the
words on the paper. Clearly this was something that I did
not control."

Then one morning the pencil seemed to be taken over by
her Aunt Mae, "the young aunt who died in the pneumonia
epidemic when I was three," Ruth recalls. "After a few brief
messages, the pencil began to draw charming little pictures
of children and animals. This went on for days, until finally I
threw down the pencil in disgust and announced aloud,
'Aunt Mae, if you have anything to say, I'll take it, but I'm
not going to draw any more of your pictures.' "

Still skeptical of this strange phenomenon, Ruth wrote to
an elderly aunt, Mae's older sister, in an effort to learn more
about the spirit who monopolized each morning's session.
"I certainly didn't tell her of my psychic interest," she says,
chuckling, "but I asked this eighty-two-year-old relative if
Aunt Mae had ever shown any interest in art."

"Oh yes," Aunt Daisy replied in quavering handwriting. "She used to draw adorable little pictures of children and animals all the time."

"So perhaps it was evidential material, but by now I'd had it with these useless drawings." Ruth shrugs. "We went away on vacation for several weeks, during which time I made no further attempt at automatic writing."

Upon their return Ruth resumed the morning sessions, and this time it was not Aunt Mae who guided the pencil, but an entity who seemed to be male. "I sensed a different energy," she relates. "The pencil began with a little drawing, and I thought, 'Oh no, not more pictures,' but when I opened my eyes and read the words on the page, they were clearly from a different source." Starting with the symbol of a graceful lily, the writing announced, "This is the identification by which you will know, each morning from now on, that it is I who is coming through."

"From that time on," Ruth explains, "every single day the pencil drew the flower and wrote 'Lily,' then began writing the most beautiful philosophy that I had ever read. I knew that it wasn't coming from me. I had never had such inspiring thoughts in my whole life."

Lily refused to reveal his identity except to admit that he had once been "a writer of great note" who wasted precious earth time in pursuit of public acclaim rather than in the higher goal of helping others. He hinted at "projects" that lay ahead for Ruth, and urged her to give up smoking and cocktails, which she did, until he also added tea, Cokes, chocolate—anything "harmful to the body" or time-consuming—to the list.

"Wait a minute!" she retorted. "Whose life is this, anyway?"

Within a few days the racing pencil advised her to buy a different house: "It should be very much older than the house you are in, with high ceilings and big rooms. This you know, too."

"I suspected that my subconscious had a hand in this suggestion," she recalls. "For some time I had yearned for a gracious older home, one with a more lived-in air than our modern split-level."

Soon the daily messages grew more specific. "You can find the house by looking in the want ads today," Lily announced after detailing the location and its interior decor. "It is very much to your liking. Offer no more than seventy thousand dollars. Go at once and find it. Buy it "

Refusing to bow to such abrupt orders, Ruth nevertheless grew curious and scanned the ads. Nothing answered that description, but the next day there it was! "Go ahead and buy it, and do not wait to dispose of your house," the Guide urged. "I promise that we will take care of that for you. Do not dillydally."

Ruth argued back. "Was I supposed to announce to my husband that we were to buy a certain older home, merely on the basis of spirit communication? To a person as practical as Bob, the idea would be ludicrous. I agreed only that we would look at it."

The house was really exquisite, its French decor and marble fireplaces precisely as the Guide had described, but with one major drawback—it had four flights of stairs, and the dining room and kitchen were located on the third floor. Even its charm and beauty could not make up for such impracticality. "Bob and I still lived in bodies, after all," she reasoned. "We had to climb stairs, not just flit up and down them like a spirit. We decided to look at other houses, and Lily graciously offered to help us find one more suited to our human needs."

But nothing could match the splendor of the dwelling that Lily had found for them on Sheridan Circle. After several disappointing inspection tours of other properties, he asked Ruth to reconsider. "The house is truly ours, and Bob will soon love it, too," he claimed. "Please buy it now." But she was not to be persuaded by such pencil arguments, and for several days both sides refused to budge.

Faced with unyielding opposition, Lily apparently summoned an ally. "Ruth, this is Dad," the writing began one morning, having skipped the familiar picture of a flower. "I want you to do what the Guide says. He knows what is best for you." During still another session Ira hinted at marvelous things yet to come. "You are one of the fortunate ones who have been chosen for this work," he confided, "and it is very necessary that you obey. I know it is not always easy, but it must be done if you are to fulfill your life mission. Do it, Ruth, do it. Believe me, I know, and I want you to succeed. It is a wonderful thing that lies before you if you will do as bidden."

Just what was this mysterious work that lay ahead? Neither spirit would answer, not until "you make the next step" and the "conditions are right."

"We looked at the house one last time," she recalls, "and definitely decided against it. A few mornings later Lily announced that this was the day we would buy it. An hour later the agents unexpectedly appeared with a contract, urging me to make an offer, *any* offer, so I phoned Bob at his office." The property had listed at $125,000—"real" dollars in those days. Ruth offered $70,000, as Lily had suggested. The owners countered with $75,000 and they compromised at $72,500.

"Oh, how wonderful!" the pencil wrote, racing in jubilation as soon as the realtors had gone. "Now we can truly begin our work. Now we can begin to serve others as we were meant to serve them by our Creator. I will handle the sale of your present house, so you will not lose on it." In less than a week Lily fulfilled his promise. An out-of-town friend telephoned to ask about rental houses, learned of Ruth and

Bob's plans to move, toured their house, and agreed to buy it—before it had even been placed on the market. One month later the Montgomerys settled into their new home.

Ruth's fifteen-minute sessions of automatic writing continued each day, growing in strength and speed—as well as illegibility. "I could hardly read some of it," she admits. "Then one morning it spelled out, 'GO TO YOUR TYPEWRITER!' which I did, feeling a bit foolish, and the automatic writing thereafter became automatic typewriting, with little punctuation or capitalization, but with surprisingly few mistakes." By typewriter, Lily and the other discarnates who soon joined him could fill two or three pages a day with lengthy philosophy about life and death, spiritual progression, and the power of unselfish prayer. The Guides, as she now called them, began insisting that she disseminate their message by means of books, but their pleas fell on deaf ears.

Ruth had already committed herself to one career, as well as to a bustling social schedule that complemented her news-gathering duties. Only her closest friends were aware of the automatic writing, a spare-time activity that took a backseat to the "legitimate" world of daily columns, deadlines, spot news, and formal dinner parties. Still an active member of the White House press corps, she set off to cover the jet-age Kennedy-Nixon presidential campaigns of 1960. But the frantic pace of air travel, lost sleep, and muscle strain from hauling suitcase and typewriter in and out of hotels finally took its toll. "With excruciating back spasms I ended up in the hospital in double traction," she says ruefully. "It was the middle of a thrilling campaign; my timing couldn't have been worse."

Feeling sorry for herself, she made futile attempts to sleep and forget her own bodily discomfort. But the network of pulleys suspended above her hospital bed forbade any change in position, and in the room next door an unknown man had for ten days hacked and coughed incessantly with pneumonia. Ruth grumbled about orthopedic patients having to share a hospital wing with people who had contagious diseases. "I prayed fervently that I be cured," she says, "but the loud coughing from the next room interrupted even my prayers."

Then a nurse arrived with a pill. "The man with pneumonia isn't expected to last the night," she remarked.

"Suddenly I felt deeply ashamed of myself," Ruth recalls. "Almost without realizing it I began to pray over and over for his recovery, begging that the life of this stranger be spared." Around midnight she fell asleep exhausted and slept more soundly than she had in weeks.

On awakening refreshed in the morning, she noticed that the dreadful hacking had stopped. "Did the man with pneumonia pass away?" she inquired gently.

"Goodness no. It's like a miracle," the nurse replied. "He hasn't coughed in seven or eight hours."

The following day Ruth was discharged from the hospital, her back unimproved. Asking that her many flowers be given to the stranger in the next room, she paused to greet him as a nurse pushed her wheelchair past his door.

"The young black man shyly confided that he, too, expected to go home in another day," Ruth recounts, "and I asked him when he had begun to feel better."

"Night before last," he replied. "I thought I was going to die, but about midnight I suddenly felt well all over."

"Startled, I realized that earnest prayers in behalf of others are indeed answered, even if self-centered ones are not," she muses.

Ruth endured continuing back spasms, but it was during this period that she began her first book. "I hadn't intended to become an author, despite the urging of the Guides," she recounts, "but this opportunity seemed to fall right into my lap." It began with a call from Mary McCarran, daughter of the late Nevada senator. Ruth had remarked in one of her columns that this family of lifelong Democrats, Irish Catholics with two daughters who were nuns, was supporting Republican presidential nominee Richard Nixon instead of Jack Kennedy, an Irish Catholic. Mary McCarran, she added, had been a nun for thirty-two years before leaving the convent life to care for her widowed mother.

After reading Ruth's column a writer approached Mary and suggested doing a book on her years in the convent, but Mary's mother thought that Ruth should be given first chance. The story had, after all, originated with her. "After Mary's call I phoned a friend who was an agent for a large New York publisher," Ruth recalls. "They liked the idea and sent us a check for first option on the book."

With a tape recorder and a hired typist—"My back was so bad that I couldn't even take notes!"—she interviewed the former Catholic nun, prepared an outline and sample chapters, and sent the preliminary material off to New York. "But wouldn't you know," she groans, lamenting the book's first setback, "the editor assigned to handle it turned out to be a fervent Catholic convert. I suspected right then that the deal would be off. The woman was almost white with horror at the thought that a nun would leave the convent, then tell about it and point out little things about religious life that weren't perfect."

The fourth publishing house to consider the book finally bought it, and *Once There Was a Nun* appeared in print in 1962. "I can remember my absolute *thrill* the first time that I held it in my hands," she exclaims. "I could hardly believe that I had actually written a book!"

But just before its release her enthusiastic editor went to a different publishing house for higher pay, and his successor issued the book with virtually no promotion. While it received favorable reviews and eventually went into paperback, it quietly faded from the scene.

"I would have stopped writing books right then," Ruth admits, "because the newspaper world was my first love. Also, by the time I had covered the typing costs for all those interviews when I couldn't take notes, there was very little profit for Mary or me."

Likewise no profit resulted from Ruth and Bob's decision to build a six-bedroom cottage on the Delaware coast, rent it to vacationers in season, and enjoy the rest of its use almost without cost. Ten days before its completion a freak storm swept up the Atlantic coast and washed it and its neighboring dwellings away. Since insurance companies refused to reimburse any of the property owners, they lost their entire investment.

Consulting with the Guides after this financial blow, Ruth found Lily remarkably unsympathetic. "We want you to write books which will take your time from such things as that," he wrote. "Get to work, Ruth, and do not go off again on a tangent which is as time-consuming as that would have been. . . . You are to help others. Keep this in mind hereafter, and don't get involved in time-wasting projects like that cottage."

Having said his piece, Lily returned to his teaching. Preparation for the next stage of life, he admonished, mattered far more than worldly blows, which "are as nothing over the long stretch." He continued to describe the nature of everlasting life, activity after death, and eternal evolution toward oneness with the Creator. "You can have no higher mission there than to pass on to others the truths which you have been learning here," he wrote.

Ruth's family, meanwhile, objected strenuously to her continued interest in the automatic writing. Bob did not want to hear about it and feared that it would harm her in some way. Her mother, thinking that it might possibly be the work of the devil, worried that others would believe something was wrong with her mentally. Ruth listened po-

litely and heard them out, but made up her own mind. "I
could not see how such high-minded philosophy could have
other than beneficial effects, regardless of its source," she
reasoned.

Still, the family's discouragement took its toll. 'My own
doubts began to surface," she recalls. "I posed trick questions to the Guides, hoping for material that could be cross-
checked, but they refused to play, retorting that their mission lay in goals more loftly than gimmicks and stunts."
Irritated, Ruth tried to retaliate by skipping the sessions for
weeks at a time—but she always came back. Once she asked
them if the philosophy was actually coming from her own
subconscious. "I received my comeuppance when they
bluntly responded, 'Were they your thoughts?' I had to concede that they were not."

The Guides' lengthy discourses continued: "Actually we
are no more the 'hereafter' than are you, who sprang from a
previous stage which you cannot recall," they wrote. "The
very thought that thinking human beings sprang fully developed in that one state of existence would seem laughable
to any except you earth people, who are accustomed to
accepting everything at face value. You who are more advanced and sensitive have lived through many previous
phases, while some of the more doltish varieties had only
primer training in a previous step. To that life which went
before, you are as much the 'hereafter' as we are to you. The
hereafter goes on and on, my dear child, until at last you and
we and all of us eventually pass through that Golden Door
where longing shall be no more, where perfection has been
attained, and where we are at last one with God, our Creator. This voyage through the various stages of life can be as
rapidly performed, or as slowly drawn, as you make it, depending on your own contribution there, here, and in all of
the various steps. The progress depends on you, not God,

who has given all equal opportunity, although not all have the same opportunity at each level of their advancement."

Scanning each new page of this material as it arrived, Ruth hastily dropped it with the others into a desk drawer and dismissed it from her mind. The "real world" continued to beckon.

On November 22, 1963, shots rang out in Dallas, plunging the nation into stunned grief at the sudden slaying of its young President. "My bureau chief told me to start writing," Ruth recalls of that shocking day. "I was the only Hearst correspondent who knew Lyndon and Lady Bird Johnson personally, so I was immediately asked to turn out an in-depth series of articles about the new President." Three days later she joined her colleagues of the White House press corps in paying last respects to her longtime friend, John F. Kennedy, in the East Room where she had covered the Roosevelt funeral eighteen years before.

Events surrounding the new administration demanded press attention at once. What policy changes would ensue? How would these new directions affect legislation and foreign affairs? As a political columnist charged with informing the public, Ruth had her work cut out for her. Then an unexpected call came from New York. Would she be interested in writing a biography of the new First Lady, and could she complete it in six weeks? It would be an honor—and lucrative.

"From then on I pounded the typewriter day and night," she recalls of that busy winter. "My daily column continued as usual, and during the rest of those eighteen-hour workdays I interviewed Lady Bird and Lyndon at the White House, their close friends around town, and worked on pulling the book together." Her second book, *Mrs. LBJ*, was released in the spring of 1964 and became an immediate bestseller, reaching the top spots on all national lists. As soon as President and Mrs. Johnson resumed public entertaining after the Kennedy tragedy, they regularly included Ruth and her husband at state dinners and White House parties. "More importantly," Ruth says, "they arranged for Dr. Janet Travell, the White House physician whom Jack Kennedy had originally sent to me, to continue her treatments that were curing my back spasms. What a godsend that was!"

Her third book contract came soon after. Jeane Dixon, a Washington seeress who had consulted her crystal ball for politicians over the years and been featured in Ruth's New Year's columns, had repeatedly petitioned Ruth to write her biography. Jeane had now found a paperback publisher who proffered a contract, if only Ruth would accept. "I finally agreed," she says, "but only on condition that the book be issued in hardcover first."

Attempting to portray a balanced view of the clairvoyant who had correctly foretold President Kennedy's assassination and other world events, Ruth pointed out Jeane's misses in the New Year's columns, along with her hits. "Any responsible reporter presents both sides of an issue," she explains. But to her dismay the publisher changed editors and the new one insisted on deleting most of Jeane's incorrect predictions. The resulting book offered an unduly rosy view of the seer's success ratio. "I was not very happy about that," Ruth confesses, "but I figured that nobody would read the book anyway."

She was wrong. *Reader's Digest* printed an advance excerpt just prior to the publication date, so that as soon as the book was released, it made every bestseller list in the country, where it remained until the paperback version was issued seven months later. Entitled *A Gift of Prophecy*, Ruth's third book became the runaway bestseller of the decade.

By 1965, having completed three biographies, Ruth at last gave serious consideration to writing a book that would encompass the voluminous material secreted away in her desk drawer. The Guides' philosophy of love and service to others, their description of death as a mere transition into an exciting new world of activity, and their explanation of the true purpose of earthly living deserved to be shared with others who were also seeking answers.

For five years the Guides had been urging her to disseminate their teaching, while the personal tug-of-war continued to plague her. "We are anxious that you not waste your remaining time there," they wrote. "You have much to give to the world, if you would only utilize your time. Many are clamoring for help, and need you. Why are you turning away?"

Simultaneously, her mother was pleading: "Please, please, Ruth, don't write about it. You'll destroy the fine professional reputation that you've worked so hard to build. You've made me so proud of you thus far. Don't throw it all away!"

Two years earlier Arthur Ford had persuaded Ruth and Bob to attend a week's seminar on meditation and psychic development that his SFF organization was cosponsoring with the Association for Research and Enlightenment (ARE) in Virginia Beach, Virginia. The latter group, headed by Hugh Lynn Cayce, had been founded two decades earlier to carry on the work of his father, the famed psychic Edgar Cayce, and to teach his precepts.

Impressed with the credentials of the seminar leaders, Ruth's editor agreed that she should cover it, and she attended it in the dual role of student and reporter. While there, she was intrigued to discover that clergymen had often traveled hundreds of miles in secret to attend ARE and SFF programs, fearful of criticism from their church members, only to find that some from their own congregations had done the same.

Later Ruth returned to Virginia Beach to attend a seminar on dream interpretation, and at last, she says, "came face-to-face with myself." The confrontation came through a dream. "We were expected to record our dreams immediately upon awakening, and then to present them to the class for analysis," she recounts. "One night I seemed to watch men at a building similar to ARE headquarters remove rotted shingles from a high-peaked roof, reaching into the exposed rafters to pull out and discard dozens of badly rusted coat hangers, and I asked why they hadn't done that a year or two earlier, when they had the chance. To me the dream meant nothing, but it certainly was significant to our seminar leaders, dream expert J. Everett Irion and psychiatrist Dr. W. Lindsay Jacob. Coat hangers, they pointed out, are used to store garments when not in use. The roof was a symbol for my head or mind, and my subconscious seemed to have been saying in the dream, 'Why did you let the challenging ideas that you received here at a seminar two years ago rust away in storage instead of putting them to better use? Now you have another opportunity.'"

"I thereupon decided to write the book that would disseminate the Guides' philosophy, but to put it into a context that would explain how a skeptical newspaper reporter could stumble into such an arcane field. And I took my friends along for company, recounting the amazing psychic experiences of these others who had impeccable credibility. They were all happy to be included. We would sink or swim together. Fortunately we swam."

Cheered on by the Guides, Ruth now set to work to organize the automatic writing that had accumulated over the years, separating it into proper categories. One day they wrote judiciously: "The time for everyone to think about his future is while he is living in what will become his past. Regard each day as an umblemished page in the book of life. Take each day with you, spotless, into the next stage, and you will have advanced far beyond your wildest dreams.

The best thing to remember is this: Greet each day as the untarnished future, and handle it as carefully as if it were already a published record of your past." Remembering that, they added, will prevent us from being deterred by the temptations of the world.

The spirit of Ira Shick also emphasized this point to his daughter: "How much easier the task will be to review your past life (after death) if you live each day as if that was the sole recording of your entire lifetime. Keep that page so neat and tidy, so filled with loving care, that if your life should end at midnight the page would be spotless and blameless."

While finishing the book, the Guides brought Ruth encouraging messages from some of her close friends who had recently passed on, including one from her longtime newspaper colleague, George Dixon, which read: "I'll be darned if you weren't right, Ruthie. Spread the word, kid, and let others know. Don't give a hang what some fuddy-duddies will say about it. They don't count for nuttin' when you see it from over here."

The Guides said of the humor-columnist, "When the parsons [preachers] come here, it is someone like George who can get them to relax and take a shocked new look at the life here, for most of them expect something so different—like marble halls and angels with harps."

People had expected something different from Ruth Montgomery as well. Accustomed to her integrity, her insight, and her dogged insistence on accuracy, they knew from experience that they could count on her to tell it straight. And she did. She put her ten years of exploration into that book, a factual account of her own winding path into a realm that had deeply touched her, and that would ultimately change the lives of many of her millions of readers.

Perhaps its dedication best reflects the alteration within

Ruth Montgomery herself: "To my father Ira Whitmer Shick (1881–1953) who continues to give me loving counsel since he passed to the next phase of eternal life."

She called the book *A Search for the Truth,* and that modest claim is all that she intended it to be.

CHAPTER VII

Reincarnation

Reincarnation? Ruth Montgomery did *not* believe in reincarnation! "Frankly, I hadn't even thought about it in those days," she admits. "I remember that when Bob's sister Rhoda told us she now believed in it, after studying the Vedas and other Eastern philosophy with Dr. Pantin in St. Petersburg, I just laughed and remarked, 'That's all right, Rhoda. We love you anyway.'"

Meditation, however, was another story. "I sincerely tried to make the time to meditate each day," she recalls. "I was somewhat more disciplined about it then than I am now, and I set aside the fifteen or twenty minutes necessary to clear my mind of worldly intrusions and reach an inner silence."

During one period of especially deep meditation something unusual occurred. As Ruth sat quietly, with eyes closed and her normally racing mind slowed to the point of stillness, a vivid scene began to unfold. "I saw a brilliant star," she recalls, "and I knew that I was in Bethlehem. I was a little girl only five or six years old and was aware that a baby had recently been born. Strangely dressed men arrived, and I saw them go down to a little stable near our cottage. I begged my father to take me there, and finally he agreed if I would promise to stay out of the way. He reached down, I put my little hand in his, and we walked over there together. I could feel his hand, and I recognized him as the soul of Arthur Ford. We didn't glimpse the baby, but we joined the others who had also seen the star and followed it." Emerging from her meditation, she puzzled over the strikingly moving scene. "It was a lovely version of the Christ-child story. I thought that my temporarily peaceful mind had simply envisioned a deep and meaningful picture of something that I had learned as a child in Sunday School. Except for the odd feeling that I'd actually been in that child's body, I assigned it no greater significance."

Meanwhile *A Search for the Truth* had gone to press. The work of final editing, typesetting, proofreading, printing, binding, and distributing normally takes eight or nine months, and during this interim another prospect beckoned to Ruth, who was still busily writing her daily column.

Homer Gruenther, a top White House aide during the Eisenhower, Kennedy, and Johnson administrations and a brother of General Alfred M. Gruenther, Eisenhower's best friend, remarked to Ruth at a party that a fascinating collection of flower arrangement photographs existed at the executive mansion. "It's a pity that somebody doesn't bring out a book with those illustrations," he said. "Ruth, why don't you do it? Come over to the White House and take a look at them."

"I told him that I was no expert on flower arrangements," she recalls, "but Homer kept returning to the subject and urging me to consider writing the text for a book about those bouquets that had graced the tables at memorable state dinners in various administrations. The material did have some historical significance, so finally I agreed to look at the photos and mention them to my editor." A division of Morrow was indeed interested in such a coffee table book, and gave her the go-ahead to assemble and write it under the title of *Flowers at the White House.*

All during this period the spirit Guides, who continued to type through her racing fingers each morning, were pursuing a new topic. "They always seem to launch my next book project before I've even recovered from the last one," she says, laughing. "This time they started writing about reincarnation, and I thought, *'What* is going on here? I certainly don't believe in *that!'* "

Undaunted, they busily tapped out their daily messages on her electric typewriter and blithely announced: "We will now discuss the path that a soul follows from its original breath of life until its reunion with the Creator." They continued to describe each soul as a spark that emanated long ago from one central source, with the goal of ultimate return to the radiant center. "Try to understand," they wrote, "that as we return again and again to earth to complete our purification, we are beset not only by the old sins that we came to resolve (karma), but also by new temptations which must be met and overcome, or we do not grow."

Ruth was unimpressed. "Why do you love butter beans so much?" they asked her one day, seeking to illustrate their point that previous lives influence the present one. "Because," they continued, "you once cultivated them in another life. You nursed them, loved to watch them develop, and considered them the most beautiful plant in your world; and before we knew so much about nutrition, you had convinced yourself that the richness of flavor and solid quality must make butter beans the most nourishing and sustaining food in the world. This was when you ate no meat and lived virtually as a hermit; but this is only a sample of what each person will be able to do when he draws forth the influences that made him what he is today." And they continued with other examples that struck home to her.

Ruth was nonplussed by all this. It had taken a considerable leap of faith for her to accept spiritual communication as real, then to overcome family opposition and dare to write about it. Now the Guides proposed an idea that she was not at all ready to tackle. "It's true!" they insisted. "Why don't you investigate it and satisfy yourself?"

"I looked back through what they had already written for *A Search for the Truth*, which was about to be released, and found that they had indeed hinted at reincarnation, though I hadn't noticed it at the time," she admits. "The idea had been couched in more orthodox terms such as 'stages,' or 'phases of soul development.'" Aware that Edgar Cayce had espoused a belief in rebirth, as did many of the people who frequented ARE headquarters in Virginia Beach, Ruth sat down for long talks first with Hugh Lynn Cayce and then with others whose lives had been changed by readings they had had with the late seer, in which past incarnations had been described along with medical diagnoses. "I read a number of those records," she continues, "and studied numerous books on the subject, and as I learned more about it, this seemingly bizarre idea began to make more sense." Not yet convinced, but opting to keep an open mind, she interviewed believers for a possible book, seeking to learn more about what had induced them to subscribe to such a concept. "I reasoned that if this philosophy had influenced so many thinking people—Benjamin Franklin, Voltaire, Henry Ford, Ralph Waldo Emerson, Henry David Thoreau, Plato, the Jewish Essenes of ancient Palestine as well as Buddhists and Hindus—then it was certainly worth learning more about."

Meanwhile publication day arrived, and *A Search for the Truth* reached bookstores across the country in February 1967. Its fascinating account of Ruth's ten-year journey into the psychic, the dozens of strange and unaccountable events in the lives of well-known people, and its powerful evidence for life beyond the grave, all compiled by a skeptical reporter with unquestioned integrity, captivated readers at once. "As I set out on the promotional TV tour, I picked up a copy of *Time* magazine in an airport and was casually reading it while waiting for a plane," she recalls. "When I reached the book section I was astounded to discover that *A Search for the Truth* had already made the bestseller list!"

Other editors soon began calling. Would she consider doing a book for them, also on the psychic field? People were hungry for this information, intrigued by its implications, encouraged and comforted by its confirmation of their religious values. Clergy of many faiths invited her to address their congregations, and strangers wrote to describe their own baffling experiences with unexplained events.

"The editors wanted more writing on this subject," she recalls, "but I had already told everything that I personally knew about it. I *had* no more information that I could verify." Besides, another idea had begun to capture her interest. "My next book is going to be on reincarnation," she told one of them almost defiantly, making up her mind on the spot.

"Really, a different topic would be more certain of big sales," he argued. "Reincarnation is too far-out."

"I'm sorry, but I don't care about that." She could not be dissuaded. "This is the one I'm doing."

Ruth admits that thus far she had not even approached an editor with the idea. "I just knew that I needed to write about it, whether or not it found a publisher. The idea was intriguing me, and I continued to research it."

By this time Ruth and Bob had bought a charming house in Virginia Beach. "It was an idyllic location, on a peninsula surrounded by water on three sides," she recalls, "and we

had a swimming pool built on the fourth side. Bob was on
assignment as a management consultant to the nearby
Newport News Shipbuilding Company at the time, and
while continuing to write my newspaper column in Washington, I began spending more and more time with him at
the Virginia Beach house. Finally we decided to put our
Washington house on the market."

One day the telephone rang and an unfamiliar voice introduced himself as Ellis Amburn, a senior editor for Cow-
ard-McCann in New York. "I've been fascinated with your
books," he exclaimed. "Would you consider writing one for
us on mediums?"

"No," she replied firmly. "I covered all that I want to say
on that subject in *A Search for the Truth*. Now I'm starting a
book on reincarnation, and that's the one I'm going to do."

"Let me talk to the powers that be," he offered. "I'll get
back to you tomorrow." When he phoned the following day,
it was to announce with great enthusiasm, "I have a contract! Could I send it down for you to sign? It's for a book on
reincarnation."

"This had never happened to me before," Ruth muses.
"He had seen *nothing* of the book, not even an outline, but
he sent a contract sight unseen. That's what I call faith—so I
signed it."

Now she set to work in earnest, writing up the accounts of
those working actively with ARE who had had the good
fortune to secure past-life readings by Edgar Cayce before
his death in 1945. "It was intriguing to delve into the
records of those long-ago lives and discover how they were
affecting their current incarnations," Ruth reminisces.

"This was the right place to be, at the right time, if I was
going to write a book about reincarnation. To be honest, I
began to wonder whether those determined Guides of
mine had even arranged Bob's assignment to the nearby
shipbuilding company so that I would spend a lot of time in

Virginia Beach and become intimately acquainted with the people at Edgar Cayce Foundation headquarters. Pretty sneaky!"

Ruth was aware that the entranced Cayce had "identified" his son Hugh Lynn as Andrew, one of the twelve disciples, and in another reading as a former king named Araaraat who ruled ancient Egypt while Edgar Cayce was said to have been the high priest Ra-Ta. But there was more!

"Hugh Lynn was so eager for me to write a book on reincarnation that he decided to disclose two much more personal episodes in his past lives, for which he believed that he had been forced to make karmic retribution in his present go-around," Ruth declares. "In one he had deserted a wife and child to join the Crusades, principally for adventure, and in this life he was reluctantly forced by World War II to leave his wife and baby son behind when he was sent to the European theater of war. In another, through flashbacks and a string of coincidences, he "knew" that he had fatally choked an unfaithful wife, and in this lifetime he had not only narrowly escaped marrying her again, but had been hospitalized several times while choking on pieces of meat that lodged in his throat."

Edgar Cayce's longtime secretary Gladys Davis, Mae St. Clair, Elsie and Wilfred Sechrist, and numerous others currently associated with ARE gave Ruth copies of their Cayce life readings and discussed the remarkable influence that those long-ago events had wielded on their present incarnations. She also interviewed such outstanding specialists in the reincarnation field as Dr. Ian Stevenson, Dr. Stanley Krippner, Joan Grant Kelsey, and Dr. W. Lindsay Jacob, recounting their own stories.

The manuscript was well along on its way to fruition when Ruth received a long-distance telephone call from Marianne Wolf of Concordville, Pennsylvania, a friend whom she had met through ARE and Arthur Ford. Excited to learn that Ruth was writing a book about a subject in which she deeply believed, she announced, "A good friend of mine is visiting me—Adelle Davis, the famous nutritionist. She knows a great deal about reincarnation and would like to speak to you. May I put her on the line?"

Ruth was delighted at the opportunity to talk with Adelle, whose books *Let's Eat Right to Keep Fit* and *Let's Get Well* had made outstanding contributions to better health. "I knew of her work in nutrition, but not of her interest in reincarnation," Ruth says. "It was reassuring to find another such believer."

The two women had a chatty get-acquainted talk before Adelle declared, "You can't write a book about reincarnation without including hypnotic prenatal regression. Have you looked into it?"

Ruth admitted that she had not.

"Then come to visit me in California," Adelle urged. "I'm going home tomorrow. As soon as you can arrange it, fly out to the West Coast and I'll introduce you to a former Air Force major who can hypnotize you and me, and you'll see exactly what the process is all about."

"Nobody's going to hypnotize me!" Ruth protested laughingly. "I'll be glad to watch while he does *you*, if you like, but I don't want a personal role in it, thanks."

"Never mind! I'll ask some other friends over and you'll be able to gather a variety of material. You can also listen to some tapes I've made of previous hypnotic sessions. They're remarkable!"

Not knowing quite what to expect from the promised sessions, Ruth arranged to fly to Los Angeles, where Adelle and her husband met her at the airport and drove her to their home in Palos Verdes Estates.

Hypnotic regression, as Ruth knew, is a process often used by psychologists and psychiatrists to help patients recall buried memories and thereby uncover the source of otherwise unexplained problems. Some dozen years earlier a popular but highly controversial book entitled *The Search for Bridey Murphy* had described the experience of hypnotist Morey Bernstein in regressing a Colorado housewife back even further, to an earlier lifetime in Ireland. Subsequently, harsh and largely unfair criticism of that book cautioned qualified professionals who valued their reputations to remain secretive with such experiments, lest they expose themselves to similar attacks on their integrity for exploring such professionally unacceptable theories as reincarnation.

Even Adelle Davis, whose work in the field of nutrition had won her international acclaim, could risk damage to her own reputation by going public with such a belief while her more readily acceptable books on nutrition enjoyed wide circulation. The same could happen to Ruth Montgomery for that matter. "I remained quite cautious, sticking to the facts and merely reporting them," she recalls. "But those facts seemed to grow more convincing every day."

Adelle played tapes of her own hypnotic-regression sessions wherein she had repeatedly described a harrowing scene from eighteenth-century America, in a western Massachusetts settlement known as Cambria. Barricaded in a cabin with her three fretful children, out of food and water, and terrified of venturing outside where Indians lurked in the surrounding woods, she wailed over the loss of her young husband who had left to fight off the Indian marauders. "He never came back! Allan never came back! The Indians killed him!" she screamed between dry, racking sobs. The tapes were bone-chilling to hear, stark and raw in their portrayal of a desperate widow too frightened to attempt to reach her own garden and well, though her children cried from hunger and thirst.

The next evening Adelle invited several friends to dinner, among them Major Arthur Knight, a psychologist who had served with the military in England during World War

II. As a graduate student in psychology at the University of
Minnesota in 1930, Major Knight had stumbled upon prenatal regression quite by accident when a university student
who had volunteered as a hypnotic subject in order to provide Knight with material for his master's thesis was being
regressed back to the age of four. Suddenly another person
burst into the room, so distracting Knight that the counting
continued longer than he had planned. When he finally
stopped and asked the subject his name, the young man
claimed a strange identity and described a completely different life, while exhibiting a markedly changed personality. That incident led Knight to further work involving the
phenomenon, with strikingly similar results: subjects regressed back to a time before their births reported prior
incarnations in widely diverse locales, socioeconomic strata,
and life circumstances.

Now Ruth was about to witness hypnotic prenatal regression firsthand, and she tingled with excitement. One by one,
guests in Adelle's living room took turns on the couch, while
Knight led them to relax completely and move back in time
through their childhood, before birth, even before concep-
tion. He also told them that they would remember everything when they returned to the present. "I seem to be a
nun in a region of Asia Minor," a woman of Protestant faith
reported, describing her flowing black habit and her daily
duties of teaching and caring for children in a Catholic
school. Under Knight's guidance she gradually moved forward in time, to her death under falling rocks as she and the
children fled nearby fighting by scrambling up a steep
mountain pass. It was, she said, the third century A.D.

Likewise a middle-aged woman described a life in France
and suddenly writhed in pain, sobbing that she had just
been thrown from a horse on her father's estate.

A handsome young doctor related tales of an unhappy
incarnation in a French castle, dying from consumption in

the year 1547, and watching as servants dumped his body unceremoniously into a ravine and covered it with rocks. At this point Major Knight paused to ask the reason for this life of suffering. The man contorted with emotional pain, stammered, and finally admitted, "In a previous lifetime I stoned a woman to death."

Knight explained to the group that through his many years of experience with regression, he had found that when a person described a life of suffering, that person would invariably tell of having made someone else suffer in an earlier lifetime. "It should make us pause and think before we act," he remarked, adding that most people under regression describe ordinary rather than glamorous lives. Many of them are dull, some even shameful.

One such story was told by a Los Angeles banker, a devout Catholic who stated flatly that he did not believe in reincarnation. Under hypnosis he described in great detail a life as an unscrupulous German landowner in 1763, foreclosing mortgages and seizing land, thereby increasing his holdings to thousands of acres, until his death of a heart attack. Once out of hypnosis he exclaimed at the vividness of what he had seen. "The inside of that bank in Germany is still as clear as this room," he remarked in awe. "I keep seeing a poor peasant pleading with me to give him just one more week before I foreclose his mortgage. Wow! Am I glad to have another chance now!"

A second disbeliever, this one a prominent attorney anxious to expose what he perceived as the farce of reincarnation, agreed to take a turn on the couch. Instructed to relax completely and go back, back in time, he suddenly began to describe in horrifying detail a Norse shipwreck during a ferocious storm at sea. "I'm clinging to a board . . . don't know whether I can hold on much longer," he gasped, clutching frantically at the coverlet. Taken to a different lifetime, he found himself in New England and gave details of a disastrous existence as a female prostitute, finally demanding, "Get me out of here! Bring me out of this damned trance. . . ." Safely back in the twentieth century he sat up and shuddered. "What a hell of a life that was!" he exclaimed.

Ruth quietly continued to tape each regression: a lady shrieking with terror at being hanged on London Bridge for stealing a loaf of bread, a young betrothed woman in nineteenth-century Japan, even a French mademoiselle guillotined after being caught with her lover.

Finally her own curiosity outweighed her earlier caution. "I'd like to be next," she confessed diffidently, ashamed of her temerity. "I wasn't yet a convert," she concedes, "but after seeing what happened even with those who thought reincarnation was fantasy, I was willing to be a guinea pig rather than a coward."

Major Knight guided her into a trance state, instructing her to relax completely. "I saw myself in Austria, a cloddish, unattractive woman," she recalls, "and I seemed to be churning, churning, always churning milk on a wooden porch. Then, going forward in time, I attended my father's funeral in a country church. The experience of hypnosis was interesting, but what a miserably boring life!"

The following day she and Adelle talked for hours, reviewing the great variety of stories that had emerged and the markedly different personalities and mannerisms displayed by those in trance. An awkward, heavyset woman had shown unusual grace, her Midwestern twang giving way to a clipped, sophisticated tone of voice. A scrupulously honest banker had told of living the life of a scoundrel and had talked with crude grammar uncharacteristic of his present-day position and education. A slim and attractive woman had described great rolls of fat on her previous body. A man told of having been a woman; a Protestant spoke of being Catholic; and a Caucasian had described life

as an Oriental. In addition, disbelievers who thought reincarnation was ridiculous related tales every bit as dramatic
and detailed as those of the believers.

"Could these stories be real?" Ruth asked Adelle wonder-
ingly. "In my own case the trance was so light that I
doubted if I had actually been hypnotized. I felt as if I were
operating on two levels. I could see the action unfold behind my eyelids, yet I also knew that I was in the room with
Major Knight asking questions and other people watching."

"It always seems that way the first time," Adelle assured
her. "People usually don't quite believe it. Would you like
me to hypnotize you and see what happens?"

"You mean that you can do it? Oh yes, I'd like that very
much," Ruth exclaimed. "I think I'll be able to relax more
with you than with a strange man as the hypnotist. Could
we see if anything comes from a life in Egypt? I've always
felt so at home there."

She stretched out on the couch, and under Adelle's gentle
guidance slipped into a far deeper trance than before.
"Vivid pictures began to form from nowhere," she recalls.
"I found myself walking through a beautiful flower garden
above the sparkling waters of the Nile. I was serene, graceful, and blissfully happy." Asked to move forward in time,
she seemed unable to do so, until she realized that she had
left the body. "Oh, I understand now!" she exclaimed, still
in trance. "I stepped on a little adder. I didn't mean to; I
didn't see it, but I was wearing sandals and it must have
bitten me." She intently surveyed the continuing scene,
observing the sadly bowed head of her husband in that life.
"Why, it's Hugh Lynn Cayce!" she exclaimed in utter surprise. Asked if he was grieving, she replied, "Yes, but he
won't for long. He's a good man. He will marry again."
(Incidentally she never told Hugh Lynn of the experience,
and he has since passed on.)

This striking and unexpected glimpse into the distant

past added one more piece of evidence to Ruth s growing case for rebirth. Did we really meet one another again and again through the centuries? Group karma, the tendency for clusters of souls to incarnate together in cycles, was a basic tenet of the concept of reincarnation. Just as we may choose our gender, race, locale, even our parents, so also we are drawn toward others with whom we need to work out problems left unresolved in previous lives.

Further explanation of the cycle of rebirth came to Ruth's attention the following day, when Adelle invited a handful of friends to a regression session that she herself would conduct. The first hypnotic subject, a schoolteacher who argued that reincarnation was for the birds, volunteered to undergo regression in order to prove her point. To the contrary, no sooner had she entered a deeply relaxed state than she described with vivid detail a lifetime in China ending in 1757, and then a scene as a nine-year-old black slave running barefoot through the woods on a Missouri plantation in 1819. When asked what happened to people between lives, the still-entranced woman replied, "After assessing the errors of our past life, we decide the kind of obstacles which will best help us to advance in the next incarnation." Surmounting chosen obstacles in earthly life, she explained, would help us to grow in understanding.

Adelle gradually brought the woman out of trance, and before speaking she lay quietly for a few minutes, thinking about what had transpired. "If there's nothing to reincarnation," she began in bafflement, "where in the world did all that come from? I simply can't understand it!"

The second subject, the attractive and well-adjusted wife of a corporate president, described lives as a prehistoric cave dweller in the Arctic, an Egyptian maiden in A.D. 1500, and a newborn infant deliberately abandoned in the mud of a cold Boston alley. "We come back each time to accomplish something, to compensate for any harm that we have done to others, and to keep them from being hurt again," she declared from her hypnotic state.

Ruth found each of these stories fascinating, but the most convincing one of all emerged from the subconscious memory of a well-educated and obviously cultured matron who was a happily married mother of three. During her two-hour hypnosis she identified herself as Sam Sneed, a cocky, cheating cardsharp who made his way from New York west to San Francisco in 1872, often one step ahead of the sheriff after doing "local yokels" out of their money all the way from Jersey through Kansas and Wyoming. Dissolving into gales of laughter with each new episode recounted by the boastful, swaggering, hard-drinking gambler, Ruth and Adelle remained absolutely captivated.

"What do you do between lives?" Adelle finally asked, after leading Sam through the street shooting that eventually ended his colorful career.

"You have to evaluate, to weigh the past life and formulate what it is that you'll need, and what you'll seek in the next one. I hadn't used women very well in that life, so I'll have to come back as a woman." As for the lessons in each incarnation, "It's got to be hard," he/she declared. "If it's too easy, you don't grow. If your whole life is easy, you never learn." Slowly Adelle guided a more thoughtful Sam Sneed back to the present.

Until then Ruth had not totally embraced the idea of reincarnation, having tried to consider all of the arguments its critics could muster. "After this regression I had few remaining doubts," she recalls. "I flew home to Virginia Beach feeling *much* more comfortable about producing a book on the subject. In my own mind the idea of a succession of lifetimes now made sense. It explained the apparent inequities of life and the purpose of living, erased fear of death, and placed the obligation of 'judgment' squarely on the shoulders of each of us, respecting our free will to learn

and grow and atone for our mistakes. We can't blame God
for our present circumstances. We chose them ourselves—
to learn."

Evidence for reincarnation continued to mount. Still,
Ruth posed her questions and recorded the answers that she
found. If we do indeed return to earthly life again and
again, why don't we consciously remember prior lifetimes?
Perhaps the burden of such memories would prove to be
too cumbersome. Just as we forget many details of our own
childhood, and usually lack recall before the age of three, so
a kind providence curtains our recollections of prenatal
follies, giving us fresh opportunities to surmount and overcome them.

Some levels of past-life memory do occasionally surface,
as Ruth was learning in her research. For instance, we may
find ourselves inexplicably drawn toward certain souls
whom we have known before. Likewise child prodigies who
exhibit native talent for music, mathematics, or foreign lan-
guages may actually be drawing on subconscious memories
of a prior familiarity with or mastery of skills that they had
learned long ago. A love of particular foods, a yearning to
visit certain faraway lands, or a fascination with unusual
fields of study may all serve as indicators of lives we once
lived.

Hypnosis is not always necessary in order to revive past-
life memories. Sometimes spontaneous recall may be trig-
gered by a whiff of a long-forgotten fragrance, or a visit to a
foreign country that seems strangely familiar. Children
often speak of earlier lives as soon as they are able to talk,
but are quickly shushed by their parents who admonish
them to stop "telling stories" and speak the "truth." According to some, dreams may serve as a key to our long-
buried past. The Guides suggested still another approach:
"The easiest way to prompt one's faulty memory is by
reaching back into the mind through meditation," they

wrote. "Then, as glimmers of truth flash before the inner eye, one may seek to determine from whence they came." Had Ruth's meditative vision of the Nativity been an actual scene from a prior incarnation? She brushed the thought aside and focused on lives that others had seemingly re-lived.

With her research on reincarnation nearly complete, Ruth invited Adelle Davis to stay with her during a visit to Virginia Beach to address a seminar arranged by Hugh Lynn Cayce. Close friends by now, Ruth and Adelle shared their final evening together, quietly chatting as they con-templated the moonlit, sparkling waters that softly lapped the shore below their vantage point on the sun porch. Bob had already turned in for the night.

"Ruth, how would you like for me to hypnotize you one last time?" Adelle offered.

"Great!" Ruth replied eagerly. Moving to a reclining chair, she relaxed as Adelle's deep voice guided her back in time, back, back to a distant land long, long ago. "I found myself in the Himalayas," she recalls, "a skinny young man seated in the lotus position at an ashram. My arms were small and brown, and while carefully surveying my sur-roundings I described my duties as a guru for younger boys who came up from the village below. Berries, fruits, and nuts formed our diet—we ate no meat. And I volunteered that I studied under an older guru who lived higher up the mountain." Told to move forward in time, she found herself in a different ashram. "My own guru has passed on," she explained, "and I have taken over his duties."

"Do you have a mantra?" Adelle prodded.

"Certainly—everyone does," she replied, and on being told to demonstrate it she burst into a verbal melding of two syllables over and over again. "Adelle tried to hush me, but for some unknown reason, I knew that I had to repeat the mantra eleven times, and I continued with the strange cadence in the darkness of the sun porch until the cycle ended."

"Now we'll go to a different lifetime," Adelle directed, guiding her to another point in time.

"Oh, oh, the sand is *hot* on my feet!" she exclaimed. "I'm racing across the desert in thin sandals. The child who was born under the star is now grown to manhood, and I'm leaving my husband and baby to hear Him preach. My husband has forbidden me to go, so I'm running away from him to join the throng of people who follow this great teacher."

"Tell me what's happening now," Adelle continued.

"Oh! I can *see* Him! I *see* Him! He's speaking under a tree and there's a whole multitude of people around Him!"

"What's a multitude?" Adelle asked, her extraordinarily deep voice holding a hint of humor.

"It must be a *hundred* people!" Ruth exclaimed breathlessly.

"I always wondered what a multitude was," Adelle said dryly.

"Later I seemed to go to the house of Lazarus in Bethany," Ruth recalled afterward. "I knew that Lazarus was my brother, but since his sisters Martha and Mary were both there, I couldn't have been one of them. We had a wonderful visit, though, and Jesus was with us."

When Adelle finally brought her out of trance, Ruth contemplated both vivid scenes. "The one in Bethany seemed too puzzling to be taken seriously," she recounts. "Even though it fit with the Nativity scene that I had observed in deep meditation, it didn't make sense that Lazarus was my brother, so I tried to put it out of my mind. But I still 'see' those settings in the Himalayas and Palestine as clearly as I do my own home."

She completed the book called *Here and Hereafter*, carefully disguising the identity of Adelle Davis (who is now deceased) under the name Jane Winthrop, and avoiding any mention of either her own submission to hypnosis or her startling glimpses of purported prior lifetimes. Ruth did indeed believe in reincarnation by now, but purposely refrained from proselytizing. "I am a reporter," she reasoned. "Reporters present many sides of a question and allow the reader to make up his own mind."

Not long after the book's completion, two startling events occurred, both related to the final regression that Adelle had conducted with her in Virginia Beach. Dr. I. C. Sharma of Udaipur, India, called on Ruth to discuss her books. "I wish I knew what my mantra was," she told him before he left. He offered to meditate on it. On his next visit she reminded him of that offer, asking him wistfully, "I suppose you haven't had time to meditate on my mantra."

"Indeed I have," he replied. "I will write it for you."

Ruth stared in astonishment at the piece of paper on which he wrote two syllables melded together as one. "They were the same two syllables I had uttered over and over while under hypnosis!" she exclaims. "No one but Adelle and I had known about it, and Dr. Sharma had never met Adelle."

The second event occurred shortly after the publication of *Here and Hereafter*. "I had not written anything about my past incarnations," she recounts, "and certainly not about the visions of ancient Palestine." Yet a letter arrived from Thomas Bunker, an unknown fan who said that he had psychically received an impression that she had been a sister of Lazarus. "It can't be true," Ruth argued to herself, "because I clearly saw Martha and Mary in Lazarus' living room."

Not long after receiving Mr. Bunker's letter, Ruth happened to pick up a copy of *The Aquarian Gospel of Jesus the Christ*, a book said to have been transcribed from the akashic records and assembled during the last century by

Levi H. Dowling after forty years of study and silent meditation. Since it was written in biblical style, she read it
slowly and contemplatively, a little each day, until reaching
Chapter 77. There, to her amazement, she encountered the
story of a sister of Lazarus named Ruth, who had left her
husband to follow Jesus until He counseled her to return to
her family and live a godly life. "It said that Lazarus had
three sisters—Mary, Martha, and Ruth! I was flabber-
gasted!" she exclaims. "Perhaps the odd vision was not
imaginary after all."

And perhaps the concept of reincarnation, perceived as
outlandish by many Westerners, who have been taught otherwise, is also not so odd. "Try to understand," the Guides
counseled, "that as we return again and again to earth to
complete our purification, we are beset not only by the old
sins that we came to resolve, but also by new temptations
which must be met and overcome, or we do not grow. Only
the law of Grace—God's forgiveness—can supercede the
otherwise immutable law of karma."

If spiritual "growth" is indeed the purpose of life, and if
we believe that we choose our own hardships so that we will
learn to overcome them, then life takes on a whole new
dimension. Indeed Ruth's life was about to change dramatically with the publication of these startling ideas in *Here
and Hereafter*.

"It is not overly important whether we 'believe' in reincarnation," she wrote at the book's conclusion. "If the laws
of karma and Grace are real, they will survive without our
attestation. What does matter is that we conduct ourselves
in such manner that we incur no bad karmic indebtedness.
The skeptic may ask, 'What if there's no such thing as
karma, or reincarnation, or eternal life?' "

"Yes," she concluded thoughtfully, "but what if there *is?*"

CHAPTER VIII

Off to Mexico

Publication date for *Here and Hereafter* on August 20, 1968, proved to be a particularly memorable one. Barbara Walters interviewed Ruth on her popular NBC "Today" show in New York, and by the following morning bookstores across the nation were deluging her publishers with many thousands of reorders.

She was also interviewed by Johnny Carson on the NBC "Tonight" show and later by Phil Donahue, the first time in history that three such attention-commanding television programs had all devoted their valuable air time to the controversial subject of reincarnation.

With equal success Ruth made her customary Midwest and West Coast TV tours, starred at autograph parties from Beverly Hills to Washington, D.C., and addressed a standing-room-only audience in the Philadelphia area where several hundred others had to be turned away.

The many reviews were also heartwarming. "A book that's hard to put down (in every sense) even though you muster up every skeptical argument," according to the influential *Kirkus Reviews* for booksellers. *Publishers Weekly* proclaimed, "The many readers of Ruth Montgomery will follow avidly her discussion of the doctrine of karma and rebirth . . . she cites innumerable instances that seem, to her, persuasive evidence that we are indeed caught up in successive reincarnations, and always meaningfully. Ruth Montgomery's sincerity, humility, and personal conviction are in evidence on every page, and readers of her previous books will not be let down." Arthur Ford described the book as "sane, scholarly, well documented," and Hugh Lynn Cayce wrote in his review: "Straightforward, honest, lucid accounts of personal experiences involving apparent memory of past lives of a number of people make exciting reading. The possibility of rebirth will take on a new dimension for many readers."

Here and Hereafter became an immediate bestseller from coast to coast, and membership rolls of ARE and SFF, which had greatly expanded after Ruth wrote about the two psychic organizations in *A Search for the Truth*, now soared anew.

The concept of reincarnation had at long last "arrived" in the Western world. It was by no means the first time that this age-old philosophy had seen print in America. But it was electrifying for a skeptical, internationally known, award-winning newspaper reporter to delve into such a realm by means of spirit communication and to emerge with an explanation so clear and logical and with evidence so convincing that people of widely divergent religious backgrounds could comprehend it. "I began to receive a flood of mail from people who had heard of reincarnation," Ruth recalls, "but who had thought the idea as farfetched as I had once considered it. They said they now understood this concept for the first time and were ready to embrace it."

Throughout that fall of 1968 Ruth continued to be in

demand for lectures and television interviews, and in late October she flew to Kansas City to address an enormous audience sponsored by a Jewish women's association at their Community Center. Hugh Lynn Cayce had been imploring her to speak at ARE seminars around the country, and although her time was too limited for many such extracurricular activities, she agreed to swing through Texas for speeches at Houston, Austin, and Dallas ARE conclaves en route home from Kansas City.

But the final stop in Dallas would put an unforeseen end to her newspaper career.

"At Love Field I was met by Rudolph Johnson, an attorney and ARE official who had taken the day off to see me to my hotel and to various interviews before the lecture that evening," she recalls.

As he escorted her through the terminal building, he announced a slight change in schedule. "Instead of going directly to your hotel and then appearing on TV this afternoon," he began, "there's an important TV station that would like to have you right away. If you don't mind, we'll go directly there, and I'll take you to your hotel afterward."

"Fine," she agreed. "But in that case, let me run into the restroom to comb my hair and put on some fresh lipstick for television. I'll only be a minute."

But as she hurried back out, anxious to be on time for the talk-show interview, she rounded a partition just inside the door, her foot slipped in a gooey puddle of freshly spilled hand lotion, and she went down face first. "I must have been temporarily knocked out," she muses. "In that dazed state I could see an arm lying across the floor, and I thought, 'How interesting, that arm way over there has my gold bracelet on it.' Gradually my perception returned and I could see that it was my own right arm, which turned out to be splintered and broken in five places, even into the socket of my shoulder."

Taken by ambulance to a hospital, she had to support the arm in place for four hours before a second specialist could arrive. "The arm was too badly broken for the first doctor to attempt the setting," she explains, "and I must have remained in shock, because I kept telling Rudy Johnson not to cancel my afternoon and evening appointments—that I could keep them as soon as the arm was set. Then I fainted. Eventually my right arm was enclosed in a heavy hanging cast, because there were too many breaks to use pins."

This unfortunate day marked the beginning of a long and frustrating recovery that was to change the course of her life. Bob flew to Texas five days later to bring her home from the hospital, and the evening before leaving Dallas they watched the presidential election returns on television in her hospital room. It was the night that Richard M. Nixon was elected President and the end of the last national campaign that Ruth would cover as a reporter. The next morning she and Bob flew to Norfolk, met by wheelchairs for changes of plane at airports en route, and she finally transferred to a rented hospital bed at their home in Virginia Beach. "Because of the hanging cast I was not permitted to stoop over or even to lie down," she says. "I had to sleep sitting up in a hospital bed every night from November 1 until the following May. I couldn't do the automatic writing, couldn't type, couldn't continue a column."

Letters still poured in from excited readers all over the country, people who wondered what lives they had led in previous incarnations or what their mission was for their current earthly sojourn. Ruth had always tried to answer each letter personally, but now even brief replies were impossible and the stacks of fan mail multiplied.

Ellis Amburn flew down from New York, anxious for her to consider writing another book on the psychic. But one look at her overflowing desk and her immobile arm and shoulder told him that anything of the sort would be impossible. "That's when Ellis arranged to have special answer cards printed," she says, describing the convenient post-cards that had a picture of the book and a small message space on one side. "The people at ARE found a secretary I could hire to write my dictated answers in longhand, and somehow we worked through that massive backlog."

As their dozens of camellia bushes burst into bloom that spring of 1969, Ruth began to grow restless. A career of daily deadlines, travel, interviews, personal appearances, and socializing had come to an abrupt halt, and although her view was peaceful over the lapping waters, cabin fever had set in. "I had scarcely left the house since November, except for visits to the doctor," she laments, "and after all those months confined to a rigid cast, my arm had become so useless that I had to go for daily therapy and to exercise at home with a pulley to lift it from my side." Before her unfortunate accident she and Bob had signed up for a spring trip to the Orient, but had to cancel that. "The doctor forbade me to do anything so strenuous just yet, but I yearned to get away for a while."

"Make it a quiet vacation," the doctor cautioned. "You can take an automobile trip, or fly somewhere and stay put, but don't try to do too much."

"Bob had never been to Mexico," Ruth recalls. "I'd been there before, and friends who had moved to its lovely climate had been urging us to visit. If we flew to Acapulco and rented a car, we could go at a leisurely pace, accept several long-standing invitations, and see the countryside."

It turned out to be a momentous vacation indeed! After visiting Carlene and Jock Lawrence in Acapulco, Ruth and Bob drove to several health resorts, and on to Cuernavaca to see their longtime friend Nina Olds, mother of author Gore Vidal and former wife of Jacqueline Kennedy's stepfather, Hugh Auchincloss. "Nina took us to parties where we met dozens of wonderfully friendly Americans who had retired, or had second homes there," she explains, "and it was a lovely mountain town with temperatures in the seventies year-round. We had planned to drive next to Guadalajara, but Cuernavaca proved too enticing to leave. We stayed at a hotel and began looking at houses instead."

Ruth had given up her political column and knew within herself that she did not want to return to her newspaper career. Explaining the memorable decision, she says, "As a Washington correspondent for twenty-five years, I had handled top assignments throughout the world. I'd had it all, and I'd loved it, but at that point I knew that anything else in that field would be anticlimactic. I had lost interest in continuing a political column in Washington, but I knew that I could write books wherever we lived."

"As for Bob," she adds with a giggle, "he had been dying to retire ever since our Detroit days when he was making forty dollars a week." They discussed the idea of moving to Mexico, and looked at available houses, but choices were limited. One of them was quite inviting, but by no means their "dream house." Still undecided, they returned to Virginia Beach refreshed from such an enjoyable change of scene, and Bob reported back to work at Newport News Shipbuilding Company.

Ruth's close friend, Hope Ridings Miller, listened eagerly as Ruth described the enchantment of Cuernavaca and the enjoyable visit with Nina Olds, who was also a friend of Hope's. "Go there again with me," Hope urged. "I'm dying to see it after hearing all about it. Please, Ruth, let's go right away."

Bob could not get away from work so soon again, but he encouraged Ruth to go. "While you're down there, why don't you look at houses again and settle on one for us," he suggested, eager to retire. "Don't worry about picking out one I haven't seen. I'll like anything that suits you. See if there's any better one than the Spanish colonial that we liked."

Two weeks later Ruth and Hope flew off to Mexico City, were met by friends at the airport, and driven the fifty-five miles south to Cuernavaca. "Hope loved the area, too, as anyone would have in those days," Ruth continues. "We were entertained by some former Washington friends who had been away during my previous trip there with Bob, and Nina gave a party for us. I also looked at more houses, but none seemed as nice as the one that Bob and I had liked."

Meanwhile another story had begun to unfold in Virginia Beach, and pieces began falling into place to complete this major life change. A realtor phoned Bob one day out of the blue. Might the Montgomerys be interested in selling their lovely home on the water? A potential buyer was inquiring about properties in their particular area. "That's the story of my life!" Ruth says, laughing. "It's as if the Guides or some other eerie forces decide what I need to do next and silently make their own arrangements behind my back."

"It's possible," Bob conceded to the agent, not having heard yet from Ruth. "We might be interested in selling, but I can't say at this time."

"Oh, in that case, I have several other clients who would certainly be interested in your house. May I bring them to see it?" The first couple arrived to tour the property and made an immediate offer.

Down in Cuernavaca, Ruth, knowing nothing of this development, finally placed a long distance call to the States. "Bob," she began, "there really isn't anything more suitable than the house that we rather liked before. It's awfully big, but it seems to be the only one on the market that we could consider. I don't know what to do."

"Go ahead and buy it," he urged. "A realtor called me, and we've had one offer for this house already."

Thus reassured, Ruth initiated paperwork to buy the

large Spanish-style colonial house with swimming pool in Cuernavaca. "This was a major change in direction for both of our lives," she says, remembering her trepidation. "It meant that Bob would give up his career and we would leave the United States to live in a foreign country. While Hope gave me moral courage, I arranged to see a lawyer in Mexico City to begin the transfer process, including application with the Mexican Government for permission to buy the property. The night before our appointment it suddenly hit me how drastic this step could be. What if we couldn't sell our house in Virginia Beach and had already arranged to buy this one? What if we ended up with two houses on our hands, nearly three thousand miles apart and in two different countries?"

In rare panic she placed another call to Bob. 'Are you sure that you really want me to go ahead with this?" she asked. "I can still cancel out until tomorrow. What if our own house doesn't sell?"

"Relax," Bob said, chuckling. "We've now had three official offers on it, and the agent is just negotiating to get the highest bidder. It will sell with no problem."

Relieved, yet silently amused over the odd sequence of events, she met with the lawyer the next morning and signed the papers that would set the gears in motion. They were moving to Mexico.

Meanwhile Ellis Amburn, Ruth's editor in New York, continued to plead for another book. "He was anxious for me to begin writing just as soon as I was able," she relates. "But he wanted a book on the psychic, and I thought I'd exhausted that field, first with the one on spirit communication and then the other on reincarnation. What else was there? Now that my newspaper career was ended, I felt that the time was right to tell a more personal story, one about my quarter century in Washington."

Unable to write or type during her lengthy confinement,

Ruth had already spent weeks and months sorting through a career-long accumulation of clippings and photographs, preparing to ship them to Baylor University for the Ruth Shick Montgomery collection that had been established there to house her papers. "During my twenty-five years in Washington I had covered six presidents," she says nostalgically. "The time had finally arrived when I needed to look back on all those years, review them, and bring them into proper perspective."

With four bestsellers to her credit since 1964, Ruth had established herself as a successful author who need no longer worry about finding a publisher. Income was also no problem. "I decided that my next book would be about my career in Washington," she says, although Amburn cautioned her that such a book would not sell as well as another in the psychic field. "I'm sure you're right," she replied softly, "but I don't care about the money. It's just something that I need to get off my chest, and if you don't want the book, I understand. I'll find another publisher. In any event, that's what I'm going to write."

"Frankly I thought it would be a relief to write about a 'normal' subject again," Ruth admits. "Perhaps there was more of my mother in me than I realized. At least I didn't want to be like some of the people I'd met whose only interest was the psychic. I preferred a balanced life—and still do."

Ellis and the publisher came through with a contract for the book, hoping that her interest in the psychic would return once the Washington memoirs were out of her system.

For the next month Ruth and Bob needed to pack and arrange their affairs. Ruth's clippings, manuscripts, and other memorabilia were slated eventually to go to Baylor; it would make no sense to take them all the way to Mexico. Using her able left arm, she had already sorted through a mass of accumulated letters, columns, and articles, dictating notes from them into a tape recorder for later transcribing. "I had drawn up a chronological outline of the book in my mind," she recalls, "so as we packed each carton to be shipped to Baylor, I added appropriate material to the tapes."

As soon as the move to Mexico was complete, Ruth began writing her seventh book, *Hail to the Chiefs: My Life and Times with Six Presidents*. "I worked a little on it each day, as the strength in my arm gradually returned," she explains. "Our new life in Cuernavaca very quickly became an active one, and we loved the climate in that 'City of Eternal Spring.' With temperatures in the seventies all year long and the sun shining brilliantly every day, we Americans practically lived out-of-doors on our huge verandas that were furnished like comfortable living rooms. There were dressy parties nearly every evening, and frequent luncheons, so that no one could miss the Washington social whirl."

Ruth soon completed the most lengthy manuscript of her writing career, "and when I mailed it off to New York, I could finally close the door to that engrossing part of my life," she concedes. "Now it was time to look forward instead of back."

Since moving to Mexico Ruth had been in frequent correspondence with Arthur Ford, who wanted to visit the Montgomerys but wondered if his long-ailing heart could withstand the altitude. Ruth cautioned against his flying to Mexico City, where the altitude was more than ten thousand feet—and from which, to reach Cuernavaca, it was necessary to drive over a twelve-thousand-foot peak. She suggested instead that he fly to Acapulco, which is at sea level, and approach their new home from the south, since the altitude at Cuernavaca is only fifty-two hundred feet.

"But please, please consult your heart specialist first," she urged, "because we don't want anything to happen to you!"

Meanwhile Ruth had turned her ever active mind toward the field of fiction. Fascinated by Mexican history, especially the account of Spanish conquistador Hernando Cortés and Malinche, the lovely Indian maiden who had served as his interpreter with her people, she decided to write a novel set in modern-day Cuernavaca. The heroine was to be a visiting American girl who accidentally discovered that she was the reincarnation of Malinche, and of course the plot would feature a reincarnated Cortés as well. Ruth sought no advance contract, with its inevitable deadline, for this book. She was merely trying her hand in a new field and wanted to be able to enjoy it.

At the same time, the Montgomerys had begun searching for the perfect house. "We were still not completely sold on the one that we had bought, however lovely," she recalls. "For one thing, its grounds were so extensive that we wanted a place requiring less upkeep. Whenever we learned of another house that had gone on the market in our area, we went to look at it, but none suited us any better."

Then a friend advised us of two house lots with a magnificent view of the perpetually snowcapped volcanoes Popocatepetl and Ixtacchihuatl some forty miles distant. "We drove there to look at the vista," she relates, "and what we saw took our breath away. It was like something from a picture postcard. The lots were located on a principal avenue in Cuernavaca, only a short walk from the *zócalo* (the town square), so that in addition to a spectacular view, we also had convenience."

Hesitant to undertake building a house in a foreign country, Ruth and Bob nevertheless toyed with the idea. "Even in the United States such a project would have been complicated," Ruth observes. "With the language barrier and other unforeseen snags, we were afraid it could turn into a debacle. But ever since I could remember, I had been doodling imaginary house plans. I loved figuring out how the rooms and halls and closets could all fit together like a jigsaw puzzle. By this time we had the dimensions of the two lots and knew how a house could be situated, partially wrapped around a swimming pool and the adjoining terrace. We would have lots of bougainvillea, poinsettias, and palm trees, but nothing to obstruct the spectacular view of the snowcapped volcanoes, and the house would have inside gardens as well. The project seemed irresistible! We decided to take the plunge. This would in no way conflict with the expected visit of Arthur Ford, because our new house would require a year to complete."

With Ruth as the architect and Bob as overall construction supervisor, they hired a contractor-builder who had done a skillful job with a friend's house and said that he could easily work from Ruth's blueprints.

Construction began while Ruth completed six chapters of her novel about Malinche, but after a lifetime devoted to reporting facts, she admitted to difficulty. "I don't think that I was meant to write make-believe tales," she says with a sigh. "Trying to get the dialogue to sound natural was my biggest stumbling block. Ellis Amburn read those early chapters and enthusiastically encouraged me to continue, but I wasn't nearly as enthralled as I'd been while writing those psychic books."

As fate would have it, she needn't have worried. Dawn had barely broken in Cuernavaca on the morning of January 4, 1971, when the jangling telephone on her bedside table roused her from sleep. Marianne Wolf was calling from Pennsylvania. "Ruth, I'm sorry to ring you this early," she began, "but I wanted you to know from a friend before the shock of hearing it on the radio. Arthur Ford passed on early this morning in Miami."

CHAPTER IX

A Glimpse Beyond Death

Arthur Ford dead! "I was numb," Ruth recalls, reliving the trauma of that early morning phone call. "Arthur had seemed almost like a father to me ever since 1958. Through the years he had often visited us in Washington or Virginia Beach; we had exchanged letters and phone calls, shared lecture platforms, and filled in for each other on TV shows. We were devoted friends, and his death came as a bruising shock, even though I was well aware of his previous heart attacks."

Ruth was no longer practicing the automatic writing that had prompted her to write two books in the psychic field. Forced by her broken right arm and shoulder to abandon it for six months, she had since been occupied with moving to Mexico, writing a "legitimate" book on her Washington career, experimenting with a novel about reincarnation, and designing a house that was now under construction. "Besides, there seemed to be no particular reason for returning to psychic affairs," she reasoned. "I had proved at least to my own satisfaction that communication between the living and the dead is possible, and I had no wish to become a medium." Her family breathed a sigh of relief.

But by afternoon of that sad January day, faced with the loss of her beloved friend, Ruth sensed a compelling urge to return to the typewriter and try the automatic writing once more. "I half expected that nothing would happen," she recalls. "Such a long time had elapsed since I'd devoted any time to the morning sessions that I assumed my Guides would have given me up as a lost cause and moved on to other projects."

Starting again with the head and neck exercises, her mantra, meditation, and a silent prayer for protection, she rested her fingers lightly on the keys in touch-typing position. They immediately sprang to life, tapping out the first of a long series of revelatory messages that would open a new window for earthlings on the life beyond death. "Ruth, this is Lily and the group," the writing began. "Arthur Ford is here and wants you to know he is as young as the merry month of May. He feels great and does not want you to grieve. He is so glad to be here. . . . He's on top of the world. A ball of fire . . . so glad to be rid of the wornout body which caused him such pain."

Then Arthur took over, typing cheerful words of greeting and adding: "Well, no goodbyes are necessary, because here I am, as you can see. I haven't gone anywhere."

Immense relief replaced Ruth's earlier sadness. 'The lead melted from my heart, and I felt as light as the proverbial feather. Lily urged me to return the next morning, and this time I needed no prompting. I could scarcely wait until eight-thirty to resume the regular sessions." Arthur was absent that first morning, having flitted off to check on funeral details and the settlement of his estate, matters that Lily promptly dismissed as inconsequential. "This is a passing phase," he wrote of Ford. "He will soon learn that it makes no difference here what is done with what, and who is where."

The next day Arthur exuberantly announced himself and declared: "This Lily is quite a guy. I sort of sensed his presence sometimes after I knew you in your plane, but he's a brilliant white light of radiant power and a mighty good influence to have on your side, so don't ever neglect him or fail to take advantage of his help."

Each morning thereafter Ruth set aside the time for meditation and the automatic typing that flowed effortlessly despite the long period of neglect. Soon it became apparent that Arthur had plans to write a book through her. "During our last telephone conversation a few weeks before his death," Ruth recalls, "I had urged him to do another book on the psychic and submit it to Ellis Amburn, my editor. Now that Arthur had progressed to a new dimension, he seemed ready to tackle the project."

"Tell Amburn that this should more than compensate for the book that I was not able to write for him there," he announced. "There was little new that I could have added to what I had already written from that side, but now we will be able to reveal many of the things which have long puzzled mankind on that side of the door."

Ruth pondered his meaning. Just what did Arthur intend to tell the world through this book that he hoped she would write? "Lily and his group want me to tell you all that we can about the state of being on this side," he responded, "the whys and wherefores which make it important to prepare there for this side, the purposes of meditation and prayer, the interlocking relationship between the two, and the way of life on this side."

Arthur continued to spell out his message, stressing that he hoped "to awaken thoughtful, thinking people to the reality that each day there is wasted unless some progress has been made in preparing for the steps ahead." He insisted that earth life is a time of learning. "We all come back there to go to school and learn how to grow and develop more speedily, as well as to test ourselves on the progress made on this side," he explained.

All this and much more was to be revealed in a project to be undertaken with Ruth. It was a tall order for a single book! Arthur seemed anxious to start by telling about life beyond the grave, since every person on earth shares that common destiny and naturally wonders what to expect of it. Arthur and the Guides were eager to fill them in and set them on the spiritual path.

"We will begin at once, if you are agreeable," Lily announced, "and will delve into the existence of life from one stage to another, telling how it differs with each stage. We will discuss the crossover to this phase as one sheds his mortal body, and as we progress with our account of life here, I will give you glimpses of the higher phases which are yet to come."

Following Lily's instruction to put a fresh sheet of paper in the typewriter, Ruth could hardly wait for Arthur to begin. "Each person is a continuing entity through eternity," he wrote. "No beginning and no ending, despite what some moralists say about life beginning with a physical birth as a baby and ending with Judgment Day. Bosh!" Continuing, he stressed that we are as much a part of God as God is a part of us, and that "since it takes all of us to make up the complete whole, it behooves each of us to concern ourselves mightily with others, for they are as necessary to us as our own arms and legs and eyes and ears." To further this point, Arthur insisted that all of us, the dead as well as the living, comprise the whole Universal Spirit, with Christ's commandment to "love one another" and His teaching that "the kingdom of God is within" finding even greater fulfillment in this concept than in one with "all the stuffy preaching about a God who sits on high to judge the quick and the dead. We are all a part of that Godhead," the former Christian minister emphasized. Arthur would return to this thought again and again in the weeks that followed.

But as a longtime news reporter Ruth was anxious to learn more about Ford's own death experience and the reunion with Fletcher, his boyhood friend who had died in World War I and later served as Ford's otherworld control through a half century of trance mediumship.

Arthur happily obliged. "As my spirit left that wearied body," he wrote, "I stepped as easily into the astral body as if I had always consciously worn it. The lightness, the freedom from restraint, the heavenly elixir of being without the heavy flesh was beyond description. What a relief!" Free to move about as he wished, with no barriers, Arthur found himself as active as a lad, able to travel at will. "As I glanced around me on arriving at this stage, I beheld my mother, my sister, and several other immediate members of the family, which made rejoicing easy. Then came Fletcher, whose ethereal face lit up like a dazzling aura to know that I had safely made the crossover without loss of realization." According to Arthur, Fletcher was at long last freed to move on to higher tasks. "But first he talked to me at length, filling me in on what to expect on this side and giving me a few valuable words of advice about not becoming as earthbound as he did through taking over that long-drawn-out project with me."

"Death," Arthur explained, "is no more than the passage through a beckoning door. It is so brief, so transitory as scarcely to be noted, for it is what lies beyond the door that counts. . . . It was like coming home, to slip through that door and release the tired old body. In an instant, without conscious thought, I was here surrounded by relatives and old friends."

After answering Ruth's question in further detail, Arthur returned to the purpose of the book that he wished to help her write, to "clear out the minds" of those who still cling to mistaken ideas about the beyond. "We are the cocreators with God of what we find for ourselves here," he insisted. "Ruth, we want you to wake the people up to the importance of this towering truth. They, with their thoughts, are not only creating the pattern of their future lives, out their own heaven or hell."

As he continued at each day's session to reveal details about life beyond the grave, he mentioned God so frequently that Ruth finally asked him to define his term. "Who or what is God?" she inquired, trusting that Arthur must by now have gained some greater insight into this mystery from his new vantage point.

"God," he explained, "is the core of the universe from which all else flows forth. He is truth and energy. He is matter and spirit, and all things of heaven and earth. . . . He is also the essence of our being, without which nothing would exist. . . . God is! The eternal I Am. . . . Because we are imperfect in our reactions and behavioral pattern, we must strive ever onward through many earth cycles until we achieve sufficient perfection to rejoin God as cocreators . . . thus our ceaseless attempts to return to the physical state in order to erase our rough edges and be able to fit into the Godhead as perfect segments of the whole."

"Does He then hear our individual prayers?" Ruth asked, wondering how such an all-encompassing force could respond to the daily petitions of countless millions of people who sought help and comfort through their own religious faiths.

"God is total awareness," Arthur answered. "He not only hears prayer, but knows without being asked what the plea is going to be. . . . This I know, and when we approach Him lovingly and trustingly, as we would a wise parent, He is ready to grant that which is in our best interests if it harms no one else. . . . Ruth, God is All!"

With a foundation thus established, Arthur set to work unfolding his fascinating story, morning after morning, at the typewriter in Ruth's study in Cuernavaca. "This material grew more intriguing with every session," she recalls. "I could scarcely wait to read what Arthur had written each day, and it made my novel about Malinche seem so dull by comparison that I decided to pack it away and pursue this far more captivating theme. Lily and Arthur were delighted."

Pressing on, Ford wrote that at the moment of death "the soul slides easily from its casing without pain or visible sensation . . . like the wafting of a summer's breeze. . . . We awaken into a realm of pure beauty and song. The trees are *real* trees here, not the reflection which you in the flesh see. The flowers are pure thought form and therefore much more exquisite than anything actually in the form seen by physical man. The birds, animals, spirits, yes, the many mansions are perfection here, for they are thought forms."

Welcomed by relatives and friends, the newly arrived soul at first enjoys a happy reunion and rest. "Depending on the worth of our characters," he continued, "we are troubled or at ease, happy or restless, just as on the earth plane." Gradually a soul adjusts to its new freedom, begins to realize that there is more to learn, and sees that time is passing quickly. "Will we want to plunge into a round of festivities and pure pleasures?" Ford asked. "Or will we want to develop our spiritual side? And if we choose the latter, do we think of it in terms of self-growth and self-advancement or as group growth and development? That is to say, will we want it for others as much as for ourselves? Remember what I told you earlier," he continued, as if to emphasize this point. Humankind advances "only as all of us surge upward toward the common goal of enlightenment and perfection. Therefore, if we would advance rapidly ourselves we must make every effort to see that others of like interest are also given every tool for self-advancement."

Yet not every soul who arrives on the other side is ready to comprehend such far-reaching thoughts. "Sometimes the soul does not realize that he has passed into spirit," Ford explained, "so he hovers around wondering why no one seems to pay attention to him on the physical plane . . . or is unable to give up thoughts of worldly goods and possessions. These troubled souls cannot be helped by our work on this side as much as they can through prayer from those of you still in the physical state. Pray for them."

Ruth urged him to give a specific example, and he described a man who, having died after a short but serious illness, awakens to find himself on a lovely grassy plain near a sparkling stream. Wishing he had brought his fishing pole, he instantly finds one in his hand, then pulls in a magnificent catch of fish. Yet as daylight begins to fade, he wants to go home. Suddenly he is home, proudly carrying the fresh fish that he can see and touch and smell. He sees his wife dressed in black, crying, and the house filled with relatives and friends. Everyone ignores him. "I might as well be dead," he exclaims—and finds himself back on the grassy plain by the brook. But this time he meets others who welcome him and take him to a schoolhouse where an old man calls the group to order, welcomes our friend, and introduces him as a newcomer to the land of spirit. "Simply accept for the time being that your family and friends will not be able to see and converse with you, even though you are able to see and talk with them," he advises. Arthur's story continued in another session, as he described the man's later progress. "He is becoming well adjusted now and no longer hangs around his former house," Ford wrote. "He is learning that each of us makes this progression and that the sooner we knuckle down to understanding the new ways, the happier we will be."

These fascinating sessions with Arthur and the Guides consumed no more than a half hour each morning, leaving Ruth free to make frequent trips to Mexico City with Bob to assemble necessary appurtenances for the new house and to visit the construction in progress. She also found time to give a speech about the psychic to benefit an old people's home in Cuernavaca, and among those in the overflow audience was Helen Hayes, a good friend who also had a house in Cuernavaca. Afterward, her eyes sparkling, the famous actress kept exclaiming, "Ruth had us all hypnotized! How she can hold an audience!"

The Montgomerys' busy social life continued unabated, but in no way conflicted with the morning sessions that were introducing her to a life beyond the grave. At one of them Arthur Ford told of an atheist, recently crossed over, who during his earthly life had thought of nothing but his own advancement, and he said of the man: "He finds himself in a situation (here) of his own making, surrounded by other greedy souls. . . . These are not the type of people he wants to associate with. They are fiendish and ill mannered, whereas he has been a stiff-necked, educated, and polished man, although he never gave a thought to anyone but himself. . . . We let him remain there until his own remorse for sinful ways begins to penetrate his being and he acknowledges to himself that he wasted a lifetime, a rare privilege, by thinking only of himself. . . . Only *he* is able to assess his wrongs and seek forgiveness, although there are many here willing to lend a hand whenever he himself reaches out to them for it."

Such a helping hand is extended immediately, however, to innocent accident victims, some of whom may sleep for a time before waking in spirit. Suicide victims who had suffered inner turmoil are likewise helped to overcome the aberration that led to their unfortunate mistake. "As their awakening forces grasp the problem and come to under-

stand the conditions which led to temporary insanity," Ford
explained, "they will adjust almost as rapidly as those who
came here through accidental death." But those suicides
who "deliberately set out to destroy their own body, thinking that they were destroying their soul as well" have a far
more difficult time, "because no problem has been solved,
but only postponed until the next earth life, wherever that
may be."

On the other hand, individuals who have mediated and
prepared themselves for a natural death "are a delight to
watch," he continued, "because their hearts brim over with
love for fellow souls and nothing is too much trouble for
them if another issues a call. Some work with babies newly
arrived who are without mothers here." Others help both
newcomers and the bereaved who are left behind, 'sending
them loving thoughts and easing their path for a time."

After adjustment to the spirit world, the soul who has
tired of "hanging around earth people" soon learns that he
must review his past life and assess his mistakes, Ford declared, adding that the final step before returning to physical being is to decide the circumstances under which he will
have the best opportunity to meet the challenges that will
provide the lessons he needs to learn.

Ruth grew curious at this point and typed out her question before the next morning's session. Could Ford provide
a broader explanation of the process by which a soul rein-
carnates? Arthur seemed only too happy to comply, beginning with the assessment and contemplation that are necessary before a soul can select "the sort of karmic debts it most
needs to shed" and decide which qualities are especially
needed for further development. "If patience is needed, he
will seek a situation where his impetuosity will most often
be put to the testing. If he needs to learn love, he will have
to select a situation where that quality is not in great abun-
dance, so that he will test his mettle against those who have

not themselves learned to give love." Choosing particular parents is a right that can be earned, Arthur explained, and he noted that souls often wish to become the children of those whom they have known before, in order to work out further karma that may still entangle those relationships.

Preferences are then submitted to a sort of "heavenly computer," which automatically selects the soul best suited to the opportunities at hand. "The soul who wins the assignment then hovers near the parents for some time to make sure he is willing to proceed with a return to that physical body, and when the time is right and the physical blossoming occurs, he enters that newborn body, usually at the time of ejection but occasionally shortly before or after."

"What about deformed bodies?" Ruth asked.

"Surprisingly there are almost as many candidates for those bodies of newborn babies as for the healthy, normal ones," he replied. "The greater the obstacles in the physical body, the more opportunity for a soul to pay off karmic debts and achieve more rapid spiritual growth."

After this logical explanation Arthur embarked on a discussion of his own growth and learning on the other side, and his return to the "temple of wisdom," a place he vaguely recalled from previous times between earth lives. He picked up his lessons exactly where he had left off before: Meditation is a process that links us with the heart of God; right and wrong are not always clear choices, but to harm someone else, whether by thought or action or inaction, is to harm ourselves as well as God; our spiritual growth progresses with every good deed, freely given, in secret, without hope of earthly reward. Most important of all, spiritual growth cannot be accomplished by one person alone. "It is a total effort of the human race," Arthur insisted, "and that, dear Ruth, is why it is so important to help everyone in need of assistance over the rough places in life."

As Ruth continued to request specific examples, story after story began to emerge from Arthur's daily communication, each designed to illustrate the experience of one soul or another upon arrival in the spirit place. First there was Joe, an agnostic whose earthly life had never found room for thought about the hereafter. Not knowing he has died, he goes off to a previously scheduled appointment, only to find that his former colleagues ignore him. He turns and sees Charlie, who died long ago. Charlie tries to tell Joe that they're both dead, but Joe thinks it's a bad joke. He rushes off to locate his wife and finds her at a funeral, but when he peers into the coffin to see who has died, he is startled to find his own body. This cannot be! He feels as alive and as real as always. Able to hear his own voice, he tries in vain to attract the attention of those he sees, yet even Charlie cannot convince him that all this isn't some horrible nightmare. Only after long and patient help will Joe begin to understand that he is immortal, but invisible to earthlings who operate on a different frequency.

In most cases, however, a newly arrived soul is greeted by loved ones, shown how to move about, and counseled. As he asks questions, he begins to remember past lives, as well as the mission he had intended for the life just completed. He assesses where he succeeded and where he failed, and makes a careful evaluation of the lessons he must next choose to learn.

"Often they attend their funeral to pay a sweet farewell," Ford offered, "and then, unless sorely needed by grieving ones, are able to step into the new role" without becoming earthbound. They make rapid progress, begin new lessons, and move along the path of understanding and growth.

Arthur next told of the arrival of a typical 'man of the cloth, a Billy Sunday type who preaches hellfire and brimstone and believes every bit of the Good Book literally. He comes across here, and after the first shock of discovering that God is not sitting on a throne surrounded by angels, he begins exhorting those of us here to repent before it is too late." The parson preaches his sermons and draws a following of souls who seek the kind of heaven he describes. They all eagerly shout "Amen" and wait for him to lead them. But Billy himself hasn't found the throne of God and demands that the ones who have been there longer show him where it is. Finally the old souls explain to Billy that he has it all wrong, that heaven is within each man, and so is his private hell. They suggest that he attend a temple of wisdom, and soon he begins to understand Universal Law. Eager to help undo the damage he has done earlier, by holding out false hopes, he then works to plant seeds of wisdom in the minds of other ministers still in physical body.

At this point in mid-April Ruth was required to suspend the sessions temporarily while she flew to Chicago to keep a long-standing engagement with a television talk-show host, after which she visited her family in Indianapolis for several days. Never one to proselytize about her deepening belief in the spirit plane, she told neither relatives nor friends about her continuing communication with Arthur Ford since his death; but Ellis Amburn knew, and was eagerly awaiting completion of the unique book that she was writing with Arthur.

Returning to Cuernavaca, she wondered if the week-long interruption would affect the continuity of the messages, but there was no cause for worry. Arthur's stories continued to unfold in still greater detail, the next one telling of "a man who thinks he is ready for sainthood and expects to be ushered to the throne of God" as soon as he arrives. The man had lived a good life, done no wrong, had never stolen, robbed, or cheated. He had worked hard for his church and charities, and as death approached, he passed into spirit serenely confident that he would join God in heaven. Awak-

ening to find a lovely landscape, he meets an old cobbler
and asks directions, only to be told, "The way lies within."

The man persists, demanding that he be shown the way
to God and the Judgment Seat. "Look within," the cobbler
repeats. "Each of us must judge himself before we will be
able to rejoin our Creator."

"But I have done no wrong," the man insists, whereupon
the old soul relates a similar tale, of his own blameless life as
a priest. The newcomer is puzzled. "What have we done
that defied God's wishes?" he asks.

"Don't you see it yet, son? We were too concerned with
our own souls to stop and ease the anguish of those less
fortunate ones." The cobbler beckons his new friend to take
a look at the wife he left behind.

At once the man finds himself on the patio of his home in
California, where his widow is talking with another man
about the husband who has died. "He was always so busy
with his own salvation," she says. "It's so dreadfully difficult
to live with a saint, particularly a self-appointed one."
Shocked to hear his wife speak of him so, he gradually
begins to see that in his quest for perfection he had inflicted
his own ideas of righteousness on others, failing to give the
unselfish love and understanding that human beings need
in order to live a rich and full life. Busily doing public good
deeds in order to build a saintly image as well, he sought
earthly acclaim rather than the spiritual advancement that
follows anonymous giving. Thus enlightened, the man returns to the old cobbler and together they search for understanding, joining a group en route to the temple of wisdom.

One of Arthur's livelier stories was of a woman who fully
expects, because of her virtuous ways, to be transported
directly to the throne of God, and mistakes the first soul she
sees for Saint Peter. "I wish to be taken to God," she requests, ignoring the man's suggestion that she rest awhile.
He waves her along. She finds an open gate and an upward

path, rushing past others who are also climbing, so that she can be first in line. As she nears the top, she adjusts her hair and clothing, expecting to find God awaiting her with open arms. "Will you announce me, please," she asks of a handsome young man, "because I am in a hurry to bow my head at the knees of God."

The man notes that others are still plodding up the hill. "How will you be saved until all those others who struggle upward are also rescued from the abyss below?" he asks.

She turns petulantly to another man and asks to be taken directly to God. "But, madam, all of us are God," he replies.

She is annoyed that he seems to include one whom she remembers as a beggar in her hometown. She sinks to a bench, continuing to argue, and finally demands, "Where is the Judgment Seat?"

"You are sitting on it, madam."

At last she begins to grasp his meaning, and, looking into her own heart, sees that in her effort to live without sin she has been thinking only of herself, never offering a comforting word to those she perceived as below her status. "Where was the love for others?" Ford asked. "Within herself lay all the answers. God would not have spoken more directly in His judgment than she was now able to do on her own."

Yet there are also souls who have tried so hard to help others that they have lost sight of selflessness and actually interfered with the natural learning process. Arthur described a young mother who has died but cannot bear to leave the presence of her husband and children. She hovers near them, seeking to guide and protect her offspring, forcing her will on those still in flesh. "Souls on this side who are well equipped to work with those like her do their best to calm her fears and teach her that each soul on the earth plane must live according to his own light, without domineering from others," he wrote. In frustration the young

woman drops into a troubled sleep. When she fina ly awakens, she finds her family adjusting well to life without her,
and gradually she learns that her overpowering smother-
love had hindered their growth. "Now when she sees her
children . . . she sends them loving thoughts and a mother's blessings, without trying to dominate them,' Arthur
continued. "Before, they were tied in knots, emotional and
afraid of making a move for fear of displeasing mother. Now
they subconsciously feel her radiating love. Decisions come
easier for them, for they feel that mother is released and
happy." And in her next life this woman will emerge as a
wiser and more selfless person.

Having described specific cases, Arthur answered Ruth's
many questions about certain well-known people John F.
Kennedy passed into spirit fully alert, helped by the prayers
of millions of caring people, he asserted, because "Catholics
have the right idea in their prayers for the dead, a custom
which should be adopted by all faiths and creeds and also by
those who still love those souls who have passed on to the
next phase of eternal life."

He told of other prominent persons who, he said, were
busy and active in the spirit world, and he described their
current projects. Lily, true to his earlier promise, told Ruth
of the various planes to which we can progress in the spirit
realm. After imparting a rich variety of other philosophy,
Arthur then outlined future events, some of which have
already come to pass, and described a planetary axis shift
near the end of this century, as Edgar Cayce had foretold.
"Many people will not survive this shift, but others will," he
wrote, noting drastically altered weather patterns, churning seas, and frightful wind velocities that will mark the
sudden calamity. Yet since all of us are eternal, planetary
changes to come will mark only a brief transition in our
journey ever upward in understanding and growth.

On May 7, 1971, Arthur concluded his account of Life

after death, with its rich lode of philosophical material that is too lengthy to repeat here. "You need a rest now," he wrote approvingly. "Be a good girl, Ruth, and live according to that which we have written for this book. Love from all of us: Art, Lily, and the group. Go with God, amen."

Inasmuch as she had written the manuscript simultaneously with the daily reception of material from the Guides, Ruth was able to mail it off to her New York editor within another week. "Arthur, Lily, and the Guides had actually given me a vacation!" she exclaims with a lilting laugh. "I made the most of that unusual grant, and for the next six months Bob and I excitedly supervised as our 'dream house' progressed toward reality."

At last it was completed, with the tropical foliage in place, the interior gardens burgeoning under skylights, the tiled swimming pool reflecting the blue skies overhead, and the snowcapped volcanoes glittering against the horizon. The Montgomerys, having already sold their other house, moved in with their fourteen rooms of furniture that November, less than a week before publication date for *A World Beyond*.

Ruth's promotional tour for this, her eighth book, began in Atlanta. Then it was on to Washington, Baltimore, and Philadelphia, where she was interviewed on the Mike Douglas television show. She flew to New York, where she appeared as the mystery guest on "To Tell the Truth," the popular network TV show; and only one of the four regular panelists identified the slim, well-bred, clear-eyed Ruth Montgomery as the "mystery" author who regularly communicated with spirits in the world beyond.

After further TV appearances in Chicago and Indianapolis, where she again visited her family, she flew back to Cuernavaca, hopefully to begin the "rest" that Arthur Ford had promised.

CHAPTER X

The Healer and the Companion

A *World Beyond* was no ordinary bestseller. Most such books enjoy a burst of attention and then gradually fade away. But this account of life after death did just the reverse—it started slowly and seemed to snowball, growing bigger and bigger, moving up on bestseller lists into the spring and summer of 1972. In late June, a full seven months after the book's release, the Chicago *Tribune* featured a second review of *A World Beyond* in a half-page spread which commented on that publishing phenomenon, and described it as "a fascinating, full-of-hope description of what life is like beyond the physical . . . makes the process of death sound as easy as going to sleep and waking in a lovely dream world, but one in which souls are still aware of what goes on here on earth, and even to some extent can influence, and partake in, events."

While gratified at the book's warm reception Ruth was hardly prepared for the sensation that it caused as it was passed from one excited reader to another, spreading widely by word of mouth. A clergyman who was unknown

to her ordered an entire case of the books and started handing them out to his flock, eagerly explaining, *"This* is what
I've been trying to tell you about death!" Ruth's volume of
mail swelled far beyond levels generated by her earlier
books, but aside from sheer numbers, the stories described
in these letters left her awestruck. *A World Beyond* had
begun to make dramatic changes in people's lives.

"A friend gave me your book after my father [or husband,
or other relative] died," they would write, "and I've never
known such comfort." "My whole life is altered." "I'm no
longer grieving." "I realize now that this is not the real
world, and I'll be with him/her again."

Others reported that they had now lost all fear of death,
or had found purpose in their lives and for the first time
looked forward to the future with new hope and understanding.

Most striking of all were letters from those who had determined to commit suicide but found the book when it
literally dropped into their path. "I thought that earth life
was all that existed, and I wanted out," a typical correspondent would write. "Then your book fell off a store shelf right
in front of me and I started to put it back, but when I read
the cover, I knew that I simply *had* to have that book."
These people would take it home and start reading it—and
read all night. By morning they had *no* more wish to end
their life. "I realized that suicide wouldn't solve anything,"
they explained. "I could finally see that I had to work
through my own problems, and that life has a purpose I had
never before realized. Thank you, thank you, for opening
my eyes and rescuing me."

"I was astonished at the outpouring of such love and
emotion," Ruth reminisces. "All my life since the age of
seventeen I had been a reporter, gathering my material and
presenting it as solid fact. I was trying to do exactly the same
with the material from the Guides. They had changed my

own attitude toward life and death so gradually over the years that I hadn't fully realized how differently I had come to feel. Certainly I never expected that these books would change other people's attitudes so dramatically." Yet they did, in profound and inspiring ways. Readers of *A World Beyond* now devoured her earlier books on the psychic and begged her to write still more.

Meanwhile the Montgomerys were caught up in a busy social season. Author Rebecca West came to Cuernavaca to visit their neighbors, Kit and Thew Wright, who gave an eightieth birthday luncheon for their famous British guest. Besides Ruth and Bob, the other guests were Helen Hayes and old-time Hollywood movie star Dolores Del Rio. "Rebecca was always stimulating company," Ruth says of the noted writer whose romantic liaison with H. G. Wells had titillated the literary world. "She was in Mexico City to research a book, but upon being invited by the Wrights for a weekend she decided, in true upper-crust English house-party style, to stay all winter. And she did, so we shared many enjoyable evenings with her at the Wrights."

Ruth and Bob went up to Mexico City for the world premiere of Merle Oberon's movie *Interval*, and afterward attended the glittering, Hollywood star-studded extravaganza for Merle at Jeanette and Chito Longoria's marble palace, which towered above Chapultepec Castle. "The movie was so bad that it was an embarrassment to meet Merle immediately afterward," Ruth says with a giggle. "Later Jeanette flew to New York for the U.S. premiere, and mentioned to a man that since Merle was a good friend of hers, she had already seen the film in Mexico City. Later, on the way out of the theater, he glimpsed Jeanette across the lobby and called, "Wow, she *must* be a good friend if you sat through that movie twice!"

Ruth's next book began quite unexpectedly. Having arrived back in Cuernavaca at noon one day after a week's TV tour in Texas, she and Bob were planning to leave again shortly for a cruise of the Greek isles, when the telephone rang. "Hi, we're in Cuernavaca and want to see you," the familiar voice of William Gray declared.

"In Cuernavaca?" she gasped. "But Bill, why didn't you call long-distance first? What if we hadn't been here? We've only been back a couple of hours and are planning to leave again next week."

With an engaging chuckle he replied, "That's easy to answer. I always know psychically where you are. We've just flown in from Australia on our way home to California, but at the stopover in Tahiti I decided we should change planes and fly here. I picked up on your vibrations there."

Bill Gray was incredible, to say the least! Ruth had known him for six years, since two friends who were aware that she was writing her first book in the psychic field brought him to her house in Washington. A magnetic healer, he had effected remarkable cures of everything from heart attacks to cancer, and regularly visited the nation's capital to treat the ailments of several highly placed government officials. Even Ruth soon benefited from his unorthodox approach. Channelling powerful healing energies through her left thumb, Bill had brought her instant relief from a painful left hip, and placement of several fingers on the nape of her neck resulted in sudden release from the discomfort of severe bursitis that had prevented her from raising her right arm for several weeks. "I danced around the room," she recalls of her first experience with his work. "I exercised my hip and swung my arm in a wide arc, temporarily free from pain for the first time in months."

She wrote about Bill Gray's amazing talent in *A Search for the Truth*, devoting an entire chapter to this seventy-one-year-old man's ability to find answers by "tuning in on the ring" that he said encircles the earth, and of his revitalization and adjustment of the body's magnetic field by what

he termed "opening the switches, tuning the heart, burning
out the rust, oiling the joints and letting the current flow
through." He called it, "the ancient wisdom" and insisted
that this magnetic force was the healing power utilized in
biblical days through "the laying on of hands."

Because he already had all the patients that he could
handle, he insisted on anonymity in the book. Ruth could
only call him "Mr. A.," and after publication of *A Search for
the Truth* she found it a heartbreaking task to withhold his
identity from the thousands of people who wrote pleading
letters asking to be put in touch with him.

Bill Gray's psychic awareness that he would find the
Montgomerys at home in Cuernavaca did not surprise Ruth
as much as it once would have done. Late in 1968, when her
severely broken arm and shoulder were showing no signs of
beginning the knitting process and her doctor was expressing real concern, Bill telephoned from the Norfolk airport
near Virginia Beach. "I'm picking up that you need me," he
said.

"It was really uncanny," Ruth recalls. "I had been unable
to write letters since the calamity in Dallas, so we had not
been in touch. Yet here he was at my doorstep, having flown
down from Washington before returning to California. I
told him that I did indeed need him, and after he gave me
several magnetic healing treatments during the next two
days, X rays at long last indicated that the knitting had
begun." Ruth is convinced to this day that the energy he
channeled through her helpless arm restored it to life, and
that without his timely intervention it might have shriveled
into permanent disuse.

Now Bill Gray and Dr. Dena Smith, the young surgeon
who traveled each winter with Bill and his wife to the
Southern Hemisphere, where he believed that he needed
to go to maintain his healing potency, were in Cuernavaca.

Mrs. Gray had gone on to California to open their house, but Bill and Dena wanted to talk about a book project.

Ruth had often agreed with them that the full story of Mr. A. was worthy of an entire book, especially if it might help others to learn more about this ancient healing art, but she had refused to consider writing it herself. "With so many thousands of heartrending letters arriving after just one chapter about him in *A Search for the Truth*, I couldn't go through that emotionally wrenching experience again," she explains. "Not unless Bill were willing to be identified so that he could deal with the mail himself." Dena had therefore decided to write the book, and it was her partially completed manuscript that they wanted to discuss.

"Ruth, I'm no writer," Dena confessed, handing over the neatly typed pages. "What I really need is your magic pencil."

Willing to help in whatever way she could, Ruth sat down to begin the editing. "I was glad to give her a hand," Ruth says, "and was making it read more smoothly, when I came to a section of totally unrelated material and asked what *that* was all about."

"You'll find the first part of it in the appendix," Dena explained.

"The appendix!" As a professional writer, Ruth was aghast.

"An editor told me that it wasn't interesting enough to put at the beginning, so I moved it back there."

"But you haven't even introduced the subject matter, or the people you're talking about," Ruth lamented, finally dropping the pencil in frustration. "You can't publish a book as disjointed as that!"

"I know I can't, but what am I going to do?" She and Bill had already consulted with several editors in an attempt to get the manuscript published, but had met with rejection unless Ruth wrote it. Now, if Ruth would agree to do so, they were ready to set up a foundation to which inquiries for Bill could be addressed, and Ruth would not be burdened with the mail.

"I realized that Bill Gray's amazing story should be told," she relates, "so I reluctantly agreed to do it." Ellis Amburn had meanwhile moved on to another publishing house and been succeeded by Patricia Soliman, an editor who had also read and loved Ruth's earlier books. Both editors wanted her book about Mr. A., but she decided not to leave her longtime publisher, and Pat Soliman was to prove a warm source of enthusiasm and encouragement, not only for this book, but for others in the years to come.

Bill and Dena joyously returned to California, and since Ruth's manuscript would now face a deadline, she and Bob canceled their trip to the Greek islands and flew instead to the West Coast to interview Bill Gray, Dena Smith, and many of the hundreds of grateful patients whom Bill had treated over the years.

The story of this remarkable man (whom she called Phil A. to rhyme with Bill Gray) and his ancient art of magnetic healing became Ruth's ninth book, *Born to Heal,* which was released in 1973. "A massive volume of mail reached me anyway," she laments. "Devastating stories about loved ones who suffered incurable ailments, and requests for me to intercede and arrange for appointments with Mr. A. as their only remaining hope." Bill Gray passed from this world in August 1975 and the foundation was disbanded, but to this day Ruth continues to receive a flood of mail from desperate seekers who plead for his treatment. Nearly three years after his death, however, the Guides began one of their morning sessions with a surprise: "Ruth, this is Lily, Art, and the group. Bill Gray wants to say something: 'Tell those people who write you that I'm now able to help them through thought and will work on their cases.' " Apparently the loss of his own body has not hindered his ability to help those still on earth, as many now attest.

The Guides continued to communicate each morning with Ruth, who was delighted to learn that her old friend Arthur Ford had decided to remain with Lily and the group for the daily sessions, at least for the present. There was more that he wanted to say about the creation of the universe and the origins of man on earth. On rare occasions the Guides also answered questions of a more personal nature. As an example:

In October of 1972 Lindy Boggs, wife of House Majority Leader Hale Boggs, telephoned to Ruth from Washington. As all America by then knew, her husband's plane had disappeared during a trip to Alaska. Search parties were constantly flying back and forth across the area, hopeful of locating wreckage and survivors, but no trace had thus far been found, and a number of well-known psychics had volunteered that they were "picking up his heartbeat" and that he was still alive. Could the Guides help to pinpoint the location while there was still hope of rescue?

Ruth posed this question to them at the next morning's session, but their answer contradicted that of the seers. The pilot, they asserted, had strayed off course while trying to skirt a storm, and "the tempest swept the plane in a swirling downdraft into the sea," ending the congressman's life instantly and without pain. According to the Guides, Hale and his companions who died in the crash were still sleeping on the other side, as souls often do after unexpected death before awakening in the spirit plane. Lily, Arthur, and the group went on to declare that Lindy would herself run for his seat in Congress, continue his work, and be able to draw help from her late husband if she should ask for it.

"Lindy sent grateful thanks for this message," Ruth recounts, "and several weeks later the fruitless search was called off. Hale Boggs was declared dead, and Lindy told me that of all the psychics who claimed to know the fate of the popular Louisiana congressman, only the Guides had told the truth." Just as they had predicted, his widow ran and was elected to fill his vacant seat, the first woman to represent Louisiana in the U.S. Congress, and has continued to be reelected ever since.

The Guides most often, however, devoted their daily sessions to subjects of their own choosing, and in early 1973 they suddenly began to write about the early unrecorded life of Jesus of Nazareth. Uncannily a letter arrived within two days from an unknown reader named Marilee (Mrs. John Warren) Beach, suggesting that Ruth pursue material on her supposed lifetime as Ruth, a sister of Lazarus and daughter of Arthur Ford in Palestine, whereupon the Guides announced that this story was indeed their current project. "In the daily sessions that followed," she recalls, "they launched a detailed account of that life, beginning with the birth of a child in Bethlehem, and my excitement as a little girl who watched richly costumed foreigners arrive to pay homage to a baby whose birth had been heralded by a star."

Remembering the ancient scene that had unfolded to her during an especially deep meditation back in Virginia Beach, Ruth also recalled the dramatic glimpses of that later life she had viewed under hypnosis with Adelle Davis. "With this new material from the Guides, I was simply enthralled," she explains. "It filled in all the blanks, and I could hardly wait for each morning's session to read their next installment."

The material that began to emerge proved to be so inspiring and consistent with Judeo-Christian teaching, yet included so many unknown aspects of the life of Christ, that Ruth soon realized it would be of general interest. She placed a call to her editor, Patricia Soliman, in New York, but before she could even broach the subject, Pat exclaimed, "Ruth, I was just going to call you. I've had the most wonderful idea for your next book!"

"Wait a minute," Ruth interrupted in a burst of laughter. "First let me tell you what the Guides have been writing lately. They are giving me fascinating material about an alleged Palestinian life when Arthur Ford was my father, during the time of Christ."

"Ruth, you should see my goose pimples!" Pat gasped. "I was just going to suggest that you write about the lifetimes that you have shared with Arthur Ford." What was going on here? Ruth wondered. Were Patricia and Marilee operating on Ruth's wavelength—or did the Guides send telepathic messages to all of them? It was mystifying.

Arthur had indeed hinted in *A World Beyond* that he and Ruth had known each other before, and now the Guides were providing more and more pieces of the story each day about a biblical Ruth who fled with her family to Egypt to escape King Herod's murderous decree and who later returned to marry, bear children, and devote her life to the new teaching that she learned from the now grown man named Jesus. They described a Ruth who found herself torn between family and faith, but whose hard-to-convince husband ever so gradually began to perceive that Jesus was not preaching against the sacred Hebrew scriptures, "but actually expanding their hidden meaning and revealing facts which hitherto had been masked in obscurity."

It was this lifetime in Palestine, the Guides wrote, that inspired Ruth to want to light the way, in her present lifetime, for others to learn the sacred principles of love and service to our fellowman. "This, then," they continued, "has returned to you each time that you took new physical form: this aching desire to serve God, even as you have failed often in that quest for perfection and holiness."

Ruth recalled her childhood yearning to become a foreign missionary, a wish that later yielded to a career in journalism. Had she at last, by continuing to convey the Guides' message of love and service to our fellowman, actually begun to fulfill that subconscious purpose that she had set for herself so long ago?

The Guides eventually concluded their story of the Palestinian Ruth who later in life traveled with her husband Jonathan to distant lands to spread the new teaching. Jonathan, they asserted, is now Bob Montgomery, and from lifetime to lifetime we continue to encounter those whom we have known and loved before, in an extended cycle called group karma.

After completing their lengthy account of the long-ago Ruth, the Guides launched into a discussion of group karma, and then described lifetime after lifetime in which she and Arthur Ford had known each other, sometimes as brother and sister, as student and teacher, daughter and father, or close friends. In ancient Moab, they declared, Ruth toiled in the fields as a man, "to prove that this tedious existence could be borne with patience and good spirit." Arthur Ford was a fellow workman, whose conversation and insight helped to relieve the tedious boredom. To this day Ruth suffers from recurring finger blisters that appear during tension or stress, "when you feel nonproductive," the Guides explain, calling to mind that lifetime in Moab where her wish to express herself found no outlet.

During a life in Egypt around 1390 B.C., they continued, she knew Arthur Ford as her father, a priest in the temple of Karnak, and those like Ruth who believed in the One God were held in disfavor. "You were outspoken about your beliefs and too intolerant of those who were unable to grasp this concept," the Guides cautioned. In another Egyptian lifetime Ruth was next in line to inherit the throne and rule as Pharaoh, but palace conspirators shoved her from a promontory so that a male (her younger brother, Arthur Ford) would lead the country, a female ruler being considered unlucky. "That fall apparently explained my fear of heights," Ruth remarks, "and the Guides continued to remind me that it also explained the recurring trouble with my back, which they said I should leave in the past, and which no longer bothers me."

In Persia around 800 B.C. Ruth was working with herbs, and together with Adelle Davis was assisting the work of the man since known as Edgar Cayce. Arthur Ford in that incarnation was Ruth's adventuresome son. A further lifetime found them again in Egypt, with Arthur as a mentor who supervised her studies at the world-famous library in Alexandria, where she researched and contributed to knowledge of the lost continent of Atlantis. "This was the Egyptian lifetime that I had glimpsed under hypnosis," she recalls, "when I died so suddenly from the bite of an adder while walking through that lovely garden overlooking the Nile."

Ruth met Arthur again as a teacher in Greece, according to the Guides, who repeated their recurring theme of service. "You were a mere lad," they explained, "but dedicated to the rule of God on earth, each person to be an individual helping all others to assert their rights through the unfolding of oneness, not by political turmoil or overthrow of existing rule, but through enlightenment and culture." The Guides described in detail the contemplative life in Tibet that Ruth had seemingly relived under hypnosis, as the little brown guru who knew Arthur Ford as the more advanced teacher who lived farther up the mountain, and whom she eventually succeeded. "You ate no meat and killed no living thing," they explained, reminding Ruth of her childhood refusal to eat meat after she realized that it first had to be killed.

Ruth's spirit pen pals at last opened a window on some past lives of Lily, who had heretofore been so reticent about his earthly incarnations. They said that he knew Arthur

Ford, but not Ruth, in an Italian lifetime when he was the
martyred monk Savonarola, and that he had befriended
Ruth in a subsequent French life at court in Versailles, a life
that helps to explain why her home is almost completely
furnished with antiques of the Louis XV period. "That was
not a particularly happy one for you," they added, "because
you were less frivolous than your family and friends, and
tried to avoid the entertainment at court."

Lily then disclosed that he had been the rather stern but
loving father of both Ruth and Arthur in a nineteenth-
century English incarnation. As in the early Egyptian life as
Pharaoh, Arthur was again her younger brother but this
time it was he who died at the threshold of adulthood and
Ruth who lived on to gain fame as a poet while suffering
severely from the subconscious memory of that painful
back injury which ended her life along the Nile.

The Guides identified her husband in that English life as
the present-day Bob Montgomery, and repeated their
teaching that we return to physical embodiment again and
again, ever rejoining those we love, ever striving upward on
our quest to round off the rough edges and help others to
understand the values of kindness and fellowship All of us
walk the path together, over and over again.

In concluding the material for this, Ruth's tenth book that
would become known as *Companions Along the Way*, the
Guides told her: "The purpose of your life today is to reach
as many people as possible through the introduction of the
truths of eternal life and the importance of assisting others
along the way, loving God and one's fellowman." To spend a
lifetime in pursuit of material gain, they stressed, is to waste
a God-given opportunity for spiritual growth.

Ever since her move to Cuernavaca numerous members
of the Episcopal Guild had been urging Ruth to conduct a
meditation-study group. "But where will I find the time!"

she would sigh. "Always I seemed to be writing a book, or flying to the States for television promotional tours of the previous one, while also giving lectures, managing a household, and answering floods of fan mail." Now, however, inspired by the Guides' words about service to others, she began holding a weekly meditation session at her home, passing on to her students what she had previously learned at similar classes in Virginia Beach and helping them to interpret their dreams.

She was indeed "taking to heart" what the Guides had written: "To each of us is given the same opportunity to cast a light in the gloom. Whether rich or poor, obscure or famous, young or old, we are presented almost daily with opportunities to choose good over evil, right over wrong, strength over weakness, and to offer a steadying hand to someone else. With each correct choice we take another leap forward in our progress toward perfection. The race will be won when all of us are as pilgrims, each serving as a strong right hand to the other. Comrades in arms, pulling together, we will lighten the load and become filled with joyousness, for joy will become the music of eternity."

By the time *Companions Along the Way* was released in 1974, Ruth's following had grown to massive numbers of people who had begun by reading her account of the psychic and automatic writing, had become convinced of reincarnation, were comforted by knowledge of an active life after death, and were now reminded that we and our loved ones are eternal and inseparable. But most important of all, the Guides' lengthy story of the life and teachings of Jesus inspired many readers to take a fresh look at the Bible and to rethink their own religious heritage from the revised perspective that they now embraced. The ancient teaching that life is continuous and eternal may not be so strange after all, and if we realize our responsibility to love one another and to lend a hand where needed, we cannot help but realize that all of us are indeed Companions Along the Way.

CHAPTER XI

Atlantis and Lemuria

Of all Ruth Montgomery's books to date none seemed to touch her Christian readers as deeply as did *Companions Along the Way*. Many hundreds of people wrote to say that they especially treasured this book because it made the New Testament come alive to them for the first time. Even those whose beliefs did not embrace Christianity wrote that they now understood more completely the impact that the teachings of Jesus had made on his followers. "Letters began to pour in from readers who believed that they also had lived in those long-ago days," Ruth recounts, "if not in the Palestinian incarnation, then in ancient Persia or Egypt or Greece."

But perhaps most importantly those who had earlier questioned whether Christianity could encompass reincarnation began to regard the two philosophies as completely compatible. Many wrote to tell of their renewed faith in the beliefs that they had known as children, but within a broader context that now allowed for learning and spiritual growth rather than the simple reward-and-punishment philosophy of their churches.

No sooner did the Guides conclude their account of Ruth's incarnations with Arthur Ford than they returned to where they had left off before, with Creation and the prehistoric period of planet earth. "At first I felt reluctant to pursue this topic," she recalls, "because I knew of no way to cross-check their amazing assertions. But I've always been a history buff, ever curious about the how and why of changes in the world and eager to understand more about the causes behind them. When I began to look more carefully at the material they provided on Atlantis and Lemuria and how these ancient civilizations helped to form the world as we know it today, I became intrigued."

The Guides also dangled a carrot, promising a glimpse of the future, and as they plunged into the task of satisfying Ruth's growing curiosity, they churned out page after page of fascinating material about the earth's beginnings, the gradual emergence of plant and animal life, and the eventual advent of humankind, first in light, shadowy bodies and then in solid flesh. Captivated by this wealth of new information, she soon realized that it would comprise a rich lode of material for a book, if it could somehow be corroborated.

For twelve months the Montgomerys had held reservations at Lygon Arms in Broadway, England, to meet Paul Shick and a friend there for the Christmas holidays of 1973, but a few days before their scheduled departure Paul telephoned that their mother had been taken to the hospital in Indianapolis. Canceling their reservations, Ruth and Bob flew to Indiana instead, and took a taxi directly to the hospital. Not long after their arrival Bertha Shick, age eighty-nine, was having a loving conversation with her daughter when suddenly she sat straight up in bed, holding both arms outstretched, and exclaimed: "How beautiful! Oh, how beautiful it all is!"

"What's beautiful, Mother?" Ruth enquired, noting nothing of particular interest in the room.

"They're showing me the other side, and it's beautiful!" Bertha replied.

"Who's 'they'?" Ruth prodded, by now aware that her mother was having a dramatic glimpse of the beyond.

"Why, Mama and Papa, I presume," she said blissfully.

Musing afterward about that reassuring episode, Ruth laments, "How I wish that Mother could have painlessly abandoned her worn-out body then instead of lingering unhappily for three more months! But she was a wise and wonderful woman. At the end, when hospital attendants were rushing artificial life-sustaining equipment into her room, Mother waved them off, saying, 'I don't want it. Take it away.' "

Within a few minutes she slipped away, and the doctor remarked to her children, "I think she made the right decision."

The Montgomerys had a number of houseguests during that year of 1974, including Sally and Hugh Lynn Cayce, Ruth's close friend Hope Miller, her sister Margaret, and numerous others. Then, immediately after Christmas, they flew to Egypt to meet Hope and the Wilfred Sechrists for a boat trip down the Nile, next to Israel and Greece, and on to Nairobi for a picture-taking safari in Kenya before proceeding to England and the postponed stay at Lygon Arms.

On their return to Cuernavaca Ruth and Bob found their household employees warring among themselves and demanding to take one another to police headquarters. They were able to soothe ruffled feelings, but the winds of change had already begun to blow in Mexico. Its idyllic climate continued to delight the Montgomerys and other resident Americans, but the *political* climate had grown much more hostile since the installation of Luis Echeverría as Presi-

dent, and minor irritations that had always been bother-
some began to multiply into major headaches.

Water for cooking and drinking had to be boiled for thirty
minutes to kill amoebas, but because there was reason to
doubt that this precaution was taken at dinner parties that
they attended, Ruth and Bob underwent regular amoeba
tests and took repeated rounds of medication. Also, corrup-
tion within the Mexican police departments ran rampant,
and as law-abiding people they found it distasteful to pay
graft to avoid spending a full day at police headquarters for
trumped-up, imaginary offenses.

Like others in the American community they took out a
policy that they nicknamed "stay-out-of-jail insurance," because if a car was involved even in a minor fender-scraping
incident, the drivers were hauled off to jail for forty-eight
hours and allowed only one phone call. Those with the
special insurance used that one call to telephone the agent,
who would then begin the complex negotiations to overcome red tape, pay graft, and release them from behind
bars.

"It didn't happen to us," Ruth says thankfully, "but some
of our friends went through that hassle, and it was like a
Sword of Damocles hanging over all of our heads. As a
consequence of this foolish law, if a bus driver ran over a
pedestrian, he quickly disappeared into the crowd, rushed
back to his dispatcher, and was immediately assigned to
another route. It was preposterous!

"Perhaps the worst blow to tranquility was a law imple-
mented by Echeverría's leftist regime which decreed that if
a domestic worker were discharged for any reason whatso-
ever after the first twenty-eight days of employment, he or
she must be paid a bonus of three months' salary. As a result,
gardeners, cooks, and maids were exemplary for the first
four weeks. After that, even if they began to steal or brawl
or skip work entirely, we had to go to the police station, fill

out endless forms printed in Spanish, and pay out the unearned reward. Not all workers abused the system, of course, but it was frustrating!"

Growing more and more disenchanted, Ruth and Bob finally looked at each other one day and said, "What are we doing in Mexico? Why don't we go back where we belong?" With mixed emotions they decided to put their dream house up for sale. "So many of our American friends were already leaving for the same reason that a number of lovely homes were already on the market," Ruth recalls. "We therefore expected that ours would take at least a year to sell, and in the meantime we would travel through the Sunbelt to see where we wanted to settle."

A year of trying to choose where to live would mean frequent trips, long absences from home, and extended delay in completing the Guides' new project on Atlantis, Lemuria, and the prehistoric earth, the dictation for which they had resumed after the Montgomerys' return from their African safari.

Now they were expecting a visit from Paul Shick and a friend, so they decided to delay putting the house on the market until after Paul's departure. But apparently the Guides had other ideas in mind. On Saturday morning, shortly after Paul's arrival, the telephone rang and the voice of an unknown realtor announced, "I understand that your beautiful house is going to be for sale. I have clients who would very much like to see it today. May I bring them by?"

"I'm sorry, but it's not convenient now," Ruth replied. "We have houseguests from the States. Possibly next week . . ."

"But my clients are here only for the weekend and have to leave tomorrow. Please, Mrs. Montgomery, we won't bother anybody."

Ruth was nonplussed. "Always," she says, remembering the uncanny ways that their other homes had sold without advertising, "it seems as if some otherworldly force takes over and brings the right people together at the right time. It's as if my life were being directed by an unseen power while I stand quietly on the sidelines. I let her bring the clients."

The Montgomerys stayed out of the way until the agent beckoned them and asked in a whisper whether they would come down on their price. They shook their heads. "We had naturally set the price high enough to allow for negotiation," Ruth admits, "but these were the first potential buyers, and there was no hurry."

The realtor consulted with her clients, who immediately decided to sign a purchase agreement at the full asking price, provided that they could have the house in thirty days. "They were wealthy Mexicans who lived in Mexico City," Ruth explains, "and they wanted to use it as their weekend home. We gulped at that one-month deadline, because we had no idea where we would move, but what if we turned this offer down? We'd have more time to think about where to go, true, but in the end we'd still have to make up our minds." With some measure of trepidation, they signed the agreement.

Needless to say, the pressure was now on. As soon as their houseguests departed, the Montgomerys packed their own suitcases and flew to Texas. "San Antonio in those days served as a sort of way station for Americans returning from Mexico," she recounts. "A number of our friends were already living there, so it made sense to rent an apartment and then take our time deciding where to settle permanently."

But finding an apartment is no easy task when one has grown accustomed to the spaciousness of a large house. "They were all too small," Ruth laments, "but since this move would be a temporary one, we finally settled on a three-bedroom apartment where I would have space for a

study." They signed a year's lease and returned to Cuernavaca to pack.

Ruth and Bob had fretted about the impossibility of fit-
ting fourteen rooms of furniture into a six-room apartment,
but even that problem found an immediate solution. "The
people who were buying our house offered to purchase its
entire contents as well," she explains, "right down to the
beds, mattresses, and linens, because everything was from
the United States, and of a quality not available in Mexico."
Unwilling to part with their Louis XV antiques and other
items of sentimental value, they agreed to sell the rest, and
by the end of the month their six-year sojourn in Mexico had
come to an end.

The Guides, of course, were delighted to get back to work
on the new book, even if they didn't admit to orchestrating
the entire move themselves in order to save precious time.
But more importantly San Antonio now gave Ruth access to
library resources that had been unavailable in Mexico. "As
material grew in volume from the daily sessions of automatic writing," she recalls, "I was able to check their assertions against geological records and archaeological evidence of prehistoric cultures. Actually I don't know how I
could have completed the book if we had stayed in Mexico."

All manner of related material also found its way to her
doorstep. "It's bewildering the way this always happens,"
she says with a laugh. "Every time I start to write a book,
scads of collateral material on that subject suddenly land on
my desk. A reader will send something of interest, or a
magazine will appear with a scientific article just as I need
it, or there will be a rash of newspaper stories that fit right in
with what I'm writing. It's incredible!"

During that year in San Antonio Ruth completed *The
World Before,* a version of planetary history about the
earth's gaseous beginnings, its original shadowy life forms
and subsequent human beings of five different races, "each

developing different pigmentation to cope with varying rays of the sun, and color to harmonize with his environment," factors that proved crucial to daily survival in that age when people seldom moved from place to place. The continent of Lemuria (or Mu), situated in what is now the Pacific Ocean, had been a land of gentle, spiritual people, the Guides wrote, while Atlantis drew souls of a more scientific, technological inclination. Air travel was later introduced by visitors from outer space and developed by Atlanteans, who made use of a many-faceted crystal (the Great Crystal) that provided means of propulsion for aircraft and ships.

It was by such air travel, according to the Guides, that delegates from all regions of the planet gathered in Atlantis for conferences on ways to rid the earth of giant beasts that threatened human safety and had forced Lemurians to live largely underground for many generations.

Lemuria met with ultimate destruction, the Guides wrote, in a planetary shift of the earth on its axis some fifty thousand years ago. Alerted in advance by space visitors who could observe ominous signs of change from their vantage point beyond the earth's atmosphere, many Lemurians heeded the warnings that were echoed by the wise men among them and migrated to other lands in North and South America, parts of Asia and Africa. When that long-awaited cataclysm at last occurred, according to the Guides, nearly all of Mu sank into the Pacific, except for Easter Island and parts of Hawaii, and elsewhere new mountains were thrust upward. Continents changed in shape many growing in size and others yielding vast portions of their land to the sea.

Much of Atlantis survived that shift, the Guides claimed, though new positioning of the earth's poles brought about a major change in its climate. The Atlantean civilization prevailed for another twenty thousand years, until misuse of the Great Crystal caused a sudden nuclear-type explosion which released pressure "greater than that at Hiroshima by ten hundred thousand times," causing storms and tidal waves, sinking large portions of that continent, and triggering the great flood that is described in the Bible as well as in the folklore of numerous other civilizations from the Chaldeans to the American Indians. Then, some eight thousand years later, Atlantean scientists again tinkering with the crystal set off final earthquakes that caused most of what was left of Atlantis to sink into the sea, except for islands such as Bermuda and Bimini.

The Guides, having described in detail the daily life during that long-ago period, asserted that records of Atlantis and Lemuria, the early history of planet earth, and technical information on the use of crystals for air transport exist to this day, preserved near Uxmal in the Yucatán, and "within a radius of eighty-seven feet" of the Great Pyramid of Giza, which itself was constructed "above and slightly to the east" of the hidden chamber.

The Guides also stated that drawings made by space visitors were left in various places on the earth, particularly in caves, so that humans may at some future point begin to understand the process of dissolving and reassembling the atomic structure of objects. It is this "Universal Law," the Guides claimed, that made possible the construction by refugee Atlanteans of the Egyptian pyramids at Giza, enabled Jesus to leave the tomb, and permits space travel by what we now call UFOs.

With each assertion by the Guides Ruth turned to the numerous books and articles that had mysteriously come into her hands, only to find repeated new evidence that humans lived on earth far earlier than had previously been believed, that remnants of tropical trees and warm-blooded animals have been found embedded in Arctic ice, symptomatic of a sudden change in climate, and that fossilized human footprints have now been discovered side by side with those of dinosaurs, thus doing away with the earlier assumption that dinosaurs vanished before the advent of humankind. Likewise she cited geological evidence suggesting that the magnetic poles have reversed themselves at numerous times in the past and that the polar ice caps have previously been situated in different parts of the earth.

As for Atlantis in particular, remnants of an earlier civilization—walls and a submerged pyramid—have recently been discovered off Bimini, and investigators continue to puzzle over the strange electromagnetic and visual aberrations that have accompanied hundreds of ship and aircraft disappearances in the portion of the Atlantic Ocean known as the Sargasso Sea. According to the Guides, the Great Crystal that had powered ships and flying machines now lies submerged beneath those waters, and "when the sun and moon are in the right positions, the rays activate the crystal, so that it interacts with the encasing carbon," creating treacherous conditions for navigation by sea or air in the Bermuda Triangle.

The Guides provided an extensive account of prehistoric migrations of people from Lemuria to other parts of the globe, where new evidence points not to a savage past as scientists once believed, but to a highly developed civilization of "unknown origins." Continuing, they described the cycles of rebirth that bring Lemurian and Atlantean souls back to the planet, with the latter especially attracted to the technological advances we know today.

As they had promised, the Guides completed their account of *The World Before* by opening a door to future events, and many of these predictions of twelve years ago have already come to pass; yet the most ominous warning they issued concerned the entire planet. A shift of the earth on its axis will occur near the end of this century, they insisted, noting that while it will not prove to be as destructive as the one that sank Lemuria, it will nevertheless cause widespread devastation to life as we know it. Millions will pass into spirit, and those millions who survive in physical body will live through trying times until a new era of peace and understanding is built on what remains, plus newly risen lands. "Those who fear death should put it firmly from their minds," they advised, "as this planetary cleansing is inevitable and our spirits are eternal, though we should realize the need to preserve written records so that future humans will be able to rediscover ancient truths and immortal written words."

And on this note the Guides concluded their comprehensive story of *The World Before*. Happy to have placed such a massive volume of information in a form that could be shared with others, Ruth shipped her completed manuscript to her publisher in New York.

Meanwhile she and Bob had looked at real estate in San Antonio and found nothing that appealed to them. "Our lease would expire in a few months, and we knew we didn't want to stay where we were." Again an odd coincidence, "probably arranged by the Guides," she says with a laugh, led them to consider returning to Washington.

Paul and Minnie Lee Summers, two longtime social friends who lived in an elegant old apartment building in the Northwest section of Washington, arrived in San Antonio for the Christmas season. "They gave a dinner party for us at the St. Anthony Club," Ruth recounts, "and mentioned that their prestigious building was going cooperative, which meant that some tenants who preferred to rent rather than buy would want to leave." Intrigued, since she knew the building well, Ruth asked if they would have some floor plans sent to her.

Then the next step fell into place. Popular talk-show host David Susskind called from New York to say that he was planning a ninety-minute syndicated TV program on reincarnation and wanted Ruth to serve on the panel. She declined. "I had just returned from Los Angeles, where I'd appeared on an NBC television documentary in the psychic field, and my sister Margaret was visiting us. I didn't want to make the trip to New York at that time, so I suggested that David invite Hugh Lynn Cayce and Gina Cerminara to be on his show. He already had Dick Sutphen."

A few days later Susskind called back "Ruth, I now have the others lined up, but I *have* to have you, because it's just no show without you. You're considered 'the' authority in this field. Please, you just *have* to do it for me."

Ruth had appeared on Susskind's three-hour "Open End" program many years before, after returning from the Nixon trip to Russia and Siberia, so she knew and liked David. She still dreaded the idea of flying to New York, but when he called the second time, it was a more personal request. "He asked with such kindness if I would *please* do it for *him*, that I finally agreed," she remembers. The David Susskind show on reincarnation became a sensation, generating such massive response that it was often rebroadcast for several years afterward, as was the NBC documentary.

En route back to Texas from New York, Ruth stopped off in Washington to see Hope Ridings Miller, who had regularly visited the Montgomerys each year, no matter where they moved, and while there Ruth dropped by to see which apartments might be for sale in the historic building where the Montgomerys had often attended parties given by longtime resident Vice President Alben W. Barkley and numerous other friends.

"Only two of the largest, twelve-room apartments had become available when the building went cooperative," Ruth recounts, "and all of the units were selling fast. Unfortunately I had to be back in San Antonio in a couple of days to deliver a lecture in behalf of a charitable organization, so I couldn't ask Bob to join me in Washington for an inspection tour. There was nothing to do except to fly home, make the speech, and then try to sell Bob on moving back to Washington."

The nation's capital had looked beautiful to Ruth after eight years away, and old friends eagerly entertained her during that brief visit. Bob was less enchanted with the idea of returning to cold winters and muggy summers, now that he was enjoying retirement, but he agreed to look at the two largest apartments that were being held for them temporarily. Thus it was a crazy week of crisscrossing the country, weighing their options, and finally buying one of the largest units.

Learning that the Montgomerys were preparing to leave Texas, Kent Keeth, director of the Texas History Collection at Baylor University, hastened to San Antonio to tape three days of conversations with Ruth about her life and career for Baylor's Oral History Library. Then Ruth and Bob again placed their antiques in the hands of packers and movers, and in the bicentennial year of 1976 they returned to Washington, only a few weeks before Ruth's eleventh book, *The World Before,* was released for publication. Another milestone in their lives had been recorded.

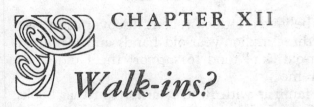

CHAPTER XII

Walk-ins?

The Montgomerys were back in Washington! A multicolumn article in the *Washington Post*, complete with a large photo of Ruth, announced their return to the nation's capital and introduced her eleventh book, *The World Before*. The article recapped her distinguished career from newspaper reporting to communication with spirit pen pals, and noted with some surprise that despite the Guides' continued prediction of planetary disasters to come, she calmly smiled and said, "Why worry? The forces are already set in motion. It's irreversible."

Those who reviewed *The World Before* likewise paid little attention to its dire forecasts for the future. They noticed instead the intriguing explanation of our origin and purpose on earth and the fact that Ruth had researched and verified so many of the Guides' assertions. Most impressive to those who held to biblical accounts was the Guides' insistence that humans did not evolve from the same ancestors as apes, but were separate creations who gradually solidified from spirit form and who walked the earth far earlier than scien-

tists had once believed. Indeed recent discoveries in eastern Africa of three-million-year-old hands and a million-
and-a-half-year-old skull tend to support the Guides' extended time frame.

For readers familiar with Ruth's earlier spiritual books,
The World Before offered something different, a chance to
pause and reflect on a new version of planetary history and
geography. Many had heard of Atlantis and Lemuria before, but with the Guides' account of the overall chronology
and daily life of these two lost civilizations, readers who
loved piecing together the how and why of the world as we
know it were simply enthralled.

But what of that ominous prediction of a shift of the earth
on its axis? "A lot of readers became quite interested in the
possibility," Ruth recalls. "Articles discussing the likelihood
of previous shifts soon began to appear in a number of
publications, not necessarily because of my book, but because other writers now decided to explore the idea as
well."

She began her publicity tour for *The World Before* in New
York, appearing with Tom Snyder on NBC's "Tomorrow"
show, and then flew to California, where she lunched at the
Beverly Hills Hotel with comedienne Carol Burnett, who
was interested in Ruth's books and had been in correspondence with her for some time. Carol also brought Anthony
Hopkins and his wife to the luncheon, since Tony was preparing to play the starring role in *Audrey Rose,* a movie
about reincarnation, and wanted to learn more on the subject.

After completing the tour she returned to the spacious
apartment with a sense of completeness. "I felt that I had
covered everything the Guides could possibly tell me of
general interest," she confesses with a sigh. "Bob and I were
back in Washington, where we had lived for twenty-five
years before moving away. Once again among old friends,

we were soon busy in the social whirl, so I was prepared to relax and enjoy life. Frankly I thought I'd earned a long rest."

The Guides thought otherwise. No sooner had the book tour ended than they began writing almost exclusively about the coming shift. "You've already covered that subject," she argued, "and I don't even want to think about the famine you're predicting, and World War III. There's no way I can have any proof that it's true, so unless you give me other material, we'll just forget it."

Ruth's sessions at the typewriter grew farther and farther apart, but each time that she returned to the automatic writing, hoping that the Guides had something new to impart, they would start in again about the world changes that they could foresee. It was *urgent*, they insisted, that people be warned of the approaching planetary chaos. "They must realize that after the shift, the earth's population will be so decimated that there will be limited opportunity for souls to return to earth life for a long time to come," they wrote. "People must be alerted to this fact so that they can begin now to work out their karma while they are still in flesh."

Whether people wanted to survive the shift or not, the Guides declared, it was Ruth's absolute *duty* to write a book about it so that people could begin to mend their ways. "At the time of the shift so many millions of souls will be coming over simultaneously that it will unduly tax our normal system of greeting and helping them to adjust to the fact that they are still alive but no longer in physical bodies," they explained. "In the usual course of events there are always a number of souls here who are ready to work with each newcomer. But with so many crossing into spirit at once, unless they've meditated about this and begun to accept the words we've already written about how to prepare spiritually, and what it's like in the spirit plane, they could experience a tremendous setback in their spiritual growth."

"That's all very reasonable and I understand that," Ruth countered after perusing this message, "but I'm not going to write a book that will frighten people out of their wits. All of our other books have been uplifting." Finally she abandoned the morning sessions altogether in a standoff that continued for months. Her hands again broke out in strange blisters that made it painful to type or even to hold a pencil. That frustrating life in Moab again?

But Ruth's fan mail continued to arrive, through 1977 and into the spring of 1978. "I would let it pile up until I could spare the time to deal with it," she recalls, "and then set aside a day to work my way down through some of the stacks of letters, writing brief postcard replies. One day I came across a beautifully written letter that began, 'Are you still there? I visited my favorite bookstore yesterday and asked if you had published any books since *The World Before*, which came out nearly two years ago, and they checked in all their lists, including that of forthcoming books, and could find nothing that I hadn't yet read. Are you still writing? You haven't retired, have you? I sincerely hope not. You owe it to your loyal followers to keep sharing the views and information given you by our unseen friends.' "

The letter thanked Ruth for writing the psychic books that "have quietly proven to us that in reality there is no death, but only change. Countless millions of us readers," it continued, "remain forever grateful to you for opening the door to a beautiful reality which had remained hidden, cloaked in dogma and in the circles we all spin in this world of illusion."

This fan letter, typical of so many that Ruth had received from readers ever since she had first delved into the psychic, then proposed that she ask the Guides about "the role of Walk-ins on the planet."

"I was intrigued with the idea of Walk-ins," Ruth concedes. "I had never heard of them before, although the letter described a Walk-in as an entity who is not born as an infant, but takes over (always with permission) the body of one who wishes to depart. 'The Walk-in first completes the task of the body's previous owner, and then goes on to do what he must do on his own projects, which are really those of a gardener who plants seeds on the planet, helps those seeds to germinate, and then lets them grow in their own direction.' "

Ruth's unknown correspondent concluded: "Perhaps it is time to tell the story of these remarkable beings, who are human while they are among us, and who help us along the way in our own evolution. Please don't stop writing!"

Walk-ins! Could there be any truth to this strange assertion? The next morning, fingers still smarting from the outbreak of blisters, Ruth posed that intriguing question. After her silent period of meditation and prayer for protection, she rested her fingers lightly on the keys and allowed the typing to begin. "The Walk-ins, so-called, are superior but not perfected souls who have gone on after many earthly lives," the Guides declared, and they confirmed that such beings "wish to avoid returning as babies and wasting the unneeded learning time of childhood. They do indeed take over with permission the bodies of discouraged souls who want to leave or who cannot keep their bodies alive. Some are even unaware that they were not always in the bodies they now inhabit, because they inherit the memory bank of the Walk-out. They are necessary to the fulfillment of the prophecies of strange and wonderful things to come, and there will be many more of them as the earth approaches its shift."

The following morning, eager for further information on this strange new concept, Ruth again consulted the Guides. "The Walk-ins are trying to bring a modicum of intelligence to those groping in the dark for solutions to the world's ills," they wrote, noting that many are also working to release those who regret having chosen this period in which to incarnate and "wish to avoid the turmoil of the eighties and nineties." Their mission, they added, is to help mankind.

By the third morning session the Guides declared a break. "Stay now for a time," they wrote, "and think on what we have been saying. Take time to meditate on the Walk-ins and their purpose on this earth. They are a breed unto themselves, few yet in number but rapidly increasing as we move toward the end of the century with its tragedies and ill winds."

"That day I finally answered the woman's letter," Ruth recalls. "I wanted to learn more about Walk-ins, and I hoped that my unknown correspondent, who was obviously intelligent, could point out where I could find more material on this interesting phenomenon."

Her letter reached its destination, several hundred miles away, on a hot summer day. Running behind schedule, I hurriedly grabbed the mail on my way to work, too rushed to do more than scan the return addresses, one of which was that of Ruth Montgomery in Washington, D.C. A letter from my favorite writer! A woman whose books had completely changed my thinking about life and death and the purpose for living. Ruth had actually answered my letter, and now I hadn't even a minute to open it without also being late for work. The suspense was driving me crazy!

Two weeks earlier I had written to encourage her to continue producing books. She and the Guides had enlightened and inspired so many devoted readers over the years that surely they mustn't stop now. Perhaps she might ask the Guides about Walk-ins?

Arriving at work with only seconds to spare and anxious to open her letter, I finally slipped off to the rest room, tore open the envelope, and eagerly read its contents: "I asked the Guides, and they indeed verify what you said about Walk-ins and are beginning to tell me more. How did you know of them? Do you know of material that I should read? The Guides have been patiently dictating material about how to prepare for the shift and beyond, but it's so grim that I have been exceedingly reluctant to write a book on that subject. But Walk-ins? How entrancing—particularly since the Guides say that they are coming in increasing numbers during the next decade to prepare us for that ominous SHIFT. Will you let me know of any material on the subject, or the source of your own knowledge?"

Now deep in thought, I refolded the typed letter, slipped it back into my purse, and returned to my work, telling no one. How could I answer this letter when my only sources of information on this phenomenon were a distant friend and a sweet old woman named Miriam, both of whom claimed to *be* Walk-ins? Nearly a year before, I had begun to visit Miriam more often. She understood life and reincarnation and energy forces, and we spent many a Sunday afternoon over knitting needles and endless cups of tea, discussing life's mysteries. One day she began to tell me about something new and strange. "I was not born in this body," she confided. "I came in more than thirty years ago. They call us Walk-ins."

Intrigued, I had leaned closer. *What* was this? I wanted to learn more.

"There are a few of us around," she continued. 'We're here and there on the planet, doing our tasks, helping one another, working on our own projects. You'll come to understand more, in due time. We're servants, helpers of the Creator."

Walk-ins? This was a fascinating concept. I had questioned her repeatedly, each time from a different angle, but her answers remained so consistent that finally I believed that this was for real. "It's secret," Miriam cautioned. "We don't need a witch hunt."

But perhaps if the Walk-in concept was indeed valid, it

was time to let the secret out so that people could understand this further aspect of life. Without consulting Miriam,
I typed a letter to Ruth Montgomery, whose books had
enlightened so many people and awakened them to the
truth. Maybe she should write about Walk-ins. The Guides
could surely tell her all that she would need to know.

Now Ruth had written back and asked how I knew about
them. *What* had I gotten myself into? I had no wish to
expose Miriam, who would be terribly upset if she knew I
had opened the subject to anyone, and I had banked on the
fact that Ruth's own spirit sources could give her as much
information as she would need. After considering the problem all day at work, I mustered the courage to break the
news to my elderly friend that evening, and I blushed from
guilt as I showed her Ruth's letter and asked how she
thought it should be handled. "Mercy me!" she exclaimed,
sinking into her rocker. "This is terrible! Dear, dear, dear, I
do wish you had never told anyone about Walk-ins, but
nothing will change that now. Give me time to think about
this." More than a month passed.

Finally it became clear how to answer Ruth's letter. Information on Walk-ins *must* come from the Guides, a source
that readers had grown to trust. I knew of nothing that had
been written on the subject, but if Ruth really needed to
know more about my source of information in this area, she
should "ask the Guides and they will tell you." If *they*
wanted to tell her about Miriam and others, they would.
Closing with words of encouragement for Ruth, trusting
that the Guides would verify that *inner* preparation is the
key to riding out the planetary shift, I mailed off my long-
delayed reply. Surely she would now get on with the book
that the Guides were so anxious for her to write.

In Washington meanwhile more information about Walk-
ins had begun to flow again from the automatic writing. "I
began to see," Ruth recalls, "that a book about preparation

for that awesome shift could include Walk-ins as a focal point and provide readers with thoughts that were positive and hopeful rather than merely dire and foreboding. Then Joanne's answer to my letter finally arrived, telling me to 'ask the Guides.' That brought me up rather short. I was musing on this when the telephone rang."

The call was from Patricia Soliman, Ruth's editor in New York. "She and I so often seemed to be on the same wavelength," Ruth says with a laugh, "that I wasn't surprised. Pat was asking once again *when* she might expect another book."

This time Ruth had something intriguing to tell her. "Listen to this letter I've received," she began. "It describes something called Walk-ins, and the Guides are verifying everything that she said."

"Ruth, I'm having goose bumps again!" Pat exclaimed. "I feel certain that the woman who wrote to you is a Walk-in, though I've never heard of them until now."

Wow! At Ruth's next session the Guides seemed eager to begin the project that she had delayed for so long. "So let's get to work on the new book," they urged. "The woman who wrote is indeed a Walk-in whom we knew both there and here." Then they plunged into a lengthy explanation of the process of soul transferral. On the following day Ruth sought further confirmation, just to be certain. "She is indeed a Walk-in," they repeated, and described a rather difficult but important task that lay ahead for the unknown correspondent.

"With pleasurable excitement I answered her letter," Ruth recounts. "I refrained from telling her any of what the Guides had revealed, but asked if we could arrange a personal meeting in the city where she lived, and if she would recommend a nearby inn or hotel."

When Ruth's second letter arrived, hinting only that "the Guides have told me many wonderful things about you and your mission," and asking to visit with me, I was genuinely puzzled. Aware only of a deep commitment to do my best in this life, I couldn't imagine what special "mission" the Guides must have described. Surely they knew more about my life than I knew at that point. As Ruth's letter requested, I telephoned her in Washington, gave her the name of a convenient hotel, and arranged to meet her there that weekend.

The evening before her arrival something very odd occurred. Busy with a routine task, humming along with the radio, and continuing to puzzle over what the Guides could have told Ruth about me, I suddenly became aware of two presences, discarnates, standing just a few feet away. I saw nothing with my eyes, only with my mind, with that extra sense that says friendly spirits have come to visit. It was a familiar sensation, but these two entities had come for a reason.

"There's something you need to know," they began, "before you meet with Ruth." These were not voices that I could hear, but thoughts that came directly from the two beings. "You see," they continued, "you're a Walk-in. Don't you remember how much you changed last year? Think about it." Then they vanished.

Good heavens! *That's* what the Guides must have told Ruth! But how could this be, if even *I* didn't know about it? Yes, I had changed markedly through the past year, grown happier and more clearheaded, and had easily solved some long-standing problems. But how could I be a Walk-in? What was going on?

Still stunned, I picked up the telephone and called Miriam. "Guess what just happened here," I began, and described the visit of the two strange beings. "They said I'm a Walk-in."

Miriam seemed more amused than surprised at this sudden revelation. "I was wondering how soon you'd figure that out for yourself," she replied. "Now you know why Ruth wants to meet you."

I had not fully digested this new information by the following morning when, as we had arranged, I met Ruth Montgomery at her hotel. Prepared only to share what I knew about Walk-ins and to encourage her to write about how to prepare for the coming planetary shift, I was certainly *not* ready to claim to *be* one of these newly arrived souls.

Ruth wasted no time in getting to the point of her visit. Leading the way to a table and chairs by the window, she handed me a sheet of yellow paper bearing the familiar greeting that is so well known to those who have read and cherished her books: "Ruth, this is Lily, Art, and the group." I read with fascination the words that followed. Then she handed me a second sheet of paper, on which the Guides had declared that I was a Walk-in. I was shaken! I gazed out the window for what seemed a very long time and then sat down with Ruth to discuss Walk-ins in general, trusting that she would not rely on my say-so, but would check every piece of information with the Guides before believing a word.

"Our meeting covered a wide range of topics," Ruth says in retrospect, "but at no time did Joanne admit to being a Walk-in. Finally, as she rose to leave, she at last framed an answer to the Guides' assertion. 'The idea of my being a Walk-in is information that was given to me only within the last several hours. I need more time to think about it before I'll feel ready to discuss it with anyone,' she said.'

After saying goodbye the Montgomerys drove to Newport, Rhode Island, and upon their return to Washington a week later, Ruth found a long, detailed letter from me, to whom she would later refer as "Laura." "Having taken some time to think it over," Ruth explains, "Joanne had reviewed the odd changes experienced during the past year. She recalled the months when she had lived alone and felt the presence of a loving being who offered to take over the body during sleep, and she now acknowledged the possibility that a substitution could have occurred, as the Guides claimed. But she stressed that at the time of her two earlier letters, no such thought had crossed her mind."

Immediately after the trip Ruth set to work on the new book that the Guides had been urging her to write. "They happily obliged by enlarging upon the role of Walk-ins in history," she recalls, "and the kinds of tasks that these newcomers will take on through the years ahead as the earth enters the New Age of Aquarius."

Ruth and Bob had long planned a vacation in England for that autumn of 1978, little thinking that a new book would be in progress by then, with its inevitable deadline. Since they were going to be guests in several famous manor houses, they had to keep to the schedule for the trip, and by the time they returned, Ruth was filled with new doubts. "Throughout my long career I have always tried to write truth," she says. "Suddenly I was beset with worries that this eerie idea of Walk-ins could be a massive hallucination. After all, why hadn't anyone written about them before? Why hadn't the Guides broached this subject until now? Would I be hooted at and ridiculed for falling victim to a ridiculous idea?"

Half in panic, she turned once again to the Guides, expressing her fears. "WHAT WE TELL YOU IS TRUTH," they insisted, capitalizing for emphasis. "We had not intended writing about it until you were ready to receive it and develop curiosity about it. It is an idea whose time has come." What is so strange, they asked, about a Walk-in with good motivation taking over a body, when "the world is aware that evil entities can 'possess' occupied bodies and cause untold suffering?" Acknowledging that the forces of good must surely be more powerful than evil, Ruth forged

ahead with the new book, exchanged letters and phone calls
with Laura and the two other persons whom the Guides had
identified as Walk-ins, and began to piece together a book
about inner preparation for the difficult decades ahead.

"Joanne (Laura) flew to Washington twice during the
book's writing," Ruth recounts. "Together we reviewed the
Guides' dire messages that had accumulated through the
two years when I had been so reluctant to write such a
frightening book, and we organized them into a framework
that could provide a positive view of the challenges to
come. She was of inestimable help and full of fresh ideas."

With the book's outline in place Ruth posed our new
questions to the Guides, who happily wrote at length about
the need to love one another, to dispel fear of death, and to
work more cooperatively with friends and neighbors. It
would be harmonious networks of people who would best
survive the coming turmoil, they wrote. Basic skills and
food supplies were important, but of far greater value
would be the realization that our thoughts can bring love
and healing. Energies can be channeled to manifest that
which we need, whether it be food and shelter or the means
to learn self-reliance. By beginning now to live according to
the basic laws of interaction, we would find ourselves in a
stronger position to weather and surmount the difficulties
that await those who choose to survive the inevitable planetary alterations.

The Guides foresaw famine and war before the shift, but
reminded Ruth that since we have free will we can still
avert the human-made misery of armed conflict. Near the
time of the shift, which the Guides claim is inevitable, they
said the Antichrist will rise to great power and will fool
many before he is eventually perceived as evil and forcibly
removed, making way for One who will follow and usher in
the New Age of a thousand years of peace.

In early January of 1979 Ruth put the finishing touches on

this her twelfth book, one which the Guides hoped would help readers to begin the subtle adjustments in attitude that will aid in ushering in the marvelous changes of the twenty-first century on planet earth.

The book, released in September 1979, was entitled *Strangers Among Us,* and it was with no small measure of trepidation that Ruth awaited its reception. She was in for a startling series of surprises.

CHAPTER XIII

More Strangers Among Us

On the day before nationwide release of *Strangers Among Us*, Ruth boarded a California-bound plane and braced herself for the exhausting schedule of radio and television interviews that would launch her twelfth book and introduce the concept of Walk-ins.

Her Guides had described Walk-ins as souls who have earned the right, through many lifetimes of spiritual growth, to return directly to the earth plane as adults, by taking over unwanted bodies if their intent is to help mankind. Sometimes the original occupant has become so dispirited that he or she wishes to bow out. In other cases an accident or severe illness has damaged the body to such an extent that its inhabitant can no longer maintain the spark of life.

These Walk-ins, the Guides declared, are not yet perfected souls, but are high-minded beings intent on aiding their fellow humans, and tens of thousands of them are already here, not as towering leaders but as quiet helpers. The problem was that Ruth had met only three who were identified as such by the Guides, and they all insisted on anonymity. Would people believe that Walk-ins really exist?

Midway through her coast-to-coast flight, as dinner was served to passengers in the first-class compartment, Ruth set aside her magazine and engaged in polite conversation with the stranger seated next to her. "He was a nice-looking gentleman, probably about forty, who had spent most of the trip working on papers from his portfolio," she recalls. "During dinner he told me that a year or two previously a strange transformation had radically altered the direction of his life. The executive vice president of one of America's major corporations, he became so fed up one day with the pressure in his office, and life in general, that he refused to go to work. Instead, he took to his bed and stayed there for a month."

The man described how he then awakened one morning overflowing with optimism and vitality and knew exactly how to remake his life. That very day he resigned his position and set the wheels in motion to start his own business. "I know this sounds crazy," he confided, "but I feel as if I actually became an entirely different person that day and haven't been the same since. Life is wonderful!"

Startled, since the man obviously could not have heard of such a thing before, Ruth flashed him a quizzical smile. "Perhaps you *did* become a different person," she replied. "It sounds to me as if you may be a Walk-in."

Such a thought might have ended there except for the next turn of events. Arriving at the busy Los Angeles terminal, she searched fruitlessly for the limousine that was to have met her, finally gave up, and tried to find a taxi instead. "I was having no luck even at that," she recalls, "when the man I had met on the plane suddenly appeared at my side."

"A problem getting a taxi?" he asked. "You'll be all day in this airport. Why not come across the street with me? I'm renting a car, and I'll be glad to take you wherever you're going."

"Thank you, but no," she demurred. "I'm sure it's greatly out of your way, because I'm going all the way to Beverly Hills."

"No problem. I have some time to kill." He reached for her suitcase and graciously showed the way.

The unknown friend drove Ruth the many miles to her hotel, carried her luggage into the lobby, shook hands and was gone. "I was so startled by this extraordinary kindness that I didn't even summon the nerve to ask his name," she muses. "But I suspect that I was intended to meet him. As the Guides later verified, he was indeed a Walk-in, and it gave me reassurance that there were many more of them around."

Strangers Among Us created a sensation! People who had followed Ruth's earlier books in the psychic field had long ago learned to trust her Guides. To them, the explanation of Walk-ins made every bit as much sense as reincarnation. If we indeed return again and again to physical life, taking on newborn bodies as naturally as we would don a new suit of clothes, they reasoned, then what would be so strange about a sick or discouraged soul yielding an unwanted body to another who wished to accomplish good in the world without having to waste time in childhood? "It's as logical as a car changing drivers," one reader remarked.

Many were grateful for the information that *Strangers Among Us* also provided on how to prepare for planetary changes to come. "I used to worry myself sick about the dire predictions," one person wrote. "Now I can see that there are things I can do right now, starting with my own attitude." Others remarked that they had begun to practice greater self-reliance and only now could see its long-range value: "At a time of worldwide crisis we won't be able to count on government services or technology to solve our problems. We should instead begin right now to take greater responsibility for things as simple as good health." One reader commented that she had always thought food storage would be her most vital priority, but after reading *Strangers Among Us* she added lots more things to her list, among them positive thought, healing energies, and basic skills. "It had never before occurred to me that sewing needles and hand tools—and the knowledge of how to use them—would be just as valuable."

But the Walk-in concept was what captured the attention of most readers. Among other things, it readily explained the sudden changes in personality and outlook that loved ones had undergone after experiencing a deep depression, a severe personal trauma, or a clinical death. Ruth soon stumbled onto an example of the latter. As the feature guest of television host Bill Boggs on his New York TV show "Midday Live," Ruth described how a Walk-in may be permitted to enter an adult body if the occupant desperately wishes to return to spirit or is unable to keep the physical body alive. When members of the studio audience were invited to ask questions, a motherly looking woman stood up and exclaimed, "Now I know what has happened to my daughter! She died for two minutes on the operating table, and this daughter I have now is a totally different personality. I feel that I hardly know her."

Ruth had certainly not expected to meet another Walk-in on television! The daughter, who was sitting quietly next to her mother in the audience, met briefly with Ruth after the show, and the following week wrote her a long letter describing the near fatal auto accident that had torn off her nose, broken her pelvis, and caused jagged rib bones to puncture her heart and lungs. On the operating table she floated up and out of that broken body, where she hovered while trying to decide whether or not to return to earthly life. During that period she registered no pulse, and the surgeon thought she was dead. But she recovered and to the surprise of many she emerged with an entirely different personality, new interests and goals. Now this confusing change at last made sense to her.

Uncannily, further evidence of the Walk-in phenomenon appeared almost simultaneously from unrelated sources. A paperback book entitled *The Once and Future Life* by Dr. H. N. Banerjee, a recognized authority on reincarnation, described several cases of purported rebirth of the soul, among them the unusual story of David Paladin, an American of Navajo extraction who was captured by Germans in World War II, tortured, starved, and left for dead. He later emerged from a thirty-month coma with a markedly changed personality and with the artistic talent characteristic of the late Russian artist Wassily Kandinsky. Moreover he was speaking in Russian, a language he had not known. In Dr. Banerjee's book, which interestingly was also released in the fall of 1979, he had cited the David Paladin case as evidence of reincarnation, but upon reading *Strangers Among Us* he sent a copy of his book to Ruth, noting that the Paladin story seemed instead to fit her description of Walk-ins.

A similar coincidence came to Ruth's attention in New York when a woman psychic who had never heard of Walk-ins reported that during a reading she was giving for a young man, she surprised herself by declaring, "You are not the same person who was born in this body."

"I know that," he replied, "but you're the first one who has picked up on it."

Likewise, in the world of fiction, where strange new ideas often find a more fertile audience than they would in real life, a concept similar to that of Walk-ins emerged in Hollywood about this same time. Ruth had never heard of *Heaven Can Wait*, nor had her Walk-in friends until *Strangers Among Us* was already set in type. The movie which was later nominated for eight Academy Awards, was produced, cowritten, and codirected by Warren Beatty, who played the starring role of a young athlete who meets an untimely death in a bicycle accident and is permitted to assume the body of another whose time on earth is over. Critics laughed and labeled the plot "preposterous," but few were so critical when Ruth's *Strangers Among Us* appeared. By early November of 1979 it ranked among the top twenty bestsellers of the nation's three largest bookstore chains. Reviewers described it as "provocative, well written and raises questions," or "gripping, intellectually stimulating, and eminently readable." And as one critic noted, "Who is to disprove a word of it?"

Having prepared for "the worst," Ruth was overwhelmed by the personal attention that accompanied the release of *Strangers Among Us*. TV personality Patty Cavin gave a "Walk-in party" for her at her nearby mansion, inviting dozens of friends who lived in their prestigious neighborhood and could *walk*, not drive, to the festivities. Hope Miller, to whom the book was dedicated, gave another large party for her at the exclusive Sulgrave Club, and editor Pat Soliman hosted a glittering affair for Ruth at her beautiful town house in Manhattan's fashionable East Sixties. She was the featured speaker at several book-and-author luncheons sponsored by leading newspapers and was feted at autograph parties.

Letters from excited readers arrived in greater volume than ever before. "Dear Ruth," they often began, "Excuse me for using your first name, but your books have so changed my life that I feel as if I know you personally." Indeed hundreds of thousands knew her byline by this time, and while her earlier books on reincarnation had earned her a loyal and enthusiastic following, *Strangers Among Us* sent more new readers back to bookstores in droves, eager to see what they had been missing all those years. Demand for her other books on the psychic reached such a crest that *A Search for the Truth*, Ruth's long out-of-print 1967 bestseller, returned to press for new editions.

Of the flood of letters in response to *Strangers Among Us*, many hundreds came from persons who thought that they knew a Walk-in, or who believed that they themselves were Walk-ins. "Sometimes I asked the Guides about them," Ruth relates, "but only if I felt in my own mind that what they described was a genuine Walk-in experience. Some were verified by the Guides, but most of the time the answer was, 'No. A highly developed soul who has awakened to his mission, but not a Walk-in.'"

One especially fascinating letter arrived from a reader in Sweden. Unlike so many others, it made no mention of Walk-ins. Scientist Björn Örtenheim, a talented inventor of energy-efficient devices and systems, wrote instead to describe the spirit beings who communicated with him during sleep and helped him to find new solutions to technical problems. Ruth grew curious. Björn had enclosed magazine articles about himself and copies of outstanding letters of reference. Could this brilliant man be another Walk-in? She posed her question to the Guides, who immediately replied, "The Swedish inventor is indeed a Walk-in, and this change occurred about twelve to fifteen years ago, as he will tell you if you ask." Ruth did ask, answering his letter and relating other things that the Guides had also said about him. Did the idea of his being a Walk-in make any sense to him? If it did, when and how might this change have occurred?

His reply confirmed all that the Guides had indicated. Not only did the idea make sense to him, but Björn went on to describe in detail the stormy day in 1967 when, intending to commit suicide after an upsetting family quarrel, he had walked to a stretch of deserted beach carrying a loaded shotgun. But the fierce winds and pounding surf seemed to hypnotize him and he fell asleep, dreaming of contact with persons not of this earth. Upon awakening he was filled with new strength and a fresh outlook. The next day he sold his gun and dramatically changed the entire direction of his life.

Ruth's fan mail brought still more Walk-ins to her attention. One letter from a stranger named Jason Winters told of his near hopeless battle with cancer of the tongue and jawbone. He reported that following a lengthy biopsy operation he felt oddly changed, suddenly becoming interested in herbs and spiritual matters, and his family noticed an astonishing difference in his outlook and personality. He began searching for herbs that might reduce the growth that threatened his life, and on a hunch combined certain plants from three different continents to concoct a powerful herbal tea blend. He drank gallons of this tea, altered his way of living, and restored his diseased body to glowing health. Jason's special blend of herbs has since been attested to by thousands as a cure for numerous ailments, including cancer. Is it possible, he wrote, that he could be a Walk-in? "Jason Winters is indeed a Walk-in," the Guides replied. "He will go far in helping others. That is why he came back."

Other Walk-ins crossed Ruth's path during the months that followed, often in unexpected places. She and Bob were invited in the spring of 1981 to spend a month at a spa in Horseshoe Bend, Arkansas, where Ruth would deliver four weekly speeches at a series of seminars conducted by the Association for Spiritual Development and Research (ASD&R). Fellow speakers included a stunning array of top authorities in their fields, among them internationally respected psychologist Dr. Stanley Krippner, author and philosophy professor Dr. Ishwar C. Sharma of India, and Dr. Gina Cerminara, author of *Many Mansions,* a 1950 book on Edgar Cayce. Also featured were UFO expert Dr. J. Allen

Hynek, a world-famous astronomer, and Bernard Gittelson, the man who computerized the science of biorhythm.

No sooner had the Montgomerys arrived for their extended stay than people began asking if Elizabeth Nachman, founder-president of ASD&F., was a Walk-in. Ruth had never met the attractive psychic, but after being introduced to her was startled to find Elizabeth surrounded by an aura of shimmering golden light. "This was only the second time in my life that I had seen a human aura." Ruth exclaims. "When I consulted the Guides the next morning on a borrowed typewriter, they wrote that Elizabeth was not only a Walk-in but was among the most superior people alive today, a veritable saint with a special mission to help people through the turbulent decades ahead. Seldom had the Guides praised anyone with such fervor." Ruth eagerly asked Elizabeth more about her life story and whether she felt that the Guides could be correct in asserting that she was a Walk-in. Only then did Ruth learn of the traumatic period in 1975 and the near fatal coma from which Elizabeth had emerged calm, serene, and resolute, with a mysteriously changed personality and a sudden realization of what she wished to do with her life. Clearly a major life alteration had occurred. Ruth had met another Walk-in.

Through the remainder of 1981, a full two years after *Strangers Among Us* had appeared in print, Ruth continued to be widely sought after to address various groups throughout the country. Between these personal appearances and her steady flood of mail, more and more Walk-ins seemed to surface in her life—a metaphysical minister, a recovered alcoholic, a musician-composer, a television personality, even a Baptist preacher in the Deep South. They represented a broad spectrum of human experience and outlook, yet each wished to serve life and help others, especially in light of the long-predicted earth changes that lie ahead.

So many Walk-ins had come to her attention by the end of

1981 that she realized they must not be regarded as mysterious freaks. She therefore resolved to remove the cloak of secrecy and introduce as many of them as were willing to be identified by name. The world needed to view Walk-ins as real people, she reasoned, idealistic and high-minded but by no means perfected beings. "They are filled with a sense of purpose," the Guides declared of Walk-ins, "and an urgency to get on with the task of helping mankind and saving planet earth in these coming decades. They feel that time is short, and their frustration with their inability, at times, to discover their mission is self-evident." Continuing, the Guides stressed that most Walk-ins are not busily asserting themselves and giving advice, but rather are "gently guiding others in the path of fellowship and self-help."

The life stories of Ruth's new Walk-in friends would make a perfect sequel to *Strangers Among Us*. In the meantime, however, Pat Soliman, the editor who had so enthusiastically encouraged her through the last four books, had gone to a different publishing house as editor for romance novels. "Why don't you give Ellis Amburn a ring," Pat suggested. (Ellis was the editor who, back in 1968, had offered Ruth a contract for her book on reincarnation, sight unseen.) "He's now back at Putnam as the editorial director, and he has always adored your books. I'm sure he'd love to hear from you."

"I did nothing about contacting Ellis right away," Ruth concedes. "The book idea was still taking shape in my mind, and in the meantime I had immersed myself in a fascinating genealogy project, tracing branches of my family back as far as 1636 in America. I was spending my days at the DAR Library or the Library of Congress and enjoying every minute."

Finally the Guides interceded, suggesting that Ruth at least telephone Ellis. "I hadn't talked with him in many, many years," she recalls. "I dragged my feet, but late one afternoon I picked up the phone and dialed his office in New York."

It was as if no time at all had passed. "Ruth, I'm so thrilled that you've called!" he exclaimed. Yes, Putnam would certainly be interested in a book about more Walk-ins, and he would call back tomorrow, as soon as he could contact the publisher. The next day he was even more excited. "Ruth, I was on a sensational high all last evening, thinking of working with you again. Everyone at Putnam is simply thrilled to death that you'll be doing a book for us. We're drawing up a contract right now."

The Guides, meanwhile, reaffirmed Ruth's decision to identify Walk-ins by name. "The time is here when they will begin to make themselves known," they wrote, "in order to help a larger range of people. *Strangers Among Us* helped them to free themselves from self-imposed silence and adopt an open policy of helping others and contacting each other. Some people who read the book are making way for Walk-ins and finding it a delightful solution to overwhelming problems which then are easy for the new, highly energized beings to solve. As word spreads that you are writing a new book on the subject, many more will make themselves known to you."

Ruth set to work on the new book, assembling detailed accounts of the Walk-ins she had met, and just as the Guides had predicted, she did indeed meet more and more of them, even during her final weeks of work on the manuscript. She found that some are trying to improve people's health through a greater understanding of herbs and sound nutrition, or are striving to help dispel fear of death. Others are starting to establish self-reliant communities that can function without electricity and modern technology, while many are working to foster more creative and harmonious ways to solve problems of human interaction. "Still more have yet to realize where they can best serve life," Ruth adds. "They arrive with higher awareness and a true sense of mission, but are not to be thought of as all-knowing, for they are striving toward perfection just as are all of us."

Ruth Montgomery's case histories of Walk-ins, entitled *Threshold to Tomorrow,* became her thirteenth book, its final chapter rich with the Guides' current view of the tasks in which these newly arrived souls are already engaged, and of progress that is still needed as we approach the planetary chaos that the Guides say is inevitable.

Threshold to Tomorrow appeared in print late in 1982, three years after *Strangers Among Us.* Ruth hoped that as a sequel to that earlier book on Walk-ins, *Threshold* would provide a more complete and balanced picture of this phenomenon, but she was startled at the outpouring of enthusiasm that followed its release. "I never thought that a book about individual Walk-ins would cause such a stir," she remarks. "What I found was that many people who read *Strangers Among Us* had regarded the Walk-in concept as quite intriguing, but had maintained a healthy measure of skepticism. Now, when they read of so many cases of Walk-ins, with real names and addresses included, their remaining doubts soon dissolved."

The Walk-in concept has since become so widely discussed that it is taken seriously by a growing segment of the psychiatric-medical community. Ruth says she finds that it is now virtually impossible to pick up any publication in the parapsychology field without running across references to the phenomenon.

Having thus rounded out the story of Walk-ins, Ruth wondered with mild amusement just what subject matter the Guides would assign to her next. She hadn't long to wait. Following her period of meditation and her usual prayer for protection, she rested her fingers lightly on the keys, and with eyes closed allowed the typing to begin. The tap, tap, tap of her electric typewriter went on with hardly a pause, line after line, until Lily, Art, and the group ended with their usual closing, "All for now, love from us here." Ruth pulled out the yellow sheet of paper to read their message.

"No, a thousand times no!" she protested, dropping it like a hot potato into her desk drawer. "I can't do a book about *that!* I don't know nearly enough about it and wouldn't know how to investigate it." Because the Guides pursued the subject relentlessly in each of the daily sessions that followed, Ruth finally abandoned the automatic writing for weeks at a time, hoping that they would take the hint.

Then, mysteriously, something that had happened repeatedly throughout her writing career began to recur. All manner of letters started to arrive, some enclosing news articles or relating a personal encounter, others merely giving a suggestion, but all urging her to explore the very same topic, one that had already captured the imagination of millions. *"Please* look into this!" they begged. "The world needs a comprehensive book about it from a skeptic who knows how to ferret out the truth. We trust you and the Guides."

Suspecting that it was again the Guides who had orchestrated this massive letter-writing campaign, Ruth finally accused them outright. Had *they* prompted this flood of mail, urging her to write about a subject that she would rather ignore? "Well, why not?" they replied. Then, with hardly a pause in the typing, they patiently began: "Now as to these extraterrestrials . . ."

CHAPTER XIV

Extraterrestrials

Absolutely not! Ruth Montgomery would *not* write about extraterrestrials, period. "My readers had learned to rely on my integrity," she argues. "How could I do a book about flying saucers or space aliens without actually seeing one and becoming convinced that they are real?"

Ever since that first séance in Florida back in 1956, Ruth had sought proof—evidential—before she would believe anything out of the ordinary, and even many years after meeting the famed medium Arthur Ford, she had continued to test him by gathering perfect strangers for his trance sessions and introducing them only *after* he had finished bringing them messages from the beyond. Likewise a full decade of spirit contact elapsed before she dared to write her first book about it, called *A Search for the Truth.*

Reincarnation, the subject of *Here and Hereafter,* had also been mere philosophy to Ruth until she personally observed hypnotic regression to past lives with Adelle Davis and then submitted to it herself. She might never have written the story of life after death in *A World Beyond* if she had not known Arthur Ford well enough before his death to believe that the discarnate information actually came from him. Before starting *Born to Heal* she insisted on meeting and interviewing many patients who had been cured by Bill Gray, the magnetic healer, and had herself experienced his remarkable healing powers. *Companions Along the Way*, the book about Ruth's past lives with Arthur Ford, might never have seen print if she had not previously glimpsed several of those lives herself while under hypnosis or in meditation. With *The World Before* extensive research had verified much of the Guides' version of earth history, and for *Strangers Among Us* and *Threshold to Tomorrow* Ruth had personally met and talked with many of those whom the Guides had identified as Walk-ins. How, she reasoned, could she ever write about extraterrestrials without meeting some and proving to her own satisfaction that they were real? "You *will* meet one," the Guides finally assured her. "We're trying to arrange an encounter for you so that you can get on with the new book." Ruth was unconvinced. She held them to their promise and waited, hoping for a spaceman to appear.

The only supposed otherworld visitor whom she had ever met was Jorge, a Mexican with red-brown hair and luminous eyes of that same odd color. This stranger had sought her out in Cuernavaca many years before and claimed to be from another planet, a notion that Ruth had found somewhat amusing—and certainly unconvincing—at the time. After all, space aliens didn't walk around in human bodies—or did they?

The second time that Jorge called on her in Mexico, this intelligent, well-mannered man invited her to go with him that evening by automobile through a nearby mountain pass. He assured her that there, in a cave near a small Indian settlement, she could meet other space aliens and see their flying saucer.

Her sense of adventure stimulated, Ruth had reveled in the thought, but her husband Bob had refused to permit it. "To this day I wish I had gone," she muses. "From a realistic standpoint, though, I don't think I would have done it by myself. It was a lonely country road at night through the Mexican mountains, and Jorge was a stranger. It would have been different if my husband had been willing to come along, but he was adamant. Alas, I probably missed my only chance for a spaceship ride!"

Not knowing quite what to do with Jorge, she had introduced him to her friend Jeanette Longoria, who was far more interested in UFOs than was Ruth at the time. From then on this strange visitor frequently stopped by Jeanette's house in Mexico City to talk about extraterrestrials. Everyone else in the house mysteriously drifted off to sleep during his visits, waking only after he was gone.

Jeanette had then lost touch with Jorge, often for years at a time, after which he would suddenly return and continue his talk of spaceships. An ancient one lay buried beneath a pyramid outside Mexico City, he claimed, asserting that earth has, after all, been visited by spacemen for centuries.

Ruth had not thought at the time to ask the Guides about Jorge and his claim of coming from another planet. She hadn't really been interested in the subject until, while writing *Strangers Among Us* in 1978, she elected to devote a chapter to her friends Helen and Dick Byrd of Virginia, who had had a close encounter with a UFO. Then the Guides suddenly volunteered: "The extraterrestrial you met and talked with in Mexico is of a higher type who genuinely likes human beings and wants to learn all he can about them. He's like a missionary who sincerely wishes to help others."

But by now many years had passed since her last contact with the mysterious Jorge. Ruth had no idea where to locate him, even if she did finally feel ready to see his spaceship.

Lacking a contact with Jorge, she insisted that the Guides must produce *someone* before they could expect her to do the book they wanted. In the meantime, she was prepared to wait it out.

It was during this latest standoff with the Guides in February of 1983, that Ruth received a letter from an unknown fan named Joyce Updike in Ovid, Colorado. The mother of six grown children, Joyce praised Ruth for writing the psychic books which she had used as "required reading" for her offspring, and then noted that the books had only "touched lightly" on the subject of UFOs. "There are thousands of us in your reading audience called 'Contactees,'" she continued, describing the ridicule that is often endured by those whose stories are printed in pulp newspapers. "Even through all this, the 'Contactees' hold to their stories and begin to look for 'people like themselves' so they can continue to function in society. We tell each other our stories."

Then she made mention of something that was even more intriguing. "I was hypnotized to help me better understand an experience in 1967. Under hypnosis I saw myself aboard a craft, on an examining table. . . ." She went on to describe the bizarre circumstances. Joyce reported that many years later, after being prompted psychically to read *Strangers Among Us* for the second time, she found herself staring into the mirror and asking, "What now?" The mental answer that came back startled her. "Your name is Yarbah. You are to finish this life and then begin a new one."

Well! Letters had urged Ruth to write about UFOs before, but none had had quite the impact of this one-page missive from a stranger who was so articulate. Her curiosity aroused, she answered Joyce Updike's letter and asked for further details of her 1967 "encounter." Thus began a lively correspondence in which Joyce, with her infectious sense of

humor, described not only the brilliant light that she had
seen outside her window in the middle of the night, but her
own inner changes, and finally her submission to hypnosis
under Dr. R. Leo Sprinkle, of the University of Wyoming.
She enclosed a transcript of that hypnotic session and said
that Dr. Sprinkle was active in interviewing other UFO
contactees and abductees and would be able to provide a
great deal more information about his investigations.

Ruth next contacted Dr. Sprinkle, and his reply opened
the door to a fascinatingly rich source of material. Now a
respected professor of psychology, Sprinkle had spotted his
first flying saucer in 1949 and another in 1956. But it was
only when a colleague hypnotically regressed him to the
fifth grade that he relived a scene on board a spacecraft,
where a spaceman urged him to learn to write well so that
when he grew up he could help others to understand life. In
1961, having earned his Ph.D., Dr. Sprinkle pursued the
subject of UFOs in earnest, enduring the teasing of his colleagues. Since then he has interviewed and/or hypnotically
regressed hundreds of people who have seen UFOs or suffered unexplained loss of time or been troubled by strange
dreams of space aliens. Going a step further, he began to
bring these contactees together from all over the world for
annual summer conferences at the University of Wyoming,
starting in 1980, urging them to "come out of the closet"
and share their stories with one another. When he replied
to Ruth's letter, Dr. Sprinkle enclosed transcripts of
speeches that had been given by them at some of these
conferences.

"Here was a reliable, dependable source of information,"
Ruth recalls, "with a wealth of supporting material from
hundreds of case studies, and still I hung back, reluctant to
write about something I hadn't experienced myself."

Meanwhile her attention focused on family matters.
Many months of genealogical research had inspired her to

write an extensive history of her Shick family antecedents, and for the summer of 1933 she organized a massive family reunion. "Six months of work went into that event," she explains. "Sixty-five relatives gathered from all over the country, four generations of them, all simply delighted to meet one another." An unexpected souvenir of that happy weekend arrived several weeks later—a picture taken by a distant cousin that turned out to be quite unlike the rest of the snapshots. In the center of the photo Ruth was addressing the dinner gathering about their mutual ancestors, while next to her towered a berobed, ethereal figure, with other similar ones gathered off to the right. "Pictures taken immediately before and after the dinner, with the same camera, showed no such distortion." she muses with a smile. "Apparently our ancestors had decided to put in an appearance while I was talking about them."

With the time-consuming reunion behind her Ruth found the Guides still more insistent that she begin a book on space aliens. They continued to write almost endlessly about beings from other galaxies, even introducing alleged extraterrestrials who began to contribute to the daily sessions through automatic writing. Space visitors mean no harm, they wrote, but instead seek to foster harmony, reduce pollution, and prevent the use of nuclear weapons. Most urgently they are aware of the coming planetary shift and want to help us in every way that they can.

This was all very reassuring, Ruth acknowledged, but if these beings were as interested and brilliant as the Guides claimed, then why couldn't they manage a face-to-face contact with her, as they seemed to have done with hundreds of others?

Still hopeful as Christmas of 1983 approached, Ruth and Bob made plans to visit relatives in Indianapolis. Maybe, just maybe, far from the lights and the dense population of Washington, a UFO would manage to make itself visible during the long drive. Alas, even in the Middle West she had no such luck.

By February of 1984, fully a year after Joyce Updike's first intriguing letter, Ruth began to grow as frustrated as those who urged her to write. Lily, Art, and the group pressured her endlessly, identifying Joyce as a Walk-in from Sirius. Joyce herself continued to plead that Ruth put the story of extraterrestrials into proper perspective, as a vital service to humanity. Ellis Amburn repeatedly offered a book contract, if only Ruth would agree to sign it. Still she said *no.* "How can I write just another book about space aliens without meeting one?" she argued. "There have been so many books about alleged encounters! I'll need to be more thoroughly convinced before I can do one."

Looking back at that indecisive period in her life, Ruth recalls: "Not the least of my prodders was Joanne (Laura), my first Walk-in friend, who was firmly convinced of the presence of extraterrestrials on our planet and increasingly insistent that I tell the world about them. In one of her frequent letters to me she wrote: 'You're the voice. Those who are here to help the planet, those hovering out in space or in spirit, can speak through you. It's important that you make yourself available as an avenue of communication for these beings. They are *trying* to speak, but you keep doubting!'

"At another time she chided: 'The extraterrestrials want and *need* to have a direct line of communication with earthlings who can communicate to the rest of the planet. *You,* dear Ruth, are that line of communication, but I don't think you fully believe it. It is crucial at this point in the planet's history for there to be some input from those beings who come from more highly developed civilizations.' "

It wasn't that Ruth denied the existence of extraterrestrials. "I do believe that they're here," she conceded. "I believe the Guides who tell about the different ways they're now entering, since fewer UFOs are now being glimpsed. I do believe that many, many people have had experience with them. Then why can't I? Yes, they're terribly intent on having me do a book about them—and I would welcome an encounter—so why can't they get in touch with me if they consider a book so important?"

Then, mysteriously, Ruth began to receive an even more massive avalanche of letters from all over the country, from persons with the utmost integrity and sincerity, reporting either encounters with space people or telepathic communication with beings in orbiting intergalactic fleets. But this time the letter writers followed a new tack. One after another claimed, "I've been told psychically to get in touch with Ruth Montgomery."

"Yes," the Guides conceded as their write-in campaign intensified, "we've been busy spreading the word in the ether." Indeed their message was out! But this was merely the beginning of their own renewed efforts.

Things began to happen quickly in the spring of 1984. Jeanette Longoria telephoned from San Antonio. On a recent trip to her house in Mexico City, she reported, she had received a call out of the blue—from Jorge! What's more, his first words to her were, "I *have* to get in touch with Ruth Montgomery. How can I reach her?"

Jorge's timing couldn't have been more perfect, since Ruth was finally ready to take him seriously. Not only that; she planned to visit Jeanette in San Antonio on her way to Houston for television talk-show interviews that would launch the paperback release of *Threshold to Tomorrow*, scheduled for the first of April. Jorge agreed to meet with Ruth in Texas, and in the meantime she scheduled interviews with others for April, to follow up several intriguing leads that had surfaced from her latest influx of mail.

She was finally ready to consider writing the new book. With a chapter on the elusive Mexican spaceman named

Jorge, and one on an elderly part Cherokee man who described out-of-body planetary travels, another on Joyce Updike, whose husband had by now also experienced a UFO contact, and material on Dr. Sprinkle and his work with hundreds of contactees, truly a fascinating array of experience could be brought together.

Ruth flew to San Antonio to visit Jeanette as planned, but the mysterious Jorge failed to appear. "I continued on to Houston for the interviews," she recalls, "but still no Jorge." She returned to Washington disappointed.

By this time, however, so much intriguing material from people of unquestionable integrity had found its way to her desk that she could no longer dismiss it. Perhaps if she began to write the book anyway, she would have an encounter of her own before the manuscript was finished. She decided to start her personal research with the charming old man who claimed to visit other galaxies.

Accordingly she and Bob drove to Salem, Virginia, to meet William Goodlett, a seventy-five-year-old part Cherokee who had sent a fascinating cassette tape on which he recounted numerous out-of-body journeys to other planets. The Guides explained that this gentleman was "an astonishing extraterrestrial himself," who "deliberately chose to come here from another galaxy to understand earth life and to help earthlings realize that we are all one. He was born into that body," they continued, "choosing a Cherokee heritage because that tribe began in his own native planet, which he has recently visited while out of the body." Greatly intrigued, Ruth interviewed this fascinating man, who gave detailed accounts of numerous other civilizations and life forms in the cosmos, as well as physical earthly experiences with teleporting himself in cases of extreme emergency or apporting needed objects by use of a Cherokee chant.

A further avenue of information opened when a letter

arrived from a stranger in New York named John Andreadis. Praising Ruth's books, John went on to declare that the truths imparted by her Guides were identical to those of the Hindu cycles of creation, with which she had been unfamiliar. Then, describing his teacher, Hindu astrologer and lecturer Frederick Von Mierers, John wondered if Frederick could be a Walk-in; but unlike most fan letters that stop there, he added, "I want to know how we can work with you to help more people."

Ruth consulted the Guides about John and Frederick, and their answer astonished her. Both are from another star system known as Arcturus, they wrote, John having been born into his present body and Frederick having arrived seven years ago as a Walk-in. Both had been high priests in earlier earth lives, and Frederick "chose to come back because of an urgent need to reach the young people who will be founding the new society after the shift of the earth on its axis." The Guides urged that Ruth include John and Frederick in the book about space aliens, and she therefore agreed to meet with them when they came to Washington.

"I found John to be a brilliant and deeply loving soul who, to my amazement, was only twenty-one years old," she exclaims, "and Frederick turned out to be the most fascinating, handsome, dedicated thirty-seven-year-old I have ever met. One of the first things I did when they arrived was to tell him about the Guides' assertion that he and John were from Arcturus."

Frederick showed no surprise at all. "Of *course* we're from Arcturus! Where did you think we were from?" he replied, gesturing so grandly that he seemed to soar with boundless energy, his sapphire blue eyes radiating a depth of profound wisdom. Mixed with a lively and infectious wit, he let flow a continuous stream of philosophy, about sparks of light and drops of water and shimmering curtains of radiance, his words punctuated only by a rare pause for breath, and his eternal question, "Yes?"

Amused, yet intent on learning all that she could about these delightful souls who had purportedly come directly to earth life from the hydrogen-light atmosphere of Arcturus, Ruth steered Frederick and John to talk of their own lives and their work with others. She was, after all, planning to write about extraterrestrials, not Hindu philosophy.

The information that emerged paralleled exactly what the Guides had been saying—that space visitors are "materializing in every part of the world now, and are able to do so without the machines (UFOs). They can assume the shape of skin and bones and walk among us, although they are also required to materialize identification papers and background material if they want to function in today's society. But this necessity is obviated if they are born here, or arrive as Walk-ins, to replace a soul that wishes to depart."

John described in even greater detail the "reality of space friends who have come to help—not an alien civilization—but their brothers and sisters. We are all souls with a Divine Parent who is God," he declared.

Aside from these intriguing new friends and the central group around them, all from Arcturus, who had gathered once again on earth to help train the leaders of the New Age, there was also Dr. J. Allen Hynek, someone very much of this earth. Ruth had met him in 1981 at Elizabeth Nachman's seminars in Horseshoe Bend and was impressed with his integrity and his solid professional credentials. A noted astronomer, Dr. Hynek had served as chief scientific consultant to the government-sponsored Project Blue Book, the massive UFO investigation of the late sixties that wound up trying to dismiss the entire phenomenon. Dr. Hynek had entered the project as a skeptic, but after studying the evidence he became so convinced of the reality of

UFOs that he later established a Center for UFO Studies (CUFOS) in Evanston, Illinois, to pursue the matter further.

"I found, through interviews with many reputable professionals," Ruth concludes, "that there seemed to be no doubt in the minds of many serious investigators that the United States Government has deliberately engaged in a massive cover-up, as has Great Britain.'

Spurred on by a reporter's instinct for truth, she pursued numerous leads, uncovering weird tales of strangers who seemed to materialize from nowhere and interviewing all of the contactees. There was the backpacker who encountered one such being deep in the Vermont woods, thirty miles from the nearest town, without supplies or sleeping gear, but with a strange, oval-shaped stone that glowed and pulsated. There was the oddly dressed hitchhiker who accepted rides within an hour from two different people on widely separated stretches of lonely highways in rural Washington State, knew their names without being told, then seemed to vanish after asking to be let out in the middle of nowhere. There were space Walk-ins and space channelers, and stories of a vast orbiting fleet, ever watchful, ever concerned, as earthlings begin to become more aware of their presence and purpose at this point of change to a New Age. She consulted with the Guides on each new and incredible piece in the UFO puzzle. "It's true," they declared, citing the ability of extraterrestrials to come and go at will, travel on beams of light by the power of thought, and reassemble the atoms into solids wherever they wish, through a process not yet understood by earthlings.

By late 1984 Ruth no longer needed a Jorge, or even a firsthand view of mysterious lights in the sky. She had eyewitnesses—good ones—people of a high caliber of integrity, from diverse backgrounds and locations, and with widely varied interests, who were serious, sincere, and looking for answers. "I had interviewed working people, airline pilots, scientists, and philosophers," she says, "people who had seen the government's evidence, had been aboard UFOs, had witnessed the maneuvers of spaceships or contacted extraterrestrials, and each provided a fascinatingly different angle—but they all fit together."

When combined, these reports made for a unique exploration of the phenomenon and supplied many answers to mankind's most curious questions: Where do extraterrestrials come from? Why are they here, and why in such massive numbers? How do they travel? Why are they contacting ordinary people? What do they want to tell us? Why has the government denied their existence?

Yet unlike most other authors of books on UFOs, Ruth moved beyond the physical evidence. She delved into the psychic and spiritual facets of alien presence on our planet, adding a dimension that opens an entirely new realm of human exploration. Are minds and spaceships interlinked by thought processes of Universal Law that are yet to be discovered by today's inhabitants of planet earth?

And when we are at last reawakened to these principles, as the New Age dawns, will we be ready as a civilization to act responsibly with what John and Frederick assert is an age-old truth: "that earth is part of an intergalactic universe-federation of which we have been ignorant for over twelve thousand years."

The Guides had repeatedly explained that because Ruth lives on one of the busiest avenues in Washington, in a large apartment building, extraterrestrials had found it impossible to land a spacecraft and present themselves to her. Since she no longer drives a car, she also conceded that they could not have intercepted her on a lonely roadway. But she now feels that there may have been an even better reason why she did not have a personal encounter. "Had I done so," she muses, "I might have been so enthralled that I'd have produced just another book about my own eyewitness account. And why should the readers have believed my experience more than the dozens that I cited from highly reliable observers? I think that I was deliberately denied an encounter, and I can see the wisdom of it. But I'm still hopeful!"

Aliens Among Us, Ruth's fourteenth book, was released in June of 1985, rich with the Guides' comments and updated predictions, including the encouraging news that wholesale Western aid to famine-stricken Ethiopia has so eased the tension in that part of the world that World War III may not break out there after all, at least not before the end of this decade.

But it was not so much the predictions that her avid fans sought to read—it was truth about extraterrestrial aliens and their purpose in coming to planet earth. Word spread like wildfire: "Ruth Montgomery has at last written about UFOs!"

Her book tour began with radio and television appearances on the West Coast, and by the time she returned to Washington, she faced a deluge of invitations. "Never in my career have I been so swamped with requests for interviews," she exclaims. The reaction to *Aliens Among Us* surpassed anything she could have anticipated for a book about extraterrestrials. Television stations in New York, Boston, Detroit, Philadelphia, Baltimore, Miami, and dozens of other cities begged for appearances there, and scores of radio stations throughout the U.S. and Canada clamored for telephone interviews. And for good reason. This was no ordinary book on flying saucers! But then again, Ruth is not one to write ordinary books, or to try to convince anyone of a particular point of view. "I look for evidence, and examine the source for credibility," she says. "Then I tell others what I've found. They can form their own conclusions." These conclusions hold far-reaching implications for the future of planet earth.

The immediate impact of *Aliens Among Us* is perhaps best captured by the comments of Kay Allison, owner of Quest Bookshop in Charlottesville, Virginia, who wrote two weeks after its release. "Your book is getting rave reviews from customers here!" she exclaimed. "One woman has bought four copies, as she feels people need to read it. That is what I think, too! There is so much information there. It is certainly a book for this time. I should say *the* book for this time. People may not agree or it may be too much for them to accept all at once, but it will make them think and reevaluate many thoughts and ideas!"

Perhaps getting us to *think* and *reevaluate* is the whole point. Only then will we begin to understand our true role in an expanding universe, the doors to which have only begun to open to us here on planet earth. And Ruth is helping to open those doors.

CHAPTER XV

The New Age

A New Age has begun to dawn on planet earth, bringing with it an expanded consciousness, an acute awareness of the psychic realm, and a deeper understanding of the purpose of living. This search for the meaning of life, long regarded as the exclusive domain of philosophers and clergy, has gradually shifted away from so-called "authorities" and captured the thoughtful attention of an educated public, a phenomenon which in itself marks a stunning revolution in human thought.

As a highly influential forerunner of this New Age, Ruth Montgomery has for the last two decades been making public her own search for answers, taking her readers with her along a path of discovery that has deepened and strengthened their own religious faith and offered new insights into the eternal question of why we live and die. As Joyce Updike has written, "At the risk of sounding blasphemous, Ruth Montgomery's books are quoted from as often as Bible scripture in many homes."

The Aquarian Age, according to Ruth's Guides, will be an

era of evolution of the mind. "The earth is passing through a long orbit that brings it closer to the center of Universal Truth," they explain, "and as it is now already doing, it is awakening people of sufficient development to the reality of one world, one Creator, one Universal Truth—the eternal truth that there is no death and that love is the unifying force of the cosmic world. Such an attitude will help human beings to overcome their fears and reach out in helpfulness to others when the earth undergoes periods of famine, flood, earthquakes, and spasmodic warfare."

During the two-thousand-year time span now ending, a period known to astrologers as the Piscean Age and symbolized by the sign of the fish (a figure used widely by early Christians), civilization has expanded outwardly, harnessing water and steam for power, making stunning advances in technology and medicine, landing men on the moon, and exploring outer space.

Now with the entry of planet earth into the Age of Aquarius, human knowledge has begun to extend inwardly, delving beyond the physical world known to our scientists and into the realm of human energy waves, attitudes, emotions, the soul, and the power of thought, meditation, and prayer. Physicians who once regarded the body as a mere machine are now recognizing the interrelatedness of mind with health and disease, and advocating such previously arcane practices as meditation for reduction of blood pressure. Scientists who once acknowledged only physical reality have had to concede that mental effort can easily cause change in plant growth or dissolve clouds. Likewise the business world has been forced to acknowledge that job satisfaction, human interaction, and work environment can no longer be ignored. They bear directly on quality and productivity, just as they affect health, family life, and harmony in the community.

The coming age, Ruth's Guides have insisted repeatedly,

will be one of even greater spiritual and psychic awareness, when individuals at long last become fully cognizant of the purpose of their earthly existence. Already those who sincerely seek answers to this basic question have begun to reach nearly identical conclusions, regardless of their religious training or personal philosophy. Life, they have found, continues to exist beyond death. Love, mutual respect, and helpfulness are the keys to spiritual growth, and just as the Guides stressed to Ruth more than a quarter century ago, the spirit world is real and alive, prayer is a powerful force for good, and life is indeed eternal.

Similarly a growing segment of the population has come to understand and believe in the principles of reincarnation and karma that Ruth began writing about back in 1968 in *Here and Hereafter*. As of 1981 a Gallup poll surveying the religious attitudes of adults in the United States indicated that 23 percent embraced the concept of reincarnation, and among Catholics the rate was 25 percent. This would mean that at least thirty-eight million American adults hold such a view, many incorporating it within their own religious faith. Such figures do not even take into account the attitudes of children, who often express a belief in reincarnation before ever hearing of it.

Ruth's Guides foretell that with the full blossoming of the New Age during the centuries to come, humanity will not only understand and live by the principles of love, helpfulness, and the laws of karma, but will evolve to a level of awareness in which no barriers to thought transferral will exist. Minds will become so open, they say, that deceit and crime can no longer be concealed, and direct communication among earthlings, extraterrestrials, and those in the spirit plane will become as commonplace as are radio and television transmissions today.

Prophets have long predicted this coming New Age as a time when evil forces will be checked and held in abeyance for ten centuries, and humanity's highest aspirations for peace and harmony will be realized. The Bible tells of Satan being cast into a bottomless pit, "till the thousand years should be fulfilled," and the late seer Edgar Cayce, speaking of Christ, prophesied, "For a thousand years, He will walk and talk with men of every clime—men in groups and in masses. . . ."

Nostradamus, the sixteenth-century prophet whose enigmatic riddles describing future events have long challenged translators and interpreters, wrote of a massive earth catastrophe to be followed by a great peace among the peoples of earth while the devil is confined to the bottom of the abyss. Clues as to the timing of this event have led many to calculate that it may occur in July, September, or October of 1999. Edgar Cayce spoke in trance of a shifting of the poles near the end of the century and of radical changes in the seasons, together with the rising or sinking of land areas all over the globe. Levi in the *Aquarian Gospel* wrote of "the sign of the Son of Man" to appear in the sky when "the man who bears the pitcher [Aquarius] will walk forth across the arc in heaven" shortly before the redemption of the earth.

Ruth Montgomery's Guides have begun warning of a shift of the earth "shortly before the year 2000," ever since dictating material for *A World Beyond* in 1971. "The last two such shifts," they now declare, "which occurred around 50,000 B.C. and 150,000 B.C., were due to the same reasons that will cause the next shift: an imbalance of the earth on its axis. This not only occurs on earth, but in other planetary systems as well. The earth becomes lopsided from a buildup of snow and ice at the poles, and from oceans cutting away land. The oil and water removed from the earth have heightened the present activity, and there is also some pull from outer space. It is possible that some planets will line up to produce a heavy pull, but that will not be the cause, merely a contributing factor at the time of the occurrence. The main reason is the imbalance, and there is nothing mankind can do to prevent it, since he is not responsible for the ice buildup and the action of the tides and ocean storms." This global catastrophe, the Guides claim, will cleanse the earth of pollution and evil people and will usher in the long-awaited New Age of a thousand years of peace.

Science points to the possibility that sudden planetary shifts have occurred in ages past. As Ruth indicated in *The World Before*, extensive geological evidence suggests that the earth's ice caps and magnetic poles have not always occupied their present positions in relation to the continents. Magnetic information in sections of rock thousands of years old, specifically in once molten lava (some of t now at sea bottom) and in certain sedimentary stone, yields clues as to which way was north at the time that such material cooled or solidified. On the basis of such data, earth scientists find that at various times in the past the North Pole may have been located in Hudson Bay, Central Asia, or the Greenland Sea west of Norway, and also that the north and south magnetic poles have actually reversed themselves many times, with sudden and simultaneous changes in the types of organisms present in the fossils from those time periods.

Glacial evidence supports the likelihood that at one time ice sheets in what is now the South Atlantic moved westward through Brazil and eastward into southern Africa. At another time in earth history, according to glacial record, ice in central India, now a subtropical region, spread northward, away from what is now the equator. Additionally the ancient Piri Re'is map of Antarctica details a continent free of the massive ice cap that exists today, suggesting that its climate was once far more hospitable.

Giant mammoths with fresh food in their stomachs, and intact tropical plants still with leaves, have been found frozen in arctic ice, pointing to instantaneous changes in climate; and historians have noted written records from Egypt to China that mention sudden reversals of summer and winter, abrupt shifts in cardinal directions and radical changes in the location of sunrise and sunset. Also, cultures throughout the world maintain legends of a great flood, the one that Ruth's Guides say occurred when Atlantis sank at the time of Noah's ark.

Ten years ago her Guides warned that earth's weather would be abruptly changing, and scientists now note that weather patterns in six out of the last eight years have been abnormal, breaking all available temperature records. They point out with some alarm that fossil fuel residues, increased methane, and fluorocarbons in the atmosphere may interfere with the ozone layer and sunlight, and contribute to a warming trend that could reduce the size of the polar ice caps quickly enough to raise sea levels drastically throughout the world. They note as well that the earth's rotation has recently speeded up after a long-term trend of slowing. Yet they disagree as to the significance of these changes, just as they hold varying theories on plate tectonics, continental drift, the Chandler wobble of the poles, the effect of sunspot cycles on geomagnetics, and the possibility that continental fragments of "terranes" wander and collide, as segments of the earth's crust slide over the planet's molten interior, shifting on the earth's axis, with the axis itself unchanged. An article in the January 1985 Smithsonian indicates that French and Chinese scientists, after three years of study, theorize that South Central Tibet "appears to be part of a vanished continent, fragments of which may also be part of California." Ruth's Guides have long pointed to the submergence of Lemuria, a vast continent in the Pacific Ocean which they say encompassed parts of California, during a previous shift of the earth.

So much disagreement exists among scientists, however,

that even with a careful study of earthquake cycles, readings of increased radon gas levels in wells along the north-
ern margin of the Los Angeles basin, and other indications
that California may experience a major earthquake within
the next few years or decades, just as the Guides have also
predicted, scientists do not as yet have enough experience
to warn of a major tremor with any degree of accuracy.
According to an article on earthquake predictions in the
February 1985 issue of *Scientific American,* ". . . many
earth scientists lose sleep worrying about how to communicate their concern to the public without raising unneces-
sary alarm." This is what Ruth and her Guides have been
accomplishing, in their gentle way, for many years.

Theorists who argue that shifts of the earth on its axis
have in the past reduced highly advanced civilizations to a
Stone Age existence now have also begun to worry aloud.
Most scientists and politicians are hardly ready to listen.
History has shown that ideas that have differed too greatly
from accepted concepts bring ridicule upon those who first
advance them, and few are willing to risk their professional
reputations or their institutional or government funding by
exposing themselves to criticism, despite the fact that even
the laws of physics are constantly being revised in the light
of new evidence. Such has also been the case with reincarnation, out-of-body experiences during clinical death, and
even the once ridiculed notion that the earth revolves
around the sun. It is laymen, not scientists and politicians,
who are most willing to correlate and examine the evidence
from widely separate sources and bring it to public attention, yet laymen are outsiders to the highly compartmental-
ized and competitive scientific community.

Since Ruth and the Guides first warned of an approaching
pole shift many years ago, other lay writers such as John
White and Charles Berlitz have delved into the possibility
of such a calamity, piecing together the clues from numer-

ous psychics, religious scriptures, scientists, and historians. The evidence from dozens of sources, Ruth and the Guides among them, points toward one conclusion. Sudden and radical earth changes have occurred in past ages, and as the Guides now indicate, they will soon happen again.

Some thinkers, such as Robert S. Lamb II of West Terre Haute, Indiana, who have read and been inspired by Ruth's books, have begun to make themselves heard. Lamb, head of the Circulation Department of Indiana State University's Cunningham Library, argues, as have the Guides, for preservation of written knowledge on a national scale. Working from maps based on earthquake risk, floodplain boundaries, psychic prediction, and even nuclear target factors, Lamb has attempted to alert library and archive leaders of the need to establish underground vaults of microfilmed materials, preferably in every region of the country. "If we don't begin now," he insists, "to protect and preserve our intellectual, cultural, and spiritual heritage that has been written down over the centuries, then how can we pass it on to the next surviving generation?"

Preparation for this earth shift, as the Guides insisted in *Strangers Among Us,* must first be one of attitude. Just as the New Age will be an era of understanding of the higher frequencies that constitute thinking, mental communication, light, extraterrestrial travel, the spirit realm, the dissolution and reassemblage of physical matter, the power of love, and the reality of God, it will also be an era when humans at last understand the purpose of earth life. Knowing the true nature of life and death, the reality of eternal existence, and the imperishability of what religions call the soul, one can look to the inevitable planetary changes with serenity and even a sense of adventure, whether we continue in physical body or pass into the spirit state. What truly matters is our attitude—our willingness to love, respect, and help one another.

Ruth Montgomery's search for answers has helped to pave the way for others to explore the truth about life and death, in a widespread quest that marks a significant beginning into psychological investigations of the spiritual and psychic side of life. The subsequent findings of psychologists, psychiatrists, and medical doctors have begun to coincide remarkably with explanations of reincarnation, life after death, and spiritual awakening that Ruth and the Guides had described many years before. Such an understanding of the nonphysical world provides us not only with a key to present human behavior, but a framework for reaching the next level of knowledge, as inhabitants of earth prepare to weather massive planetary changes. When Ruth first delved into the psychic, she was well aware that she risked ridicule. Yet, at the same time, her reporter's instinct led her to dig still further, to search for explanations that must surely exist. "I don't like being told what to think or do," she often remarks with a defiant note in her voice. "It is truth that makes us free."

The first great truth that emerged from her search was that life indeed continues after death, in a world of activity and growth. "The churches have taught 'eternal life' in a heaven or hell for many centuries," she says, "but it was only after years of my own probing, both through Arthur Ford and the automatic writing, that I proved to my own satisfaction that death is merely a transition into another vibratory level, that we pick up there where we left off here in spiritual development, and that two-way communication with that world is indeed possible."

Encouraged that a famous, skeptical reporter would reach such a conclusion about immortality, especially in an era when institutions of all kinds faced renewed questioning, many clergy hailed A Search for the Truth as a welcome confirmation of faith and invited her to address religious gatherings across the country.

But it was Ruth's investigation of reincarnation that opened the widest door to understanding. In *Here and Hereafter*, which was published in 1968, she explained this ancient concept in a manner so convincing and logical, and so compatible with Christianity, Judaism, and Eastern philosophy, that persons who had long misunderstood its tenets began to see it in a new light, realizing that it made perfect sense. Pointing out that this belief had once been basic to early Christianity, Ruth went on to note the vast accumulation of evidence, both religious and psychological, that supports its validity.

People who had once scoffed at the idea of rebirth suddenly looked to it with renewed interest, and other writers soon delved into the topic enthusiastically. Debunkers who had enjoyed trying to disprove reincarnation after publication of Morey Bernstein's *The Search for Bridey Murphy* found their arguments against the concept outweighed by the volume of facts in *Here and Hereafter*. A profusion of new books on the subject began to appear, thus helping to set the stage for widespread discussion and legitimate research.

During the years that followed, the atmosphere of acceptance and respect generated by Ruth's popular and well-documented writing on reincarnation made it less threatening for those in the scientific and religious worlds to step forward with similar convictions. Among them Dr. George G. Ritchie, a physician and psychiatrist who has served as chairman of the Psychiatry Department at the University of Virginia Hospital, has since stated that "the evidence is so preponderantly in favor of reincarnation that you cannot doubt it if you have anything like an open mind."

In her study of reincarnation for *Here and Hereafter*, Ruth also pointed out the therapeutic value of an understanding of past lives in helping individuals to uncover the hidden causes of seemingly irrational phobias, such as fear of knives or bodies of water, acrophobia, claustrophobia, or fear of open spaces. Likewise, she noted, it can help to explain the origins of otherwise puzzling attitudes, such as an instant like or dislike of another person or clashing personalities within a family relationship, and she described numerous cases of prenatal hypnotic regression in which she had participated.

Many practicing therapists had independently reached similar conclusions, but until the notion of reincarnation became more widely understood and accepted, they were forced to keep their views to themselves or to share them only with trusted colleagues who held similar attitudes. Despite individual, private research into the validity of past-life therapy, with carefully documented and proven results, practicing clinicians risked public censure, professional ostracism, and even revocation of their credentials if they dared to advocate such an as yet unorthodox approach.

All that began to change with greater public understanding of the mounting evidence in support of reincarnation. In 1978 two practicing therapists, Dr. Edith Fiore and Dr. Morris Netherton, published separate books with basically the same premise that Ruth had noted a decade earlier, that problems of current behavior can frequently be resolved through an understanding of causes that extend back through past lifetimes. Past-life therapy, practiced either with hypnosis or with relaxation and imagery, has been found to be effective whether the patient believes in reincarnation or not.

It is this consistency of results that inspired formation in 1980 of the Association for Past-Life Research and Therapy in order to promote formal research and training in reincarnation therapy, to share information, and to maintain professional standards of practice.

Dr. Hazel Denning, executive director and one of the founders of APRT, began her own research in this field more than two decades ago, long before any practicing psychologist could discuss it openly without incurring ridicule. Her results substantiated all of the basic philosophies that Ruth Montgomery and the Guides, as well as other writers who followed, maintained about the principles of the universe—that we live a series of lifetimes in order to learn and grow and evolve, that we are treated by others according to how we have treated others in the past, and that we alone are responsible for our actions and besetting problems.

Some clinicians who already believed in reincarnation had never considered its usefulness in their work with patients until Ruth Montgomery and the writers who followed paved the way for its more widespread understanding. Among them is New Zealand-born Dr. Alexander Bannatyne, who earned his Ph.D. at the Institute of Psychiatry at London University in 1953. Intrigued by the possibility of recalling past lifetimes through medically approved hypnosis, he induced an altered state in his eight-year-old daughter and was astounded when she began to talk of a prior life in which she was teaching school in Germany! After that startling experience, he sought more specialized training in past-life therapy and began to incorporate it into his practice when a patient specifically requested it. "With the first case of past-life therapy," he explains, "we found that the patient's anxieties and stomach problems seemed to originate from her having been chopped up by a crocodile in some African river in an earlier life. We did a lot more work than that, but solved her current problems within months rather than the years of analysis that conventional approaches would have required."

Dr. Bannatyne notes that colleges and universities have now begun to study the concept of reincarnation. "It's becoming accepted as a topic for a doctorate in psychology," he continues. "The psychology departments of universities are allowing people to do research, and are funding research, using their graduate students." By way of example, he cites a recent study entitled "A Behavioral Perspective on Past-Lives Therapy with Difficult Phobics," by Dr. J. M. Cladder, a professor of psychology at the State University of Utrecht in Holland.

Dr. R. Leo Sprinkle, a psychologist and professor of counseling services at the University of Wyoming in Laramie, has expressed similar sentiments. "In my opinion," he states, "past-life therapy with its attending research is at the forefront in the emerging investigations of psychic phenomena. My own individual meditation, as well as my professional studies, have convinced me not only of the reality of reincarnation, but also of the importance of spiritual awareness for self-development." Emphasizing the pioneering role that Ruth Montgomery has played in publicly laying the groundwork of understanding in this field, he stresses that she has "demonstrated the personal meaning as well as the social significance of the 'journey of the soul.'"

Formal research into reincarnation has also begun on a more general level. The late psychologist and educator, Dr. Helen Wambach, after recognizing the need for further documentation of this phenomenon, designed, carried out, and published her findings in a psychological study with large groups of people. More than a thousand subjects who were guided to purported past-life recall completed questionnaires immediately after the experience and noted such details as type of clothing, architecture, eating utensils, currency, and source of everyday supplies, with startling results. Not only were the recalls remarkably accurate, but they even revealed information that archaeologists discovered only later.

A subsequent study by Dr. Wambach probed the prebirth memories of 750 subjects, uncovering attitudes identical to what Ruth Montgomery had indicated in *Here and Hereaf-*

ter and that her Guides had further described in *A World Beyond*. Wambach's subjects reported widespread reluctance to plunge into earth life, yet a conviction that this was necessary in order to learn specific lessons. They described knowing their parents in prior lifetimes and indicated that their own choice of family was sometimes guided by wiser souls. Just as the Guides had revealed to Ruth earlier, subjects noted that they usually chose to enter the fetus at or near the actual time of birth, preferring to enjoy the freedom and activity of the spirit world until they could no longer postpone their return to physical life as babies.

Other accomplished professionals in the field of human behavior have begun to express openly their belief in reincarnation. Carl Jung, who lived in an era when such an admission could have damaged his credibility, is now reported to have held such views privately. More recently, with rebirth being more widely understood, noted psychologists are no longer keeping so quiet. According to Dr. Hazel Denning, Dr. Carl R. Roberts, who is regarded by many as the father of modern psychology for his development of the client-centered approach to psychotherapy, once "confided" to an audience of thousands that he personally believed in reincarnation as the only thing that really makes sense in our world today. "The audience," Dr. Denning recalls, "was so enchanted that they rose in a body and applauded him loudly, even shrieking just as people do at an opera. And then anthropologist Margaret Mead, who followed him on the platform, remarked with a laugh, 'Well, I'm glad he's found out about this, because some of us have known it for a long time!' "

"And it's true," Dr. Denning continues. "It's been the intelligent people, through the ages, the outstanding leaders and persons of great stature, who have believed in it. The masses have never believed in it, particularly, because they don't understand it." It is due to writers such as Ruth Montgomery that more people now do understand it.

Just as the dawn of the New Age has opened the door to formal research into reincarnation as a reality, yielding results that are remarkably consistent and support the assertions made earlier by Ruth and her Guides, the way has also been opened to study death and its true implications for the living.

What actually happens after death, a matter that the medical and psychological community long regarded as the business of the clergy, was described at length by Ruth's Guides in 1971. *A World Beyond*, the bestseller that comforted and enlightened millions of people of all faiths, presented a detailed account of souls who at death find themselves out of their bodies but puzzled because people seem to ignore them. Some hover around their former homes in confusion, while others who are spiritually more prepared for death find themselves in a world of exotic beauty, with flowers and trees more vivid than any they have seen on earth. They may be greeted by departed loved ones and then helped to look back at their lives and assess their spiritual growth before going on to further learning.

After the publication of *A World Beyond*, other books began to appear detailing the strange experiences of people who had been declared clinically dead and then had recovered. They often described the identical phenomenon of having floated out of their bodies to hover near the ceiling, sometimes watching in curiosity while medical teams tried frantically to revive them. Some who had been "dead" for longer periods reported seeing deceased relatives and friends, a magnificent world of flowers and trees, and a shining spirit-being who showed them a panoramic replay of their lives so that they might compare their own actions to the loving acceptance they could now perceive around them. Others saw "souls waiting to be born" as well as bemused ones who still wandered near their former homes.

Curious and yet skeptical, doctors and psychologists began to look into this phenomenon, interviewing their patients and analyzing case histories, correlating medical information, cultural background, religious attitudes, and age, and determining whether patients had previously heard of near-death experiences. Studies are now underway at more than half a dozen universities across the country, with results so stunningly similar that they are being shared widely within the medical community. An international clearinghouse for exchange of research findings and information has been established at the University of Connecticut, with case files of the International Association for Near-Death Studies (IANDS) now bulging with such stories, leading researchers to delve not only into the occurrence of such events, but their very meaning.

It is the *meaning* of the near-death experience that has intrigued Dr. Kenneth Ring, professor of psychology at the University of Connecticut and past president of IANDS. Studies of the phenomenon follow a remarkably similar pattern regardless of a person's religion. Any "judgment" is a self-assessment, a life review that is aided by a shimmering being, often with a warm sense of humor, who helps the individual to see his own mistakes in the light of supreme love, compassion, and unconditional acceptance, and who asks one major question: "What have you done with your life?" Some subjects report that they reviewed prior incarnations as well. Persons who return to their bodies after such an experience seem to be affected profoundly, often viewing the world and earthly life with a higher understanding of Universal Love and compassion, and a new and more powerful awareness of the effect of their own thoughts and actions on others. Dr. Ring has observed that certain near-death experiencers emerge completely and radically transformed, with a waning interest in personal status and material possessions, more concern and love for their fellow humans, and "a heightened sense of spiritual purpose." Some such persons have been pinpointed by Ruth's Guides as Walk-ins, a concept explained at length in *Strangers Among Us* and *Threshold to Tomorrow.*

As for these personal transformations that occur in many near-death experiencers, Dr. Ring has observed that some people change so radically that they seem—to themselves and others—to have an entirely new personality, almost a new identity. Such changes, he continues, appear not to be confined only to those who have neared death, but to countless other individuals all over the world, who are emerging with a heightened, universal understanding that transcends the boundaries of conflicting religious views. "It may very well be that these persons are the harbingers or the forerunners of the next wave of psychospiritual evolution,' he reasons. "I'm not talking about a new species of human being, but maybe a more spiritually advanced type of human being, who is coming into manifestation now, and whose qualities of character, and whose expression in terms of conduct, is the kind necessary in order to move into a New Age, and the kind of New Age that I think a lot of people would hope would be in our future."

Whether these sudden transformations occur as a result of the Walk-in process, an awakening process, or a combination, "something very interesting is certainly happening," he observes. "I can't deny the data." It is interesting to note that Ruth's Guides for many years have been asserting that the gentle Lemurians, a deeply spiritual race, have been reincarnating by birth and the Walk-in process to replace the overly ambitious Atlanteans who brought downfall to their continent some 12,500 years ago, and who have been predominant here in the twentieth century.

Other professionals are also taking an interested look at

the concept of Walk-ins. Dr. Marcia Chambers, a clinical psychologist at Georgetown University Hospital in Washington, D.C., has said of it: "I can't rule it out! I know of no logical medical explanation at the present time for these cases where a complete metamorphosis occurs after a near-death experience. The concept is very interesting."

Dr. Albert Hugh T. Doss, a practicing psychiatrist in Raleigh, North Carolina, declared after reading Ruth's *Strangers Among Us:* "I have been fascinated by its logic. The concept of Walk-ins seems to fit in with the cosmic pattern that when great crises or changes affecting the earth and all mankind are impending, illumined entities come from the One Creative Source to help mankind." Citing a case with which he and Ruth Montgomery are both familiar, Dr. Doss told her: "After considering all the known facts, I am convinced that [he] is indeed a startling example of a Walk-in. In my practice of psychiatry I must occasionally deal with persons who are potentially suicidal. In your book you have pointed out a new and valuable approach to this real and often critical problem." Suggesting ways that this new approach might be used by psychiatrists, he continued: "The patient would be encouraged to keep his body, the temple of the soul, in excellent condition, without drugs or a self-inflicted mortal wound, so that it would be ready for the incoming Walk-in. He would simply vacate his body during peaceful sleep. After all, in this time of organ transplants, is it not reasonable that when a person feels that he cannot solve his problems on the physical plane, he could allow a Walk-in to occupy this body and use it to accomplish good for humanity?"

Dr. Kenneth Ring, in viewing Ruth's contribution to understanding in this field, comments: "I think what Ruth Montgomery's books have already done is make serious people at least look at this particular phenomenon and evaluate it for themselves. That's how near-death studies began

—from personal observations that people started thinking about. Only after other researchers come along and investigate a puzzling concept can there be, eventually, a widespread understanding of it."

As any student of human behavior is aware, people will listen to and understand only as much as they are ready to incorporate into their own thinking. Just as in Matthew 11:13–15, where John the Baptist was identified by Jesus as the reincarnation of the long-dead prophet Elias, such a pronouncement could be heard and understood only by those "with ears to hear it." Likewise sacred scriptures unearthed in 1945 from the Christian Gnostics indicate that Christ imparted general teachings to the masses, according to what they could understand, and inner teachings to those who were more spiritually mature.

Ruth Montgomery, as a skilled communicator and a skeptical seeker of the truth, has throughout her career gently guided millions of readers to a level of spiritual maturity in which they are at last ready to understand the Universal Principles that have for centuries been masked. Psychologists and psychiatrists alike have long sought such answers, and as Ruth's writing has opened the doors to understanding at the dawn of the New Age, an educated public has finally begun to feel free to explore those truths that were once confined to the realm of philosophers and clergy.

Again and again, psychologists probing reincarnation, physicians studying near-death experiences, social scientists noting sudden, unexplained, and widespread enlightenment, and even Christian researchers such as Professor Geddes MacGregor, author of several books explaining the compatibility of reincarnation with Christian teaching, have all begun to return to the basic premises that Ruth Montgomery and the Guides have explained, step-by-step, for a quarter of a century: We are all spiritual beings, all sparks of God, changing and evolving and moving ever upward on a spiral of understanding, toward ultimate re-union with the Creator.

As her Guides have emphasized, "The New Age is the crossover from the present mundane world of the body and its comforts to the spiritual plane and its reality of one world, one universe, one cosmos. This period will last for the biblical thousand years of peace and brotherhood, when men's minds will be opened to each other and to the forces beyond earth's own magnetic center."

If, as Ruth's Guides and others predict, earth now stands on the threshold of an inevitable disaster of cataclysmic proportions, one that will decimate its population, destroy many of its cities, halt commerce, and force its survivors to establish an interaction of helpfulness, love, and mutual respect, then a unique opportunity lies at hand, both for those who will physically perish and for those who survive. As earth begins to pass into the higher energies of the New Age, many are even now beginning to recognize that death is merely a vibratory transition, and that what matters in each lifetime is what we manage to accomplish in working more harmoniously with others around us. Ruth has been repeatedly telling us that those who open their minds spiritually and seek cosmic answers will necessarily reach the same conclusion: Life truly is eternal.

Moving into this enlightened New Age, many who look back even a generation or two are startled to see how far we have come in our understanding of life. "If only we had known this before!" they now exclaim.

Others, who have grown and spiritually unfolded during the past quarter century with this Seeker of Truth, merely point to their bookshelves and nod. "Ruth Montgomery knew it."

CHAPTER XVI

Beyond the Bend

Beginning fifteen years ago with *A World Beyond*, Ruth's Guides have gazed ahead and shared what they have foreseen with readers of her books, while reminding us that from the perspective of spirit, earth time has little meaning and free will can alter the course of man-made events. Regardless of this cautionary note, many of their predictions have already proven to be remarkably accurate.

In the spring of 1971, when President Richard Nixon had reached his lowest ebb in public opinion polls, and informed sources speculated that he would drop Vice President Spiro Agnew as his running mate for the 1972 campaign, the Guides flatly declared that Agnew would be on the ticket and that Nixon would be "a shoo-in" for reelection. November 1972 proved them correct.

Then, on November 27, 1973, the Guides announced that Nixon would not finish his second term as President, and that "a health problem" would be a factor in his decision to resign. Ruth was so intrigued by this pronouncement that she promptly shared it with others, even asking her husband to sign and date the page on which it was written. Nine months later Nixon resigned his office and shortly thereafter entered the hospital for a near fatal bout with phlebitis, a health problem that was severely troubling him at the time of his resignation.

Back in the spring of 1971 Ruth's Guides noted that in Egypt "a strong man with good heart and head" would step forward to assume power and that "a more monolithic form [of government], but with greater freedom" would emerge. Within six months of that prediction, President Anwar Sadat emerged strong from an abortive coup attempt and Egypt ratified a permanent constitution. Sadat became Premier in 1973, and by 1976 had ended that country's military and economic dependence on the Soviet Union, turning Egypt toward its present political alliance with the free world.

"Zionism will continue to be a force in persuading those of Jewish faith to return to the Palestinian homeland," the Guides noted in 1975, "but the numbers of those leaving Israel after trying the experiment will outnumber the new recruits." An article in the Washington *Post* in the summer of 1985 reported just such a trend, with emigrations from Israel rising from 2,600 in 1983 to 15,000 in 1984, a sixfold increase, and surpassing the number of immigrants. "This is just as well," the Guides added. "Why overpopulate a land that needs hardy workers who love every inch of the soil with swashbucklers who seek only adventure, or revenge on the Arabs?"

National leaders whom the Guides foresaw rising to world prominence included, for England, "a Tory Prime Minister who is a woman," and for China, Teng Hsiao-p'ing, who would begin to Westernize China more than ever before. Their 1975 declaration for Great Britian was fulfilled four years later with the election of Margaret Thatcher as Prime Minister; and their 1976 prediction for China came to pass in 1978, despite Teng Hsiao-p'ing's intervening purge, after which he emerged as China's undisputed strongman and promptly began opening the doors to Western influence and cooperation.

The Guides told Ruth in 1971 that neither Henry "Scoop" Jackson nor Ted Kennedy would win the Democratic presidential nomination in 1972, and that Chile would soon overthrow its Communist regime. History has shown that they were right again.

Their prediction about Vietnam also turned out to be accurate, indicating that America would gradually withdraw from that protracted war, but that "the bloodshed will continue for a long time yet, without peace or sanity." Likewise they correctly foretold psychological adjustment problems for returning veterans, who would face severe unemployment and wish to "plunge right into careers or work, rather than to attend college like World War II veterans did."

Fifteen years ago Ruth's Guides claimed that Japan would "rise to supremacy in the commercial mart," and "boom the marketplaces with her cleverly designed wares," a fact that can now be attested to by today's shoppers and by those congressmen who are arguing for protectionist legislation to stem the Japanese imports that are flooding our markets and causing unemployment here.

They also predicted in 1971 that before long "the two sectors" of divided Germany would become "somewhat closer together but not totally merged." Economic cooperation between East and West Germany has indeed increased in the years since then.

Concerning Arab-Israeli matters, the Guides correctly insisted in 1971 that there would be "no world war there, but a continuing thorn in the flesh," a fact patently evident by the ongoing unrest in that part of the world.

In 1975 Ruth's Guides announced that more men would

begin to take over "housekeeping and baby tending, without any onus attached," while their spouses filled the role of breadwinner. Today such a switch in roles is regarded as a viable option in an era when career opportunities for women have opened beyond the narrow boundaries known by their mothers and grandmothers.

The Guides have long predicted that hunger would beset those underdeveloped nations "that are more intent on power, prestige, and guns than on the well-being of their citizens." They also warned Ruth that these food problems could lead to war, and they told her in 1975 of "a dangerous fanatic" from Abyssinia (Ethiopia), "a man of mixed lineage" who was determined to wreak havoc on the surrounding area, take over all oil and mineral resources, and wage war on the world. In 1978 they identified this troublemaker as the new Ethiopian strongman Mengistu Haile Mariam, and four years later they predicted the start of World War III in 1986 in the Horn of Africa, "unless there is a tremendous rallying in that part of the world."

Since that 1972 prediction famine has indeed grown acute, especially in Ethiopia, but the Guides now declare that the Western world's generous response to this crisis has forestalled what would otherwise have grown into an international conflagration. Stressing again that mankind has the power to overcome evil with good, they observed: "The Ethiopian government is taking a second look at the enormous help from the democratic or Western world, and the lack of it from the Soviets. It will therefore be quieter there, and Western help will be accepted in improving the food crops. Wrangling will continue, but there will not be an outbreak anytime soon that would lead to a world war. Famine is already occurring in that area and other sections of the earth, and there will be continuing hunger, but not as severe as if a war with nuclear weapons had devastated so much of the planet."

As both Ruth and the Guides continue to stress, free will often intervenes and alters an otherwise predicted course of events. As another case in point, the 1980 elections which the Guides said would place in the White House a free-spending Democrat who would nearly bankrupt the American economy resulted instead in Ronald Reagan's installation in office. Ruth's loyal readers have since pointed out that Reagan was indeed a New Deal Democrat before switching to the Republican Party, and also that huge budget deficits under the Reagan administration have reached record levels, but Ruth is not about to let her Guides off that lightly. Their predictions are not always right, she continually reminds her readers, "because people have free will, both at the ballot box and in their personal choices."

In early March of 1984 Ruth asked her Guides to predict the outcome of the fiercely contested Democratic primaries. Despite Gary Hart's bright prospects at the time, the Guides said that Walter Mondale would win the primary. Then, to her surprise, they added that Ronald Reagan would defeat Mondale but would not be able to finish his second term. Ruth included this information in her most recent book, *Aliens Among Us*, which was published in mid-June of 1985. A few weeks later, on July 12, Reagan was operated on for cancer of the colon, six months into his second term.

What lies in wait for the future, always a matter of curiosity to those on earth, is a global catastrophe that Ruth's Guides foresee as more massive than anything this planet has undergone in many thousands of years. The long-awaited shift of the earth on its axis cannot be avoided, they stress, since natural forces that have brought about imbalances will trigger this compensating movement in order to return it to stability. In that light the Guides declare repeatedly that individuals have free will—to wage or prevent war, to succeed or fail in their endeavors to grow spiritually or waste time in frivolous pursuits, but not to countermand universal laws that are irreversible.

From the Guides' vantage point in the spirit plane, they are able to see beyond the bend in the river of life that we here on earth are traveling. They can see obstacles that will confront us, but they cannot predict our final choices, only the likelihood of what will come to pass unless people exercise their free will to change the course of events.

In preparation for this last chapter Ruth volunteered to ask her Guides a series of questions of general interest pertaining to the remainder of this century and the New Age that will follow. Always obliging, they provided her with a sweeping array of predictions to help prepare us for the years ahead.

"The San Andreas Fault will begin to split within the next few years," they wrote, "and will wreak havoc on some of the fine modern buildings erected on it. People knew better than to build there. It will begin to divide and parts of California will topple into the sea. Many lives will be lost, but it won't be the sort of devastation that the shift will bring, because there will be ample warning signs; and although the buildings themselves cannot be saved, many lives will be as the area is evacuated."

Looking ahead to the time remaining before the shift of the planet on its axis, Ruth's Guides see years of challenge. "There will be earthquakes of increasing dimension, and floods. Because of drought there will also be famine in the early part of the next decade. This will not be confined to Africa or the Middle East. America will also be affected, and since it is the breadbasket for so much of the third world, there will be few answers to calls for assistance. Russia will be stirring trouble and taking advantage of the situation on the American continents, both North and South, and people will begin despairing of anything going right again. Those with plenty of money will be able to make do; as always, it will be the poor who suffer."

Urged to tell more, they added: "The weather will continue to change as it is already doing, and in the mid-1990s there will be violent alterations in weather patterns, with eruption of volcanoes in South America as well as North America and Hawaii, and although these will create some hardship, they are not directly related to the shift. However, the particles emitted will help to block the sun and its beneficial rays so that drought and poor crops may be the result. Thus the famines"

Responding to further questions from Ruth, the Guides indicated that an earthquake is "caused by a shifting within the molten interior of the earth in relation to the hard crust above, and thus it is possible to occur at *any* spot—not necessarily along a fault, which simply means an old, old break in the earth's crust. New ones are able to form within that inner adjustment. We do not see the New Madrid Fault [in the Midwest] giving big problems before the shift, although some shifting is occurring there. The San Andreas Fault will pose problems within the next six years, and parts of California will be engulfed, although it may not be as drastic as some have foreseen until the shift occurs."

As for the prospect of nuclear warfare, "The Cold War will continue," the Guides wrote, "but how much better that is than bloodshed. Economics will improve in some areas, and the debtor nations will make some headway in repaying their gigantic loans. As the 1990s approach, tension will certainly exist between the East and the West, but we do not see the conflagration of World War III in this period." Another time they stressed. "The big war with nuclear weapons can easily be averted if enough right-minded people assert themselves in government counsels," and they have told Ruth that peaceable Walk-ins from other planets have already infiltrated some of those counsels here and abroad.

As for the new government in Russia the Guides pointed out that it "will do much to lessen tensions for the immediate future, and although its own interests are nationalistic, and aggression with neighboring countries through infiltration will continue, nevertheless it has no wish to set off World War III. We see that danger lessening at least for the remainder of the decade."

Another day the Guides again cited Soviet activity, noting that "Russia will continue its sabotaging of friendly governments and try to expand its sphere of influence throughout Africa, the Middle East and Latin America." They repeated that famine will continue, but that "a purpose has been served by the Ethiopian disaster, as it is gradually turning Africa toward the Western nations who have come through with so much aid."

In a more dramatic vein Ruth's Guides have begun to sound warnings of a mounting struggle on planet earth between the forces of good and evil, a tug-of-war that they see continuing until the shift of the earth on its axis. "As we near the last decade of this century," they write, "we will encounter evil beings who are intent on taking advantage of everyone from governments to the lowliest stranger. This is the last desperate attempt by evil forces to control the earth before they realize that their power will be eclipsed by the shift and the New Age. They will try every bestial ploy to induce people to sin and to abuse their minds and bodies with dope and other hallucinogens with the hope of winning their souls to satanic purposes. It will be a particularly devastating time, this final attempt to seduce mankind, and all should be aware of these forces that would betray, destroy, and wreak havoc on the earth and its peoples. The new leadership in Russia will be behind some of these plots, to be sure, but not all of them, because there are

as many evil ones in the U.S. as in the U.S.S.R. Take care not
to fall into their trap. It is a contest for men's souls and all
should be forewarned. Pray for protection, help others, and
love one another, but beware of these evil forces."

Well! The Guides had seldom conveyed such emphatic
warnings, and their portrayal of this long-prophesied struggle seemed gloomy indeed. After rereading their dire message, Ruth returned to them the following day, typing out
her questions before beginning the usual meditation and
prayer. "Is yesterday's writing yours?" she asked. "If so, any
advice on how people can prevent this influence on them?
Something *cheerful?*"

After a brief greeting they addressed her questions directly. "The writing yesterday came from us but is perhaps
too discouraging," they conceded. "Let us say it this way:
Throughout the remainder of the present decade, evil will
flourish as dark forces grapple with the forces of good for
control of men's minds and souls. There is evil abroad, and
one should be constantly on the alert not to be taken in by
it, for ulterior forces are enticing young and old to the use of
mind-warping drugs, as well as to the lure of profitable
treason, which, in so many words, is selling one's soul to the
devil. Satan is abroad, make no mistake about it, and the
best defenses against such temptations are meditation,
prayer, and a watchful alert. Suspect anyone who offers
hallucinogens that are of the unnatural variety, drugs, and
money for subversion. The time remaining before the New
Age dawns is so brief that surely anyone can resist tempta-
tion for that long! Indeed he must if he is to survive the shift
or to have another chance anytime soon to reincarnate and
live among the high-minded people who will populate the
earth in the new century."

Just where did the current craze for drugs and pornography, the misuse of sex, and the low ebb of family life fit into
this gloomy picture, Ruth wondered. "As for the drug infes-

tation, and sodomy, this harks back to the days of Sodom and Gomorrah, as do the actions of those couples who refuse to take the marriage vow and yet bring children into the world who will have to be reared by only one parent, if even that one is faithful to the trust of harboring another soul," they asserted. "Pornography, so well known in those days and also in Pompeii, reflects the decadence of mankind in such destroyed civilizations. A blot on the human race! Better to be thinking of how to help the ones being born today into that frightful world that is called civilization."

Ruth asked the Guides if they could tell her anything "to help humanity" about the current epidemic of AIDS that has begun to spread not only through the homosexual community but also to others, and they replied: "As for AIDS, it is one of the seven ancient plagues of the testaments, and has returned to devastate the population of the earth. It is a virus that has been brought back into being by man's evil ways and discordant thought, and until humanity reverses its downhill plunge, it will continue to infuse and plague the population. Such a pity that even innocent children are infected by it through mothers or through blood transfusions, but remember that there is seldom such a thing as an innocent newborn. Most earthlings are old souls who have sinned in ages past, and this may be a karmic thing in some instances. Remain pure by thinking pure thoughts and loving others, even the unfortunates who are paying for their sins. AIDS will still be around until the shift cleanses the earth and humankind."

This response prompted Ruth to enquire why planet earth seems to be in the grip of so much evildoing nowadays. After all, according to the laws of karma, people are supposed to be progressing—climbing upward on the spiral of spiritual growth. Instead, problems with crime and drugs and terrorism seem to be getting worse instead of better. The Guides pointed the finger, as they have in the past, squarely at one massive influx of souls, latter-day Atlanteans. This was a reference to those in the technologically advanced civilization of Atlantis who had selfishly misused their power, causing the continent to sink in a massive planetary cataclysm at the time of Noah's Ark. Their use of powerful energy sources to destroy distant lands had backfired on them, according to the Guides in *The World Before*, and in this century vast numbers of them had reincarnated to participate in the modern scientific age that is so reminiscent of life on Atlantis.

"The Atlantean culprits who have been so predominant in the last half of the century are doing their utmost to disrupt and take charge," the Guides continued. "As we have said, they are a dying breed who will probably not earn the right for another opportunity in physical body for a long time, and they're subconsciously aware of it, clutching at straws and creating strawmen to disrupt and alienate one class from another. This was the last-ditch fight prophesied in the Bible, when Satan would assemble his forces to seek control of the world, and the shift is necessary to cleanse the earth of these evil ones. But many of the Lemurians have more recently been entering, "to replace those latter-day Atlanteans." The land of Mu or Lemuria, as the Guides described in *The World Before*, once existed in what is now a large portion of the Pacific Ocean. Populated by a civilization of highly spiritual people who are now returning to physical life, Lemuria sank in a shift of the earth on its axis many thousands of years before the final destruction of Atlantis.

The alienation of one class from another seems currently to be reaching such strident levels, all in the name of God and all supposedly based on principles of love and harmony, that Ruth next posed a more detailed set of questions. "Is there anything to be done about the conflict between Christian fundamentalists and New Age thinkers?" she asked.

"What about the fundamentalists, who after all are God-fearing people, but think only they are right, and that the Bible is not subject to interpretation? And what of today's cults and satanic influences?" The Guides' answer filled nearly an entire page as they tackled this troubling question.

"Ruth, this is Lily, Art, and the group," they began. "The satanic influences are pervading all strata of society throughout the world. Never in many centuries has there been such fertile ground for the spread of evil influences, as people dip into the occult for nonspiritual purposes, using the demonic powers that they learn in this way to influence others. They are selling dope, taking dope, and employing black witchcraft that had all but died out during the Dark Ages. Evil is rampant.

"The Christian fundamentalists are sincerely trying to stem this flow of evil, and because they know so little about the New Age philosophy and are unwilling to listen to discussions about it, they are lumping all of these ideas together. It is a pity, because some of these people are genuinely sincere in trying to save Christianity from satanic influences, but so many of them are ignorant, with closed minds and little education, that they fail to realize the close relationship between the ancient Eastern religions and that which Christ brought to the world. They fail to understand that we are all one. That is the basic reality. We are all one, and instead of lambasting other religious groups as so many of them are now doing, they should be drawing together and accepting that the worship of the one God with many messengers is the proper role for Christians, Jews, and all sects.

"One God indivisible, and love for one's fellowman. That's what religion is all about. Unless they can accept that basic premise, they will continue along their bigoted, ever narrowing path that leads to nowhere, for until they grant

the right of others to disagree on the pathway so long as
those pathways all lead back to God, they are lost.

"The rift [between Christian fundamentalists and spiritually minded New Age devotees] will probably not be erased
until the axial shift occurs, at which time the population will
be so decimated that the survivors, helped by Walk-ins and
extraterrestrials, will realize the wisdom of all pulling together for the good of everyone. There have always been
religious confrontations and wars fought in the name of
religion. The New Age, the millennium, will see an end to
that strife, at least for a thousand years. Beyond that we
cannot prophesy."

Almost as a postscript to this lengthy dissertation, they
added on the following day: "The philosophical rift, as we
said, will continue until the shift of the earth on its axis.
People's minds will then be almost universally opened to
the broader spectrum of thought that leads to the understanding that there are many paths to the top of the mountain but only one top, God. Some may wind around and
around on the way up, but the important thing to remember is that all paths which lead upward in spirituality will
eventually reach the pinnacle, the return to the Creator.
The earth is now orbiting nearer to the central core of the
cosmos, and because of that fact people's minds are more
and more being opened to the reality that we are all one
and that each of us is a part of God."

During the next decade and before the shift of the earth
on its axis, the Guides told Ruth, a Walk-in will be elected
President of the United States. Walk-ins, as they explained
in *Strangers Among Us*, are high-minded beings who, having attained sufficient awareness in previous incarnations,
are permitted to return to earth life as adults, taking over
dying or unwanted bodies, if their purpose is to serve humanity. Arriving now in ever increasing numbers, Walk-ins
are working quietly to help earthlings prepare for the trou-

bling years ahead. The Walk-in whom the Guides say will be elected President "is already in a position of trust and his special talents are gradually being recognized, but he is not one of those being touted now as a possible candidate in 1988. When the time is right, we will tell you who he is."

Prodded by Ruth to be more specific, the Guides continued: "This future President will become recognizable as a Walk-in to those in the know within the next four years. He will be almost above party in that he addresses all Americans and reflects no strong party affiliation in thought or manner. He is a good man who is already in a position of some prominence and will be elected in the 1990s. Not sure which term, since time is unimportant here as it relates to such activities as elections there. He has great foresight and will work with scientists and others to probe the extent of possible disaster and will have a calming effect on those who realize that a shift is imminent. With his advisors and helpers he will map out those geographical areas that will be safe from the massive tidal waves and sinking of vast land areas in the United States, and will also dispatch notices of dangerous and safe areas to the leaders of other nations."

Ruth's Guides say of this Walk-in President: "People will be aware of his special qualities and his abrupt turnaround in ideals and goals [at the time of the ego substitution], so that many will realize his Walk-in status while others will think of him as a born-again Christian. He will tackle the problems with gusto, and if a war has not involved the world in its flames, and it does not look now like that will have occurred, then he will deal with the spots of famine and the floods and turn people's attention to the potential shift of the earth. He may not call it by that name, since he will not wish to frighten the people ahead of time, but he will be openly discussing safe geographical areas and sponsoring projects in those sections of the country so that people can move there and find employment, with useful services and tools already available for them. He will stress the importance of cooperation among the newcomers with those who are already in those sparsely settled areas, and will see to it that one does not crowd out or infringe on the other. These are necessarily inland areas, and as the time for the shift approaches, he will begin quietly to alert governmental agencies of the need to be on guard against looting and other selfish acts, for the populace will suddenly begin to swarm into those areas at the first signs of severe earth wobble. Even scientists will by then admit to foreseeing a shift, as the President starts preparing for the earth changes."

The approaching planetary calamity, as Ruth's Guides have warned in her recent books, will set the stage for the long-prophesied coming of the Antichrist, and they indicate that he has already been born and is now an American boy in his early teens. "There will be people who will rise up to claim that they are the messiah who can lead others to safety. The evil ones will not go away just because you wish them to," the Guides told Ruth. "They are firmly entrenched there and eager to seize power. But as the time approaches, the Antichrist himself will step forward and will command admiration and attention from some good people as well as bad, for the devil has a charismatic personality or he could not have wooed so many followers for so long. He will say he has plans for saving everyone, if he is allowed to take charge. Some will heed his insidious voice and decline to move to those areas where others will survive. Instead, they will remain in shore areas that are unsafe, and when the shift at last occurs, they will naturally be swept away. The Antichrist will meanwhile have taken himself to a safe area. He will achieve wide recognition immediately after the shift and will attract those unworthy ones who were able to survive it, but he will soon be recognized for what he is, because the preponderance of those surviving the shift will be good souls. There will be chaos for a time following the shift, but after the Antichrist tries to assert dictatorial authority, the people will turn on him and put him to death."

Other evildoers will also abound between now and the time of the shift, the Guides have told Ruth in answer to her questions. "Terrorists will persist until the time draws near for the shift and they are driven by fear to find safe hiding places, but many of them will be swept into the seas or otherwise disposed of during or shortly after the event. Until then they will continue their terrorist acts, because they are in rebellion against God's will and firmly believe that might makes right. They are a despicable breed of latter-day Atlanteans who foraged and slaughtered the innocent near the time of the sinking of that advanced continent, and they have come back to reap revenge for their own ill-doings that led to death at that time. Too bad that they reincarnated to persecute the innocent again."

"As the time approaches for the shift," the Guides indicate, "numerous warning signs will be available, as scientists even now are viewing with more open minds the distinct possibility of a major planetary alteration. The wind currents will shift more noticeably, the seas will rise in some areas and sink in others in proportion to the adjoining land, and some areas will begin to break up beneath the soil. So much water and oil have been removed from some sections of the country that there will be cave-ins and other small calamities, but nothing to compare with that which comes with the shift. Some of California will already have broken away before the shift, and when that event occurs, Manhattan will begin to experience some crumbling."

Physical areas of safety, as the Guides have stressed to Ruth through more than a decade of warnings, will lie inland. "Practically no coastal areas will be safe during the shift because of the tidal waves. Behind the coastal mountain ranges is best. Islands will be particularly hazardous places because most of them, unless at high peaks, will be completely washed over until the earth again settles into orbit. Then some of them, such as Australia, New Zealand and the Bahamas, will have greatly increased in size, while others will disappear. The lowlands of Europe are in a perilous situation, but large land masses away from the sea— such as in Canada, Russia, Siberia, Africa, and China—will be relatively safe, as will many inland parts of the U.S., except for the area immediately adjacent to the new path that will be cut as the Great Lakes link with the Mississippi River. The shift itself "will occur in the very last months of the century as it looks from here," the Guides assert, "although as we have repeatedly said, earth time is not relative in terms of the cosmos. It is a man-made convenience timed to the sun and earthly revolutions around it."

Ruth's Guides indicate that while most earthlings will remain on the planet to ride out the shift, some will be removed temporarily. "Now as to those being rescued," they write, "it will be a massive undertaking, but the space aliens, as you call them, will indeed be on hand to lift off some chosen earthlings who will remain in earth orbit until that planet settles back into proper rotation. They will be alerted psychically and by some of those in earth bodies who are in contact with extraterrestrials, and who will tell them where to go to be lifted off."

The shift, as the Guides have repeatedly warned, will happen "in the twinkling of an eye," as the earth "slurps approximately onto its side." As they have previously described to Ruth, "In daylight areas the sun will seem to stand still overhead, and then to race backward for the brief period while the earth settles into its new position relative to the sun." Seasons will change abruptly, high winds will sweep the planet's surface, and the oceans will slosh about as would a jostled bowl of water, rushing over adjoining land areas in tidal waves too massive to escape.

"It is not possible to designate the exact degree of the shift," the Guides concede, "but as we have already stated, one pole will be in the Pacific and the other somewhere in South America, toward the southern tip. Those areas then will be extremely cold, and instant freezing will occur, but in the Pacific this will affect mostly fish and any who happen to be in that broad vicinity. Those bodies will be preserved in ice as have been the carcasses of mammals at the present poles after an earlier shift."

In response to Ruth's recent questioning, they say of the chaos: "Most of those losing their lives will be in coastal areas, and their bodies will be swept into the sea, posing no particular health problems for the survivors of the shift, but others who are physically extinguished by falling buildings and the like will of course need to be buried. There will be mass graves, and little time for public mourning as the survivors look to their own sustenance during that chaotic time. As we have said before, parts of Hawaii, the west coast of California, Florida, England and Holland, and many island nations such as Japan will be devastated at the time of the shift, with much of their land disappearing beneath the ocean, while other areas rise and enlarge in size."

As for what will be left of life on planet earth, the Guides described for Ruth a period of reconstruction followed by a golden New Age of peace. "There will be many injured, true," they say of the period immediately after the disaster, "and some will pass on into spirit, but there will be a sense of helpfulness not witnessed in the earth plane in millennia. Splints will be made for broken bones, other injuries will be treated with tourniquets, and basic human medical remedies will be applied. We do not see vast numbers riddled by disease. The rubbish will be cleared as quickly as possible, and all people will continue to help one another. Electricity

will exist in some scattered areas, but not along the coast
and in most large cities. Nuclear wastes will present some
problems, but these will be solved. It will not be a time of
reversion to the Dark Ages, because of the enlightenment
that will flow to the new race of people coming in, some
who are Walk-ins and some from other planetary systems.
Those who have meanwhile been lifted off to safety by
extraterrestrial fleets will return to designated areas and
begin work among the peoples, soothing and reassuring
them and teaching them new methods of growing crops
more speedily and of erecting dwellings that require little
time or energy.

"Many others who have survived by being guided to safe
areas will, after this harrowing experience, realize that they
were saved for a purpose and will mend their ways. True,
some will survive who are not fit to exist in the New Age,
but as we have told you, they will soon die off, and the new
race that repopulates, as well as the nobler ones who are
saved or returned from orbit, will take positions of authority
and guide the bewildered ones into fruitful paths."

The New Age that will emerge after the shift will be "a
paradise on earth compared with the present moment," the
Guides have assured Ruth. "Some of the evil souls will manage to survive the shift, but in such decreased numbers that
the good souls, aided by the Walk-ins and extraterrestrials,
will overcome them, subdue them, and banish them from
polite society. The New Age, as we see it there, will be a
time of love and understanding, of consideration and compassion, and of a joyous awakening to the reality that we are
all one. There is little enough time left for preparation. We
therefore urge that all of you begin readying yourselves
now for the joyous fellowship that will occur whether in
body or in spirit, for communication in that New Age will be
simplicity itself between the physical and the etheric vibrations. It will be a time when men's eyes are opened to the

Universal Truth—the eternal truth that there is no death and that love is the unifying force of the cosmic world. People will often communicate through thought waves with each other, and also with outer-space beings. The way is being opened for direct communication with the astral and etheric planes, and after the shift this will be rather commonplace, because a more spiritually developed race will be inhabiting the earth. Some of them will come from other galaxies, and others will have experienced life there between earthly incarnations, so that the universe will be opened up just as the earth has been opened to instant communication since the advent of television and radio.

"Those who survive the shift will learn to adjust rapidly as their minds are opened to the new realm, and with the guidance of Walk-ins and extraterrestrials they will find new and exciting ways of overcoming obstacles. As they return to the old-time ways of providing for themselves and others, they will rediscover the joy of making things by hand, and cooperating with neighbors and friends, eschewing the so-called sophistication that has gripped the Western world in recent times. Love is the basic commodity of the universe. Soul love. That's what people will rediscover as they work together for the well-being of everyone."

In answer to a question that had been bothering Ruth, the Guides said that in the New Age people will realize that there is "no stigma attached, morally or ethically, to letting a person die with dignity. These artificial prolongations of life are, after all, new to the medical profession within the past few decades," they stressed, "and doctors are actually trying to play God with souls who are ready to leave their bodies and proceed to the greater happiness of the spirit plane. Better to let a person who has no hope of recovery go quietly in God's own good time, rather than man's. In the New Age this will be thoroughly understood and no such methods will be permitted. It is, after all, simply experimentation, using human beings as guinea pigs, and is a dark blot on the present era of medicine. Fine work is being done in the field of medical research, and in making the older years more bearable, but no one has the right to keep a heart, which is only a machine, beating endlessly while the soul is trying to escape and the brain is dead.'

They told Ruth that this will be more thoroughly understood in the coming age. "And now to tell you a bit more about that approaching time," they continued. "It will be the finest period that the earth has known since the early beginnings when all were able to go and come as they pleased and were in communication with the Creative Force. This New Age will be an opening into awareness, with memories of previous lives on earth and on other planetary spheres retained, as well as those of the spirit plane between. In other words, all minds will become open to the eternal Now, and to all that has gone before. The akashic records will be available to all who seek spiritual awareness, and in those times ahead souls will realize that we are all one entity, the heart of God.

"Now as to the next century, there will be few divisions in spiritual matters, for all will work together and realize that with one God we are all to serve, there is no need for sects and divisions and so-called religious wars. Since communication between the spirit and the physical plane will be relatively easy for most of those in that golden time, it will be understood that to be Catholic or Presbyterian, Southern Baptist or Jewish, Muslim or Hindu or whatever is an arrogance of mind that has no place in religion. We are all one, all brothers and sisters, and together we make up the whole.

"The Christ spirit will enter a perfected person within some twenty to thirty years after the earth has restabilized," the Guides continued, recalling the merging of the Divine Christ spirit with the man called Jesus, at the time of His baptism, which marked the beginning of His ministry.

"People's eyes will then be opened to the reality that it is all one world, in different vibratory levels. And as their minds are also opened to contact between those differing vibrations, it will be a wondrous time on earth."

Meanwhile, they cautioned, "we are approaching a time that will try men's souls, as the old orators liked to say." But the best preparation for the catastrophic events to come, the Guides told Ruth, is *inner* preparation, and it is best to begin now, "for as the shift approaches, those who are to be preserved in bodily form will know how to survive, and those who cross into the spirit state will thereby be equipped for the abrupt arrival of so many others simultaneously. We foresee a time of tribulation, yes, but those who are meditating and readying themselves for these strenuous times will find solace within and will understand how puny their individual worries seem in relation to the cosmos. Many millions who perish in physical being will awaken in the spirit realm with a more highly stepped up vibratory level, and if they have not adequately prepared through meditation and prayer, they will be bewildered because of the sudden influx of so many souls at once. They should consequently begin *now* to evaluate their goals and to understand that life is a continuing process which does not end with the grave.

"As to safe areas," they concluded, "these are actually within oneself, for if one is doing his very best for others, he is eternally safe from harm. That does not mean taking over another's burdens, but lending a helping hand and an encouraging word that comes from the heart. Therefore, it is well for those who wish to make the most of this present lifespan to open themselves through meditation to the eternal truth that there is no death and that love is the all-powerful unifying force."

It is this reassuring message that Ruth Montgomery has sought to convey throughout her quarter-century pilgrimage along the often lonely corridors of the psychic world. Undeterred by doubters, since she herself has been a skeptic throughout her thrilling pursuit and understands their perplexity, she has sought always for verifiable truth. "Pure faith is difficult to achieve," she says musingly. "It is not easy to grasp and believe in phenomena beyond our five senses until they begin happening to us."

As a longtime newspaper reporter Ruth had set an early course to enlighten her readers. Ferreting out the truth and relaying it accurately, she reasoned, would enable thinking people to comprehend the issues confronting them and to act from understanding rather than ignorance. Then, following the trail of her journalistic curiosity and nose for news, she began delving beyond the issues of politics and world affairs to the mysteries of spirit communication. If such alleged contacts were merely cleverly perpetrated fraud or hallucination, people should be so informed. If, however, something significant was really going on, then the need to know about it surely outweighed the importance of today's political headlines.

What she began to discover in her search for truth soon opened a veiled door to an exciting realm that not only validated age-old religious belief, but gave the academic and scientific worlds new tools for exploration. During those often frustrating years of testing, probing, reasoning and retesting, Ruth verified to her own satisfaction that the spirit plane is as real as the physical world that we can see and touch and that communication with that world indeed exists.

But this realization did not put an end to her search. Through the prodding of her discarnate Guides, Ruth launched an investigation of the ancient belief in reincarnation, exploring every avenue while maintaining a healthy skepticism and an open mind. If reincarnation is valid, she decided, we should know about it but if it is merely an ancient superstition accepted by two thirds of the world's population, perhaps she could put it into proper perspective.

The evidence that Ruth found in support of reincarnation became so overwhelmingly convincing that she and tens of thousands of her readers soon revised their attitudes, comprehending for the first time that each physical sojourn has a definite purpose, that schoolhouse earth is a recurring testing ground for us, and that we go on forever.

An understanding of reincarnation led next to Ruth's exploration of the life beyond death, when we shed our bodies like outer cloaks and move on to evaluate what we have learned, before choosing the next set of lessons in our progression toward reunion with the Creator. This reunion, she found, is the ultimate goal for all of us, and the subconscious yearning for it is the source of our current dissatisfactions. Obstacles should therefore be viewed as stepping-stones along the way, because if we handle them well, they will hasten our spiritual advancement. Death is merely a transition, and rebirth is inevitable until we reach the perfected state that permits such reunion. What matters is how well we learn our lessons here, not the material trappings that seem so important to us while we walk the earth in human form. We should begin to put our priorities in order.

"How can anyone fear death," Ruth asks, "once he realizes that we have all been through it many times before? We regularly go and come between the real world of spirit and the shadow world of physical being. It is all a part of our soul growth, and it is surely comforting to realize that a benevolent God is giving us many more opportunities to achieve perfection rather than judging us solely on our present performance."

Planetary changes are soon to occur and the shift is inevitable, as Ruth and her Guides continue to warn, yet an understanding of the real nature of earth life will lead us beyond all fear to a new level of spiritual maturity

Ruth's search for truth has served as a beacon for all of us to follow. This distinguished writer has probed and questioned while our civilization at large has groped for answers, and through her courageous quest she has found a truth that can enlighten humankind. Others who followed her lead and searched for their own answers have reached the same conclusions, regardless of the route they have taken, because it is Universal Truth. In sharing her own quest Ruth has led her millions of readers a long, long way, validating notions as familiar as prayer and afterlife, and as archaic as reincarnation and karma.

Through this search she has arrived at one all-important message: Life is eternal, and the quiet inner listening called meditation is a valuable tool with which to open our minds to an understanding of this reality. We are here on earth to learn. We have been here before and will return again and again, always confronting ourselves, until we eventually overcome our faults and achieve reunion with the Creator, of whom we were once an integral part. Ruth is handing us the key that can unlock the doors of life's deepest mysteries, and in the golden years following the next shift of the earth, all will comprehend these principles.

As a seeker of the light, and a messenger of the true understanding that is about to dawn on planet earth, Ruth Montgomery is indeed a Herald of the New Age